Composing
a Teaching Life

Composing a Teaching Life

Ruth Vinz

Teachers College, Columbia University

Boynton/Cook
Heinemann
Portsmouth, NH

Boynton/Cook Publishers, Inc.
A subsidiary of Reed Elsevier Inc.
361 Hanover Street, Portsmouth, NH 03801-3912

Offices and agents throughout the world

Copyright 1996 by Ruth Vinz

Library of Congress Cataloging-in-Publication Data
Vinz, Ruth
    Composing a teaching life/Ruth Vinz.
       p.   cm.
    Includes bibliographical references.
    ISBN 0-86709-379-X
    1. Teaching—Case studies. 2. English literature—Study and teaching—Case studies. 3. Knowledge, Theory of—Case studies. 4. Interaction analysis in education—Case studies. 5. Reflection (Philosophy)—Case studies. I. Title.
LB1027.V476   1996
371.1'02—dc20
                          95-47261
                          CIP

Editor: Peter Stillman
Cover designer: Gwen Frankfeldt

Printed in the United States of America on acid-free paper
99   DA   2 3 4 5 6 7 8 9

Contents

Prologue

I remember the date—April 27, 1965. The bell rang, as always, at precisely 3:02 P.M. Students ran to the one bus that transported all twenty-four of them home to face the evening chores on their ranches and farms. This was rural Montana, and I was a twenty-year-old student teacher who found myself working in a community that had one school, the grange hall, a general store, and a congregation of Christians who used the school as a church. I lived with the Millards for the semester because they had extra room since they'd quit hiring "hands" after Millard sold off some 800 acres of land where he'd harvested wheat. Most of my memories of that day in April center on Jacob Keller.

He was still in the classroom at 5:00 P.M. I watched him tear strip after strip of paper into thin white lines, then arrange and stack them. I worked at my desk in the back of the room trying to prepare for the next day's discussion of Steinbeck's *Red Pony*. I'd never known Butch Keller to be late to pick up his son, even though they lived nearly thirty miles from the school at the north end of Leonard's Gulch, which had a vein of fifteen miles of curving dirt road. "Help me carry things to my car, Jacob." I broke the rhythm of the clock's steady tick.

It was well after clouds swirled on down the valley and into the gulch, and nearly nightfall, before I'd driven Jacob to his Uncle Buster's ranch. I was assured by his aunt that she'd take care of Jake. The next morning I pieced together a story from the details given of the accident. The truck and bull were intertwined into a mangled hybrid in a sinkhole left by the tag end of a rainstorm. Butch must have been in a hurry, hit the hole without braking, and veered through the fence with full force. The bull happened to be in the way. I spent that weekend staring out at the clouds unravelling across the dark rock and sage, wondering how Jacob was coping.

His Uncle Buster, from his dead mother's side of the family, took him in. Yet, I kept thinking he must be homesick for the home he no longer had. His desk was empty for nearly two weeks. When he did return, so much was left unsaid. I tried to find ways to tell him I was sorry, but the words caught in my throat. Nights as I made lesson plans or weekends when I walked the slag heap of plowed prairie along the line of cottonwoods, I thought about this boy who was without mother and father.

"It's time to think about school," my cooperating teacher told Jake after school one day. Jacob nodded and shuffled out for the long walk ahead. He didn't come back to school, not the next day nor the next. I didn't know whether to go after him or to leave alone what I couldn't mend. I was well into interviews for my first teaching job when I heard from Jacob. He'd asked the Millards for my address. Jake wrote that he was working for his Uncle Buster on the ranch and that he'd ridden his first roundup; it was through some of the most beautiful yet forlorn country I've ever seen. He sent a picture from the Billing's stockyards where he sat on a corral smiling and waving, a cloud of crows illustrating the wide expanse of sky in the background.

Nearly a year later, as I tallied percentages for Susan, Eileen, Craig, Everett, Tom, and the other 130 students who survived my first year of teaching, I got another note from Jacob and was reminded of what Montana ranchers say about trouble never "traveling lonesome." He wrote, "I'm going to work for Bill Simmons. I'll drive the scatter rake some. Uncle Buster couldn't let me stay what with the hay crop and cattle not worth selling. We had grasshoppers and no rain. Buster got deep in loans. Jake."

His is the first name in a string of adolescents—Jacob, Richard, Terry, Stephen, Cherri, Jane, Susan, Netta, Randall—who slipped into and informed my teaching life. I'm sure you have your own list of previous students, some of whom you may have remembered as you read about Jacob. Each of their stories reminds us about who we are as teachers. Throughout my years of teaching, I kept learning about uncertainty and ambiguity and appreciating how I must continuously construct and reconstruct my teaching life.

I've begun thinking about how my beliefs have changed over the years and how those beliefs have been shaped by students, colleagues, or mentors who challenged me to think in new ways about teaching and learning. I constantly reconsider my beliefs and aspirations within the complexity of competing intentions and expectations from those people—students, parents, administrators, other teachers—who also have a vested interest in what goes on in the classrooms where I teach. As I write this Preface, I am beginning my twenty-ninth year of teaching. It's hard for me to imagine my life without a new group of students each year, or the stacks of papers and books cluttering my home and office, as well as the questions that prompt me to think about ways in which I might work more effectively in classrooms and schools. About the time I become complacent enough to trust moments of seeming success, these are inevitably followed by other events that challenge my current understandings.

Just as the proverbial blind pundits focused their attention on only one part of the elephant's body in order to define it, I too have sometimes focused my attention too narrowly on the contradictions, mysteries, or superficial subjects that were the most directly in my gaze. I'm trying to move beyond describing the constraints—how the principal validates one style of teaching and not others or how we don't have enough money for a new set of books. Yes, these are important issues, but they tend to freeze me into inaction or at least rationalization. I'm realizing that many of the key moments in my teaching life have gone unnoticed in the routines, the tiredness, and the overly demanding days. So, in this book, I'm trying to dig deeper, to refine my ways of remembering, of telling, and of invoking the meaning of our work as teachers. Subsequently, I hope that this discussion and exploration will entangle you again in the complexities of teaching and learning and will be a way for you to re-search and re-examine your teaching life.

I've divided the discussion into two major sections. Part One, "On Teachers and Teaching," has four chapters, each dealing with the different ways that our knowledge, beliefs, and understandings of teaching are formulated. Much of this section contains accounts of the influences on me and other teachers that seem to dictate or at least direct what we do or how we think about what we do in our classrooms. In Chapter One, "Shaping Images of Teachers," I examine how the images of teachers, gained from our experiences in school, from literature, and from the popular media, influence not only our, but also our students' and the general public's beliefs about us as persons, teachers, and professionals. The chapter ends with a discussion of how we might study these images as we continue to define who we are as teachers.

In Chapter Two, "The Predicaments of Learning to Teach," I point out how teaching is about beginnings: unfamiliar faces each year, clean chalkboards and the smell of new chalk, an empty grade book with a list of unfamiliar names followed by a blank matrix, and then the first bell in September. Each beginning is filled with complications that must be examined in order for any of us to take subsequent action. In this chapter, I discuss what I learned from four first-year teachers—Avis, Ben, Sarah, and Stephen—who invited me to document the issues and questions surrounding their first year of teaching. This chapter also contains a discussion of the major issues facing four student teachers—Beverly, Jennifer, Regina, and John—during their first semester of teaching.

Chapter Three, "Far More Than Technicians: Provoking Reflections on Teaching Literature," focuses on the complex negotiations among contexts, intentions, and expectations that determine teachers' purposes and practices in literature education. This chapter examines the reflective inquiry of three teachers—Beth, Jane, and Joe—who have taught for more than fifteen years each. I spent one school year documenting their understandings of teaching through interviews and classroom observations. They fine-tuned my understanding of how they put their beliefs and purposes into practice.

Chapter Four, "In Teachers' Hands," demonstrates how we might read our teaching histories in much the same way we would read any text—to open a field of inquiry. I illustrate with examples from my own classroom practices to demonstrate how I have learned to read my teaching history and how such readings subsequently inform my practices. At the end of the chapter, I suggest metaphoric ways of thinking about being a teacher. This chapter is an invitation and possibly an evocation to help you read and reread the text of your teaching life.

Part Two, "Lessons from the Classroom," offers glimpses of life in classrooms through scenarios that serve as vehicles for drawing out, articulating, questioning, and illuminating their contexts, structures, and curriculums. The scenarios are narrative reconstructions of the classrooms from the eleven teachers described in Part One. Chapter Five, "Teaching Mindfully," takes the reader into the classrooms of three experienced teachers. There we find informed practices based on the careful reflection of these teachers. This chapter illuminates one version of what I believe Robert Scholes (1985) meant when he suggested that "Our job is not to produce 'readings' for our students but to give them the tools for producing their own."[1]

Chapter Six, "Developing Habits of Mind," focuses on the classrooms of four first-year teachers. At the heart of this section is the recognition that teaching is a ceaseless activity, one that takes enormous intellectual, spiritual, and physical energy to produce the encounters with meaning that encourage learning. Chapter Seven, "Initiation into the Discourse on Teaching," documents the four student teachers' first teaching experiences. It is written as a celebration really, one that includes some unsure moments amidst those of certainty when paradox or conflict urged them to question what their work as teachers was and what it might be. Their experiences remind me how important ongoing inquiry into teaching will be if we are to raise critical questions about how our educational system might be improved.

Ours is a time when people are mindful about the role of teachers in developing the critical consciousness of a nation. For all·the rhetoric about lack of teachers' commitment, knowledge, or ability to meet diverse needs, how often are we asked what it means to teach? How often are teachers considered an important source of knowledge? And yet we are key figures in the struggle to understand more about schools. Our reflections can provide certain types of understanding about how identities, subjectivities, and political structures shape schools. Teaching is full of questions and the unexpected as well as mixed and contradictory intentions. As we struggle to define and redefine our place in schools, we discover that there is no perfect or generalized model to explain how one learns to teach. The process of composing a teaching life is one of revising and reshaping. My own life as a teacher, and those of the teachers with whom I've worked in the past several years, help me resist the impulse to simplify teaching into recipes of reified, unitary, and static treatments.

I believe that teachers' voices need to be valued in discussions on teaching and learning; teachers need to become active participants and shapers of the political, social, and ideological realities of schooling. I was made keenly aware of how unusual these premises were when Cynthia Linn, a teacher of seventeen years, told me: "It makes me feel funny, talking about my teaching. We always rolled our eyes at teachers during methods or in-service classes. You remember the ones who always talked about their classes? War stories, we'd say with an acid tone in our voices. I'm realizing how we were socialized to keep our mouths shut about what we did or didn't do in classes. Nobody wanted to hear. The idea was to sit back and let someone else tell us how we should act and think and what we should value. The message was clear: Don't waste time on war stories." Cynthia's perspective suggests how we have devalued and constrained our own knowledge. Much of our experience provides wisdom for our future teaching lives and for others' lives as well. I want to stress that the stories of individual lives and the accompanying improvisations, as Catherine Bateson (1989) suggests, help us discover "the shape of our creation along the way, rather than pursuing a vision already defined."[2] Particularized viewpoints and experiences of teachers haven't often been legitimated as central to understanding schools or teaching.

Catherine Bateson's (1989) book *Composing a Life* led me to a deeper appreciation of my own life of dissonance, watchfulness, and disorder as I lived, along with the five women Bateson details, through their ways of composing a life. Their improvisations of living led me to remember that teaching is often fraught with frustrations, dead ends, and dreams fulfilled or deflected. For me, there are moments of clear insight, adaptation, and always and forever there is life-long learning and continuously falling in love with what I do. For all these reasons, *Composing a Teaching Life* is a conceit, a direct reference to Bateson's commitment to share the lives of herself and others. I have tried to highlight several of Bateson's themes as they apply to teaching: recognizing the constant improvisation, finding path and purpose, reimagining the future, and reinterpreting the past.

I spent time with a young boy in Harlem last year, and he reminded me again of Jacob and the long list of others whose words and actions I can't get out of my heart and mind. He asked me why I liked to read books; and something in the earnest tone of his voice left me without an easy answer. I thought a few minutes before saying, "I'm not sure. I'm a snoop for one thing. I like getting involved in someone else's life. How about you, Randolph?" He looked at me for a long time before he said, "Me, I read to escape and hear some old story of hope. There be no story in these streets worth tellin' or readin'. The moon, it don't shine over Harlem." Jacob, Randolph, and all the others in the long list of names that each of us could add, have a cumulative effect on our developing history as teachers. We keep learning with and from them and the memories they give us.

I believe that these memories work with the present to help us consider and reconsider who we are as teachers. Remembrance helps us step into our futures. I'm indebted again to Mary Catherine Bateson. She suggests that the "process of improvisation that goes into composing a life is compounded in the process of remembering a life, like a patchwork quilt in a watercolor painting, rumpled and evocative. Yet it is this second process, composing a life through memory as well as through day-to-day choices, that seems to me most essential to creative living. The past empowers the present, and the groping footsteps leading to this present mark the pathways to the future."[3]

My intent is not to dwell on issues of reform or to examine past discussions of teacher productiveness or competence, or to recite a litany of all the societal and political problems that damage how teachers can work productively in the school culture. Rather, I look on *Composing a Teaching Life* as a deliberately personalized portrait of what it means to teach—one filled with memory, experience, and hope.

References

1. Scholes, Robert. 1985. *Textual Power*, p. 24.

2. Bateson, M.C. 1989. *Composing a Life*, p. 1.

3. Bateson, M.C. 1989. *Composing a Life*, p. 7.

Acknowledgments

From start to finish, *Composing a Teaching Life* required the goodwill, effort, and support of so many people. For inviting me to participate in their journeys through teaching, I wish to acknowledge the eleven teachers whose insights, struggles, and practices are discussed throughout this book—Beth, Jane, and Joe, who have spent nearly two decades in their classrooms; Avis, Stephen, Ben, and Sarah, who were in their first year of teaching at the time I collected data for this study; and Regina, Jennifer, John, and Beverly, who invited me to document their student teaching experiences. I was an interloper in all of these teachers' work and thoughts, and I hope that I have told fair and truthful stories of their experiences. They led me to respect their different purposes and practices and helped me to understand how individual possibilities of expression add rich texture to the ongoing discourse on teaching and learning. Approximately 4,195 students have survived or thrived in the classrooms in which I have taught. Digging through old file folders of their writing and listening to audio tapes of class sessions for examples to use in this book reminded me how particularly privileged I've been to collaborate with them in various learning projects. I appreciate their permission to tell the stories and to share the writing so that others may learn from it. The ideas and spirit of many colleagues shape my work. My thanks to John Mayher, Gordon Pradl, Margot Ely, Lonann Reid, Beth Brisbane, Greg Hamilton, Fran Claggett, Stephen Dunning, Pat Pieter, Bob, Barr, and Dianne Brunner. Peter Stillman, editor and friend, shepherded this book from conception to final production. His suggestions for revision, along with those of Ellen Richmond and the staff working for Heinemann Boynton/Cook, helped to focus and tighten this version of the composing story. To my husband Warren, one of the best teachers I know, who shared my past and advises my present; to Trace, Jason, and Katie, who gave me a happy history of motherhood and upscale my daily life with their presence, this book is dedicated to you.

Composing
a Teaching Life

PART ONE

ON TEACHERS AND TEACHING

Who can say what teachers think they are up to, what they take to be the point of what they are doing, what it means for teachers to teach? Who, indeed. To say that teachers are the ones who understand, know, and can say seems so obvious that it is beneath reporting. But in the often odd, sometimes upside-down world of social research, the obvious news must be reported and repeated: The secret of teaching is to be found in the local detail and the everyday life of teachers; teachers can be the richest and most useful source of knowledge about teaching; those who hope to understand teaching must turn at some point to teachers themselves.

W. Ayers, in Schubert W.H., and W. Ayers, eds., 1992
Teacher Lore, p. v.

Chapter One

Shaping Images of Teachers

Miss Lynch sticks in my mind as a tough-minded cross between Morticia of *The Addams' Family* and Miss Grundy in the *Archie* comics. I don't remember her in anything other than black, although the weight and texture of cloth changed with the seasons. She loved Dickens' *Great Expectations,* and we spent the better part of three weeks on the imagery of decaying lace, molding wedding cake, and the aging Miss Havisham. We moved on to examine how the repeating images of handcuffs, cufflinks, and the montage of hands might emphasize themes and symbolism that Miss Lynch had chosen to explicate. Then, marshes and darkness took us into the final stretch before essay writing and the dreaded test. Rumor had it that Miss Lynch had lost a lover in Flanders Field during World War I. I attributed that loss to her love of dark stories and black dresses.

Miss Lynch occasionally looked above her glasses to the back wall of the classroom and began to ask questions. I remember one incident through a blur of thirty years' time. We were reading Camus' *The Stranger.* Mersault had received news of his mother's death. "How do you feel about Mersault's reactions to his mother's death?" Jack, class president and big mouth, said, "He doesn't care. He's weird." Susan interrupted, "He's probably in shock." And the conversation began. Miss Lynch pushed us in yet another direction. "How about any of you? Are there times when you wouldn't allow yourself to feel anything for fear of how it hurts?" Silence. She waited. Miss Lynch had invited us to talk about ourselves and most of us blushed at the thought.

We weren't socialized into discussions of personal experiences in classrooms. We didn't walk over that line, and Miss Lynch, what-

3

ever her motivations, didn't push us. After the silence, she looked back at her notes and expounded on the sun, heat, and glare that surrounded Mersault. Her eyes gleamed right through the extra thick lenses with a passion and intensity I can't forget. I don't know how deliberate were her attempts to evoke personal connections with the literature. What I do know is that she introduced me to Dickens, Dickinson, Hardy, Woolf, Camus, Bishop, and Tolstoy. This past year when I reread *The Mayor of Casterbridge,* the image of Miss Lynch came to mind. I know she believed in the power of words on the page as surely as she believed in black.

Learning from Experience

Remembering teachers and reflecting on how they have influenced our constructions of teaching, may help us understand our own beliefs and practices. As Adrienne Rich (1979) writes, "Until we can understand the assumptions in which we are drenched we cannot know ourselves" (p. 35). It's easy to recognize that teachers like Miss Lynch can be influential in shaping our knowledge of what it means to be a teacher. Part of arriving at that self-understanding involves a deliberate inquiry into what we have learned and from whom. Biographical reflection fosters such an understanding. Tom Popkewitz (1984) suggests that teachers use their personal and teaching histories as texts wherein "a particular system is considered not in isolation but in relation to other aspects of society that influence its own form" (p. 48). I believe we can profit from a careful examination of our individual "texts" as teachers. My purpose throughout this chapter is to describe some of the constituent parts of those "texts" and to suggest how these can inform and influence our practices.

To engage in such an examination we must put in order our past experiences so that we virtually create a text that becomes the subject for further interpretation. We can, as it were, create a narrative accounting of our experiences. By allowing ourselves to enter the time, place, and events of the narrative, we submit ourselves to the story that we are telling. For example, Hayden White (1980) considers autobiographical narratives a means "to translate knowing into telling, the problem of fashioning human experience into a form assimilable to structures of meaning that are generally human rather than culture-specific" (p. 5). Or, as Victor Turner (1980) argues, narratives provide opportunities for "rearticulating opposing values and goals in a meaningful structure" (p. 168). Telling our stories of teaching is one way to learn more about ourselves. When *Stories Lives Tell,* edited by Witherell and Noddings, was published in 1991, I felt heartened that "the stories lives tell—in educational practice and research" were finding a central place in the dialogue on teachers' experiences (p. 1). In the same year, Donald Schön (1991) edited a collection of case studies, *The Reflective Turn: Case Studies in and on Educational Practice,* emphasizing the link between retrospective accounts and present situations. Specifically, the chapter by Clandinin and Connelly (1991), "Narrative and Story in Practice and Research," advances a series of suggestions on the uses and methods of autobiographical inquiry in education. Witherell and Noddings' book along with Schön's is a reminder that making sense of experiences may help teachers learn to "examine their own histories, those connections to the past which in part define who they are and how they mediate and function in the world" (Aronowitz and Giroux, 1985, p. 160). It seems to me that this turn inward to autobiographical accounts of educational experiences can provoke us into conversations of what comprises our teaching lives.

What we saw, heard, appreciated, or resisted in our own school experiences with teachers must have an effect on our beliefs and practices. I'm certain you have Miss Lynch stories of your own. Other images can be found in the professional literature that surrounds us. From *English Journal* wherein a teacher describes a student enactment of the witches' scene in *MacBeth* to *In The Middle* wherein we can imagine Nancie Atwell crouched in conference with an adolescent reader, our view of how English teachers practice is partly defined through the stories that we take as representative of the profession. What these teachers do and believe juxtaposes with our beliefs and practices. I suggest that by either recounting the experiences we've had with teachers or considering how the images from the professional literature influence us is a good way to begin examining who we are as teachers.

Add to this the images of teachers we've come to know through popular film or television. Who can forget Cosby playing Chet Kincaid or Glenn Ford as Dadier in *The Blackboard Jungle*? Then there is Robin Williams leading the charge across fields of poetry. Teachers have been canonized, not always in positive ways, in the very literature we teach in classrooms. Many of us have taught literature in which teachers have a role—Jean Brodie in her prime or the grim Wackford Squeers from Dickensian tradition. And, while we know these teachers as characters in a book, it is possible that the images of the teachers constructed in these texts have some influence on how we and others view the teaching profession. The historical perspective on teachers carries a mythology of its own that suggests how teachers have taught and should teach. Some of us may practice the Socratic method; others search for the wisdom of Confucius. The point is that teachers do experience themselves through the nearly invisible connections they have to others before them.

More nettlesome may be how we see ourselves as a result of the perceptions harbored by our students and their parents, our colleagues, and the community at large. Visions of school marm virgins with buns pulled tightly in place depict a lack of passion in the profession. Too often we hear stories of ineptitude. Recently, I saw on television a film clip that a student made in his classroom. The teacher sat at his desk unable or unwilling to control a classroom full of thirty students who gyrated around the room like they were slam dancing. Such depictions influence how others see us and how we see ourselves. Becoming a teacher is a continuous process and one through which a teaching identity is produced and reproduced through the particular social interactions and ideologies that inform us. To quote Maxine Greene (1978), "It is important to hold in mind, therefore, that each of us achieved contact with the world from a particular vantage point, in terms of a particular biography. All of this underlies our present perspectives and affects the way we look at things and talk about things and structure our realities. To be in touch with our landscapes is to be conscious of our evolving experiences, to be aware of the ways in which we encounter our world" (p. 2).

Teachers from Our Past

As I've been working over the past few years with prospective and in-service teachers, I have encouraged them to talk or write about their memories of particular teachers. Their inquiry into prior schooling or teaching provides them with insights through which they can develop theories about teaching and teachers' work. Through this pedagogical choice, I hope to dislodge the notion that methods courses are about finding the right theory, method, content, or curriculum. My strategy is based on the belief that for all there is to learn from others about theory and pedagogy, it is impossible to talk about teaching without questioning personal beliefs and knowledge. I want prospective teachers to think about the images they carry with them, the ghosts, if you will.

Some have found it helpful to determine why an incident occurred in class by relating it to their own past experiences. For example, Regina, who was approximately six weeks into her first student teaching experience, described a disappointing class session. She couldn't get the students to focus on the time they had for reading, writing about, and discussing the novels chosen by their small groups. "Today, they mostly squirmed, bothered each other, and looked out the window. It was awful. I'm embarrassed how many times I told them to get back to their discussions of what they'd read. I even threatened them: If you don't write at least a page in your reading journals, the groups won't meet tomorrow." As Regina described what went on in class, she began to talk about a teacher she had in eighth grade:

> I had Mrs. Jenkins and I didn't learn much about literature. We'd start out writing in our logs about what we read the night before. It was open-ended which we're now saying is good, but I often just ran out of things to say. Maybe it's better than answering questions but I felt like I was saying the same things over and over. Not only did I sit there and try to stretch out log entries to one full page, but there was a challenge to say something important. As I think about it now, it's not just keeping a reading log that counts, it's helping kids find connections between the reading, themselves, and the writing. What Jenkins seemed to believe was that keeping a log would naturally lead us to involvement with the literature. It can be artificial. Why didn't I remember how this was for me before I assigned students to do the same?

Regina recognizes that her experiences as a student can provide important information to her as a teacher. Before she can use this knowledge to influence her teaching practices, she must connect it with her beliefs about learning literature. It seems to me that she does this when she states, "It's helping these kids find connections between the reading, themselves, and the writing." Regina frames the problem of student motivation by considering her own motivation in similar circumstances. She notices that the reading log doesn't motivate or stimulate student interest and determines that the intrinsic motivation must exist before students believe the log is a useful tool. Comparing her teaching practice with her own experience as a student led her to empathize with her students' lack of involvement. By reminding herself of what a student feels like, using an incident from her past to connect with a present moment, she gained dual vision. Reliving and reconceptualizing our experiences isn't just narcissistic, it's a way to effect new connections in experience and to see that what we set out to do has some underlying pattern, which sometimes needs to be challenged.

Another way of seeing how considerations of the past inform

our teaching is to question our assumptions in relation to past events. John, who was in his first semester of student teaching, described how he challenged his assumptions about an after-school reading club he began at his school. On the surface, he suggested, it sounded like a great idea to have kids join this reading group. The problem was that the students were selected by John. Privilege was accorded to only a special few. At first he felt very good about setting up the club, but he began to recognize the implications:

> It's amazing how little I questioned assumptions about what we do with these kids. I remember that my seventh grade English teacher "invited" me into an after-school reading group. It included less than a dozen top readers. It was a big deal, and I felt special. Why not? Now I have to think again why I just assumed this group should be selective. Why only the students who the teacher thought worthy? I might have done the same thing with my students if we hadn't been provoked into thinking what this kind of thing means. It's been helpful to search through our own experiences and learn from them. It's obvious from our discussions that this is a strategy we can use to help us think more carefully.

John's experience reminds me of how important it is to consider again the things we often take for granted or that may appear to be responsible choices on the surface. This applies particularly to practices that are time-honored and seldom subject to any type of interrogation. Many of these practices we came to expect at school—tracking, teacher-only evaluation, films on the Friday before a holiday, writing-on-demand, and study guides. Not that any of these practices are "bad" or "good," but they should be examined for the implicit messages that result. Maybe, as John pointed out, we are and can become critical readers of experience through a process of discovery and rediscovery.

Portraits of Teachers in Professional Literature

As I suggested earlier, perhaps the construction of a teacher goes deeper and broader than can be accounted for in our actual experiences with teachers. Who we are as teachers is constructed within a complex network of contradictory images from various sources. In professional literature, teachers portray themselves or are characterized by other writers by giving "how-to" accounts of what goes on in classrooms or through descriptions of innovations in instructional or structural practices. Professional conference presentations leave indelible images of teachers and their classrooms. I've found that the professional literature and conferences have influenced my ways of working in the classroom and have often caused me to re-evaluate myself as a teacher. There are times when I've been badly shaken, thinking I couldn't possibly do what so-and-so did with their kids. Other times I believe that I've got some things going that are keen and sophisticated. But, it's important to go beyond these initial responses and consider that any of these accounts of teaching are simplified versions of the messiness, chaos, and false starts that are a part of teaching.

Professional literature and conferences often give us the stream-lined version. That isn't to suggest the exchange is harmful. Many times the strategies offer alternative approaches that are worthy of consideration. More often than not, other teachers' accounts pro-vide examples of renewal and redefinition that are important to our work as teachers. Yet I don't want to overlook the need to examine how these teachers inform our views of ourselves. I've heard many of the prospective teachers with whom I've worked over the past several years lament their inability to teach like Donald Murray, Tom Liner, Nancie Atwell, or Linda Rief. It is important to reorient them. Any of the approaches they read about—practical or radical, traditional or progressive—cannot be replicated. Every teacher needs to understand that the work of other teachers can become part of the dialectic on teaching, but it cannot essentialize each individ-ual teacher's work.

Here's an example that shows the spirit of inquiry rather than the following of a recipe. Jane, a veteran elementary teacher, gave this example:

> The people I come in contact with through reading, in classes, in rooms next to my own or across town, don't often give me an-swers. They raise more questions. The questions create dilemmas that take time to formulate into alternatives. I really can't accept the Lucy Calkins or the Thomas Newkirk way. I love the class-rooms they describe but wouldn't it be sort of . . . like being a part-ner who only imitates someone else's view of say . . . creation. I'm thinking of the Sistine Chapel. I'm no Michelangelo, and I wouldn't want to spend my energy or imagination or individual-ity replicating his view of the finger of God touching Adam. I have my own ways, but that means I need to solve my own problems. Sure, I find the questions through contact with others, but seldom the answers.

Do teachers yearn for right answers and success stories? Perhaps the professional literature shows too many success stories and not enough stories of the messy and chaotic work of sorting through options, interrogating values, or making hard decisions between equally valid alternatives. Accounts by other teachers help us search out our own significant questions. As Jane points out, such portraits should enable rather than constrict us.

Sarah, a first year teacher, found the professional literature daunting at times:

> I'm tired of trying to live in somebody else's house. This classroom is where my students and I must learn to live together. I'm just beginning, and I hope students are too. After reading Atwell's *In The Middle,* I thought it sounded great. I held that image in my mind and didn't live up to it. Now, I'm thinking Atwell isn't me and the kids in her class aren't my students. I need to struggle with getting to know myself as a teacher and learn how to know kids. All this takes time and constant revision. I'm more confident that I'll find my own ways.

Much depends on how we try to understand and on whether we are willing to be critically aware of the presence of ourselves and the ghosts of others in our teaching. Sarah suggests that she must bring her own meaning into being. In her first year of teaching, she reminds herself through her reflections that she can constitute her own reality. The biography that informs Sarah becomes the skeleton from which she will flesh out who she is as a teacher.

Jennifer, a student teacher, wrote:

> Maybe it is learning to be critical readers of our experiences. I'm beginning to notice that teachers create portraits of themselves. I'm thinking about what they say and write. You know, from the faculty room to *English Journal,* in-service meetings, or methods classes. Many of these people make their practice sound neutral of values and talk too much about how things should be done. It's like their practices will make me an effective teacher and that what they suggest are ways I should teach if I want to be an effective teacher.

Jennifer notes that teachers cannot become members of a knowledge community by adopting others' practices wholesale. She recognizes that she cannot be some other teacher. Someone else's experience cannot tell any of us who we are or how we might practice, for, as Foucault (1985) suggests, experience is interpreted through "the correlation between fields of knowledge, types of normativity, and forms of subjectivity in a particular culture" (p. 4).

Teachers should produce knowledge for one another. However, my concern relates to the tone and spirit in which that may be done. Texts giving descriptions of practice can be written as more than just one's authoritative account. At the heart of these accounts, I'd like to see more discussion of the teacher's particular beliefs and assumptions as well as the contexts that influenced decisions of practice. I hope the professional literature of the future will create more images of teachers that help us rethink our ideas or imagine new practices, but will not try to convert us.

Images of Teachers in Popular Culture

Another rendition of teachers is the generalized and often stereotyped portrayals found in popular culture, which offer incompatible depictions between the complexity of real life in schools and the near simplicity of day after day, as the sitcom would suggest, of being "Saved by the Bell." Oversimplified portraits may result in an incapacity to empathize with these teachers' predicaments. They often appear pathetically uninformed, treated by others as inept, and treating themselves with a dose of complacency. Few would dispute that English teacher Miss Brooks, played by Eve Arden, is more interested in capturing Mr. Boynton's attention than that of her students. What might we suggest in Bill Cosby's switch from teacher Chet Kincaid in his earlier series to that of doctor Cliff Huxtable in the much longer running series? I couldn't help but wonder whether Cosby and his writers found a teacher's life unfulfilling as they attempted to spell out its complications week after week for a television audience. Or, maybe ratings suggested that the audience just wasn't much interested in the teacher's story. Whatever the motivations, I believe that the constructions of teachers on television need to be examined and that we, as teachers, might become vocal about these depictions. I am mindful that many television situation comedies portray teachers who are weary of the fight and grow complacent. I want to challenge those images for the prospective teachers and in-service teachers with whom I work. I wish I had done it with the secondary students I worked with in previous years. As Ken Kantor (1993) suggests, "television shows about schools are potential occupational hazards to those of us who have worked in schools" (p. 176).

Films create similar false portraits. Consider the heroine in *Butch Cassidy and the Sundance Kid*. She reminds us that she might as well go to Bolivia. After all, she is twenty-three, single, and a school teacher. What is there for her to risk? She isn't alone in suggesting that teaching is a dead-end career. Teachers are often depicted as unfit to survive in the jungle where survival of the fittest counts. Richard Brooks' *Blackboard Jungle* arrived in theaters in the mid-1950s.

Dadier, played by Glenn Ford, is a Korean War veteran hired to teach English. But the urban adolescents, pulsating with tensions, face powerlessness and disillusionment because of the social structures of class and race. Dadier is insulted, mugged, slashed, and nearly killed, but he doesn't give in. That's the shame of it. As the rest of the faculty said on the first day Dadier came to the school, "They hire fools like us with college degrees to sit on that garbage can and keep them in school so women for a few hours a day can walk around the city without being attacked." Is it any more noble to stay and perpetuate the fraud than to leave? That is not made clear. By 1984, Arthur Hiller's film *Teacher* portrays Alex as a drunk whose wife left him because she wanted more than a teacher. The teacher nicknamed "Ditto" dies one day during class without any of the students noticing. His students had grown to accept his practice of giving them worksheets for the period while he slept at his desk behind the newspaper, so the students just didn't notice.

Songs such as Chuck Berry's "School Days," with a teacher who "don't know how mean she looks," and Van Halen's "Hot for Teacher," with lyrics taunting that "homework was never like this," distort the image of teachers and the profession. Yet, these popularized versions become part of the social construction of what it means to be a teacher. Giroux and Simon (1989), in their study of the pervasiveness in popular culture of negative imagery of schools and teachers, found that such images are "not insignificant in shaping how students view themselves and their own relations to various forms of pedagogy and learning" (p. 221). I suspect the media depictions influence how teachers and prospective teachers see themselves. Self-image can be obstructed by these often discouraging images of the profession. Do these artifacts of popular culture hold a mirror up to reality? Do they generate or distill the public's attitudes toward portraits of teachers? Certainly the mass media serves as a vehicle through which certain depictions and beliefs are expressed regarding teachers. Do we come to believe them? The strongest messages we received about teachers often reinforce the exaggerated portrayals that the audience or reader has come to accept or expect. The repetition of some messages takes its toll and perpetuates the adage: "Those who can, do; those who can't, teach." George Orwell (1970) suggested that "people are influenced far more than they would care to admit by novels, serial stories, films and so forth, and that from this point of view the worst books are often the most important because they are usually the ones that are read earlier in life" (p. 528). I wonder how often we examine for ourselves and with our students how these popular constructions influence our beliefs about teachers?

Teachers in Literature

Even in canonical U.S. literature, Ichabod Crane is scared out of town wearing a pumpkin over his head by the macho males in town. Lest the reader forget, I offer this reminder—Ichabod was a teacher. But, it is in the portrayals of teachers in Dickens' novels that the caricatures of teachers reach an extreme. His parade of teachers, including Creakle, Blimber, Gradgrind, Mell, Marton, Headstone, Squeers, McChoakumchild, and Wopsle's great aunt, depict the pathetic, malevolent, crazy, lunatic, or downright mad. The patterns and formulas Dickens used to shore those teachers in the world of schools have truths of their own. His creations are recognized and recognizable. McChoakumchild does just as his name suggests. He follows his utilitarian philosophy of education, leading children to learn facts until they are lifeless and less than child-like (Dickens, 1854). Indeed, the times are hard for children in a school where Gradgrind and McChoakumchild, with intentions they believe to be sound, lull children into dullness.

On the Dickensian spectrum, there are professionally trained teachers who do not harm students but remain detached and cannot enter their students' worlds, lost as they are in their own worlds of facts, numbers, or mechanistics. Dr. Strong's passion for words, manifest in the compiling of his dictionary, keeps him distanced from his students' realities and needs. Even David Copperfield and his classmates recognize that Strong lives for one thing only. "He [Adams] considered that it [the dictionary] might be done in one thousand six hundred and forty-nine years, counting from the Doctor's last, or sixty-second, birthday" (Dickens, 1850/1958, p. 228). Lacking esteem, intention, effectiveness, passion, and understanding, many of Dickens' teachers are more pathetic than they are malevolent. Bradley Headstone represents the mechanistic teacher who had "acquired mechanically a great store of teacher's knowledge. He could do mental arithmetic mechanically, sing at sight mechanically, blow various wind instruments mechanically, even play the great church organ mechanically" (Dickens, 1865/1971, p. 266).

In an extreme portrayal, Dickens (1839/1982) draws Dotheboys Hall with the sinister Wackford Squeers, who is a teacher characterized as near blind, cruel, and nearly comic in his stupidity. Under the tutelage of the near mythic Squeers "there was childhood with the light of its eye quenched, its beauty gone, and its helplessness alone remaining" (p. 152). Not that we are or believe there to be many Squeers who starve students or leave them emaciated, torn, filthy, and near death. It is the starvation of spirit we have come to worry about. Yet, Dickens' Fagin, (1838/1966) the pickpocket, knows how to teach. He motivates, models, and entertains. He nurtures, guides, and evaluates. He praises and rewards Oliver. "You're a clever boy, my dear," says the playful old gentleman, patting Oliver on the head approvingly. "I never saw a sharper lad. Here's a shilling for you. If you go on, in this way, you'll be the greatest man of the time. And now come here, and I'll show you how to take the marks out of the handkerchiefs" (p. 112).

It's interesting to consider what actual influences such depictions of teachers might have on readers. In many of the literary texts we study in school, there are depictions of teachers. Joan Rockwell (1977) operates from the basic premise that "literature neither 'reflects' nor 'arises from' society, but rather is an integral part of it and should be recognized as being as much so as any institution . . . Fiction is a social product, but it also 'produces' society . . . Fiction is not only a representation of social reality, but also paradoxically an important element in social change" (pp. vii, viii, 4). This is another argument for the need to look critically at the social product and what is produced in the construction of a teacher. Nothing else, I am convinced, will effectively counter the dissemination of beliefs about teachers that perpetuate how we are represented by others and by ourselves.

Images that Others Have of Teachers

We can't forget that the representations of teachers, whether true or false, have substantial impact on how the profession is viewed by parents, our students, and the community. I've tried to discern some of these views by interviewing parents of students in various schools considering a revision in the English curriculum. Many parents seem mystified at the changes in English curriculum and pedagogy that have occurred since the days that they were in school. I have no doubt that their experiences in school influence how they evaluate their children's education. Recently, I interviewed a group of middle school parents. Their reactions may seem typical, but I found they reveal the incongruity between our profession's changing view of what to teach regarding literature, language, and writing and what the parents believe should be taught. The following responses to a question about what they (parents) believe is stressed in the English classrooms of their children, give an idea of the issues and debates we currently face in English education.

On Literature

"My two children are reading all this adolescent literature, and it really simplifies issues. The writing isn't very good and the subject matter is often about sexual issues or AIDS or social conditions. I don't think it is universal enough. Where are the classics? Don't teachers value the classics anymore?"

"The multicultural literature isn't very good literature. I want our children reading quality work like I read. I think *Old Man and The Sea* is a must and instead our daughter is reading bad literature like *Journey of the Sparrow* just because of the PC rhetoric. I believe English teachers are brainwashed into this new view. They don't seem to stand firm on the value of good literature."

"The teachers don't seem to be teaching the correct interpretation any more. My teachers gave the meaning of the text and taught us to interpret through symbols, imagery, irony. I don't think teachers know how to do that anymore. They are probably the products of the lazy teaching that they give our kids."

On Language

"My son can't spell. Why don't teachers teach spelling? We learned to spell things right because we had drill after drill and I know it helped. Aren't these teachers learning to teach spelling? Why don't we have a spelling book?"

"The teachers don't care about the grammatical errors, and they don't stress these anymore. I find papers filled with errors and the teacher just writes something about 'A great idea' and 'Keep up the hard work.' We learned grammar through drills. I don't think the teachers know grammar anymore."

"I feel like we have Social Studies teachers rather than English teachers. The teachers seem to let the children do a lot of talking and writing about what they think is important in their lives. I feel like they are social workers rather than grammarians. English teachers should be teaching grammar. Our children need to know how to use correct English in their future jobs and for college. I think they will be at a serious disadvantage because all that happens in English is talk and more talk, writing and more writing, but the students aren't learning how to use the language."

On Writing

"My kids aren't learning how to write compositions anymore. They do all this journal writing that seems like flabby thinking, but they aren't learning to hone the skills of writing—

paragraphing, topic sentences, supporting details. They mostly write about themselves. I don't think the teachers really know how to teach writing the right way. They aren't college professors who have the right background, and I think they do more damage than good. My kids think writing means just blabbing anything on paper that they feel like saying."

"I've been glad that my child wrote in elementary school, but I wonder if that didn't damage the writing that should be done now that she is in seventh grade. She learned to just write her feelings but didn't do much with correcting the writing and that seems to be what she does now. Yes, her writing is improving in clarity and maybe structure, but there are still too many mistakes."

"I think the teachers are messing in areas where they don't have any business. The kids will learn to write in high school and college. Most of these teachers can't write themselves let alone teach writing."

Admittedly, I included quotes that would send a chill of response down your backbone. Many of the parents had positive things to say as well, but the discrepancy in how they interpreted what teachers were trying to do and how these teachers described their purposes and practices was definitely noticeable. These differences arise in part from the different perspectives from which parents and teachers look at the subject matter, the pedagogy, and the children. But I think teachers gain new insights when they hear how the parents perceive the work that is being done. I also believe it is important to educate parents to ensure that they understand that our knowledge of the discipline as well as our understanding of pedagogy keeps changing. As English teachers, we will not all agree on what or how to teach, but it is important for parents to understand that as knowledge develops, the classroom as they knew it will not be the same for their children. It seems ludicrous that parents don't understand this as a given, considering the importance of change in nearly everything else around us. But many don't, so we will need to bring them into the discussions and challenge their construction of the English classroom and the teacher's and students' work within it.

At the heart of how we see ourselves is how we believe our students see us. I interviewed elementary and secondary students about their experiences with literature, language, and writing. I've found a range of responses, but whatever the differences, from the sublime to the mundane, it is clear that teachers leave lasting impressions. Elementary students have diverse opinions. Jeffrey stated that his fifth grade teacher "is an alien because we read this

weird science fiction stuff that Mr. Brown is really psycho about."
Tanisha said her fourth grade teacher was "kind of fixed on writing.
We spend a lot of time writing and it gets boring. I don't always
know what to write about." Randall's sixth grade sensitivities were
apparent in his reaction: "My teacher's going to have a baby, and
she's sort of moody about it. She gets mad when we don't use our
reading time. I think she wants to be a mom and the teaching, well,
is something she has to do until the baby comes."

Of course, others praised their teachers. Julie, a fourth grader,
thinks her teacher is "cool because we get to work on our writing
every day. We get to write about the stuff that's important to us."
Boyd finds that his sixth grade teacher is "too focused on the spelling and if we punctuate, but we write stories and we get to choose
what we want to write about." I heard many times what Shawnie, a
fifth grader, said: "I like it when our teacher reads to us. Then, she
stops and we discuss the book. I love to hear the words out loud. I
understand a book better." Not much, however, about selfless, dedicated, and inspiring teachers as the mythographers would have it.

The results of Brian Austin-Ward's (1986) study, "English, English Teaching and English Teachers: The Perceptions of 16-Year-
Olds," is revealing. Although the study was conducted in England,
Scotland, and Wales, the general summary of responses from these
older adolescents sounds all too familiar:

> The majority of students were critical of the English they were
> taught at secondary school, and saw little purpose in much of
> what they had done. They felt teachers had either concentrated on
> a few aspects of the subject, or attempted to cover so many aspects
> that they were unable to see any "core" in the subject. Teachers
> were described as having contradictory and conflicting ap-
> proaches to English, particularly towards grammar, spelling, and
> 'correctness'. This seemed to lead in the minds of many students,
> to the strong conviction that English teachers were uncertain about
> their subject, and how to teach it (p. 39).

Elisa, a seventeen-year-old senior, told me that her English
teachers "seem to want us to feel like they do about their subject—
to get us to have a passion for the material. I appreciate the enthusiasm, but sometimes I think 'get a life.' It's pretty fuzzy, like there is
no defined subject in English." Lima, a sixteen-year-old junior, felt
he needed "more grammar and skills. I want college and my English
teacher mostly just gets us to write and write more, but I don't think
I'm learning anything from that." Becka, a senior, suggested that her
English class didn't have "a hard-core subject. I don't exactly see
what we are doing. We read a book and talk about it. We have this

independent reading thing. Then, there is the writing part where we work on a portfolio. I don't see how it all fits together." Ray, also a senior, felt much more positive: "I think in some of my English classes we've learned to have a conversation about literature. I find that I can have a conversation with my parents, especially after AP. My father is glad I'm learning something in school about literature. The family thinks it's important." Janelle believes that English teaching seems "like a fulfilling profession. I mean if what you wanna do is to be with people, and to have some effect on their lives, then that's what you're doing."

Generally, the students suggested that their English teachers offer conflicting messages. "One year it's grammar and punctuation and the next it's just write and don't worry about spelling or punctuation. It gets confusing," Stephanie complained at the end of her interview. Many expressed their general feelings of satisfaction but were concerned whether or not they were getting what they needed for the future. Oliver said, "I like to read and write. I just worry if I'm getting what I'll need later." Kerry urged that English teachers "figure out how to get more drama in. I love the drama and when we act out scenes." Some felt it just wasn't a practical subject. Erin expressed it in this way: "I don't know how all this reading and writing will help me in a job. I need to learn how to write business letters and work on a computer. This writing about my life won't help me there. Frankly, it gets a little boring."

It might be important for us to talk with our students about their impressions. I learned so much through the series of interviews and, of course, many of the students' comments made me wonder what my own students had taken away from English class. I think if I had it to do over again, I'd spend more time talking with students about the motivation behind assignments. I don't want them leaving with the attitudes about teachers that Brian Austin-Ward (1986) expresses near the end of his article:

> It is evident from the findings that the majority of students in the study were critical, to some degree, of the English teaching they had received in secondary school. The fault lay, in their eyes, with the teachers. A high standard of competence was expected and many students found this lacking.
>
> Among the most frequently mentioned criticisms of English teachers were: that they dominated lessons, imposed their views, did not appreciate how difficult English was, did not explain what was to be done, or how, or why (p. 41).

We have some work to do on reconstructing these portrayals of English teachers, possibly for ourselves as well as others. Views from the outside, painful at times and pleasurable at others, may illustrate how important it is for us as teachers to see how others perceive us. How will we counteract the images that we believe distort or falsify what we are trying to do? To compose our teaching lives, we must confront the predictable essentialism of others who believe they understand what our work should be. As Deborah Britzman (1991) suggests in her discussion on teacher identity, "Indeed, the significant, albeit hidden, work of learning to teach concerns negotiating with conflicting cultural representations of and desires for what a teacher is and does. One must ferret out how multiple interpretations of the meanings of social experience and classroom life structure one's thoughts about identity" (p. 56).

Images of Ourselves

What I'm suggesting by this near catalogue of images of teachers is that the portrayals need to be examined, whether from traditional literature, television, film, children's literature, music, or that of the students and parents with whom we are engaged in the educational enterprise. At times we can deflect what we perceive as hurtful images with the adage: "That's entertainment." After all, entertainment gets a laugh by playing on stereotypes rather than interrogating them. I am concerned that real teachers in real classrooms become implicated in the social construction of teachers through popularized portrayals. I would argue for an oppositional discourse that challenges these constructions of teachers and all that they imply. I'd suggest we analyze these images for ourselves and with our students. I taught many Dickens novels over my years in secondary schools. At the time, I didn't consider raising questions about his portrayal of teachers. What I did cover in lessons were the many other caricatures of lawyers, accountants, or convicts that Dickens created. The silence that resulted from not discussing the images of teachers may have communicated an important message. If I had this to do over again, I'd examine these portrayals and help students challenge the personal, historical, and social contingencies that affect their beliefs about teachers.

The problem of knowing ourselves as teachers goes beyond how we are constructed by others. How will we carve out the beliefs we hold about ourselves? How will we construct ourselves as more than the mirror images of others' expectations? That is, we may need to think beyond the pressures and constitute ourselves within the context of how we will work with students in classrooms. Much of the work I have done with prospective and in-service teachers draws on the dissonance within the self that underscores issues of conformity and vulnerability. Discovering tractable lessons from past experiences informs the present through a tangle of remembrances and possibilities. As one first-year teacher suggested, "I recognize how important it is for me to make sense of my past as a way of helping me cope with the present. One of the most important benefits is that I see myself in the process of becoming. I see that my inquiry needs to be continuous. Because I'm constantly changing, and each day in a classroom leads to new understandings, I can see myself thinking about what *could be* rather than *what is*." It is a long process and one that requires patience. Explicit inquiry into our experiences provides a distinct opportunity for the development of insights about teaching and can help us rethink our assumptions and beliefs. Such inquiry may contribute significantly to our developing knowledge about teaching.

Take, for example, the reflections of four first-year teachers who described what those first months of their first year were like. Avis, Stephen, Sarah, and Ben suggested that they had mostly decontextualized conceptions about teaching with the exception of their student teaching experiences. Even the student teaching, they suggested, was not the same as taking full responsibility for curriculum design, daily planning, and the structural and management issues in their classrooms. These first-year teachers assumed the classroom existed because there was a space that housed students, desks, books, curriculum guides, and a chalk board. They felt that their job was to walk through the door, into a room, and implement their plan for learning. What they discovered instead was that their teaching needed to socially organize the learning in the classroom within the context of the larger school environment.

Such a realization led Ben to state the limitations of his understanding "of the immense scope of teaching. I thought I knew how things would go together. I'd watched plenty of teachers and believed I had a good idea of what teachers do. I was successful in my student teaching. What I realize now is that even during that experience, much of the way the classroom operates was the result of all that the cooperating teacher had set into motion. Personally I'm overwhelmed emotionally and intellectually by the decisions and demands." Ben revealed in his reflections what Avis, Stephen, and Sarah said in other ways. They had taken their identity as teachers for granted, assuming they knew how they would act, respond, and teach. What they discovered were the multiple desires, demands, and interactions that they had to negotiate each day. Once they put their predetermined beliefs and plans into actual situations and interactions, they began to invent as well as question who they were becoming as teachers. But their first inventions were hesitant and faltering; their questions filled with an urgency for answers.

In September, the first-year teachers met to discuss their reactions to the first three weeks of school. They focused on how self-doubt and fear often motivated their teaching decisions. As Ben put it, "I resort to the time-honored, typical methods of dealing with students in classrooms. I find myself asking them to copy off the board just to keep them quiet. I know I said I'd never do that, but when you get in there and these are your kids and you're responsible for them, well, the fear that they'll get out of control settles in." Avis added that "I mostly focus on how I must look to students. I want to be the bearer of knowledge, to let them know that I have answers, and I didn't think I'd feel the need to do this. I know I said more than once in methods classes how comfortable I was with the idea of telling my students that I didn't have all the answers. But once I got into a classroom of my own it seemed dangerous." Stephen expressed his "feelings of inadequacy. It's like the knowledge I need is elusive. I'm in this holding pattern where I have students writing in journals and reading short stories, but I don't for the life of me know why." Sarah stated that she "explores different teaching techniques to see if they will 'work.' 'Work' for me right now means that the kids don't complain and are busy and orderly. 'Work' mostly means busy work—turning every activity in. I end up with too much grading, but I can't figure out how to motivate them."

Avis, Stephen, Sarah, and Ben were learning that they are social beings who construct their teaching identities through more than their own doings. They began to realize that their predetermined agendas dominated students' agendas, values, beliefs, and preferences. As Avis suggested, "I'm planning everything out—sort of lock step for now. I want every minute filled with my agenda. It's safe, but not realistic. I need to figure out how to work with the students rather than work upon them." Ben spoke of his hopes. "I haven't figured out exactly how to do things differently, but I'm already making slight adjustments. Little things about how to let kids know they are responsible for their learning. It's a beginning." All four of them described their continuing struggle to distinguish what they do from what they hope to do. Negotiating between the present and what was yet to come had ambiguous consequences. More pressures and tensions were added to what were already frustrating and uncertain opening days.

The inherent complexity of teaching, with all the influences that challenge our self-understanding, may also create the possibility of individual choice. But, as I have suggested throughout this chapter, we must challenge the visions of teaching that are potential sources for both truncating and enriching the work we do in classrooms.

A Framework for Understanding

It may be helpful to list a few principles that support the inquiry suggested above. Each offers a potential starting point for examining your teaching life.

Engage in Active Questioning and Reflection for Yourself and with Others

Throughout this chapter, I've presented specific examples of teachers' connecting their school histories to their present situations, but I'd like to suggest that making connections is a means rather than an end. One book that is particularly helpful in offering tools for an inquiry of this type is Connelly and Clandinin's (1988) *Teachers as Curriculum Planners: Narratives of Experience.* Although the authors admit that the process of coming to know ourselves as teachers is difficult, they believe that journal keeping, autobiographical accounts, imaging, document analysis, storytelling, letter writing, teacher-teacher conversations, and observing in someone else's classroom are methods to engage teachers in reflective inquiry. I'd recommend reading Chapters Four and Five particularly. Connelly and Clandinin caution that "tools, however, do not provide you with more than some data, some stories, parts of the whole. . . .We need a language that will permit us to talk about ourselves in situations and that will also let us tell stories of our experience. What language will let us do this? The language we, and others, have developed is a language close to experience, a language of affect, morality, and aesthetics. It is a language of images, personal philosophy, rules, practical principles, rhythms, metaphors, and narrative unity" (p. 59). The process of conscious reflection helps us understand how we develop as teachers.

A particularly resonant example of this was captured for me in a large, paisley print–covered stationary box in which Jennifer, a student teacher, stored her correspondence with her grandmother. One day when she came to meet with me she said, "You must let me read an excerpt from this letter. My grandmother, did I tell you that she's been teaching in a country school for forty years? I got this yesterday. I'd written to her about my student teaching experience and asked her some questions."

Dear Jennie -

One month now the dry farmland has been covered with snow and the winds are relentlessly harsh. The farmers tend just what they must and the rest, well...Things remain undone. It's the way of winter here. I was thinking about why I have lasted here. I could hear fear in your words. You won't fail unless you give up. Did I actually mean to stay here? To teach three generations of the Thomas and Swenson and Kelchner families? You asked me when I was certain I was making a difference and when I felt secure in what I was teaching. Did I actually give you such an impression? Here, the clapboard houses have been painted white with red trim for decades and while it may seem I'm planted in the certainty of this place, teaching is a grand adventure every year.

It is not easy to accept that we are constantly in the process of composing our lives. Yet, I found new energy from Jennifer's grandmother.

Read Other Teachers' Stories of Their Experiences

Hearing about other teachers' experiences can lead us to revisit our own and begin to see patterns in the dialogue created among multiple stories. Juxtaposing multiple stories is an inherent part of the process of conceptualizing what it is to be a teacher. I encourage teachers with whom I've worked to share their stories of teaching with others as well as to read autobiographical accounts—for example, Pat Conroy's *The Water Is Wide,* Mike Rose's *Lives on the Boundary,* Sylvia Ashton-Warner's *Teacher,* and others too numerous to mention. These stories of teaching offer examples of how professional knowledge develops and ways to examine our own teaching lives.

For example, during a year-long research study that I conducted, I asked three teachers who each had more than fifteen years of teaching experience to share some of their autobiographical accounts that might suggest how they had formed some of their beliefs about teaching literature. These three teachers—Joe, Jane, and Beth—learned from each other. For example, Beth tells her thoughts after reading several accounts of Joe's descriptions of the importance of literature in his home:

> Joe's dad's actor-wanna-be renditions reminded me that all my significant adults did that as they read aloud. They took different voices, different persona, sometimes even used props. Even my poor grandmother who had to sound out all the hard words in the newspaper would always put on an old, battered Walter Winchell hat to read the news and use Walter's radio voice—something about "all

the ships at sea." She could do what she thought Stella Dallas' voice would be like when she read the comics and her Li'l Abner was a scream. I hadn't thought of that until I read Joe's description. I love using those techniques in class, imagining how Mrs. Danvers would sound in DuMaurier's [1938] *Rebecca,* whining like Mrs. Van Daan in *Diary of Anne Frank* [1947/1952], or using Charly's bumbling monotone at the beginning and end of Keyes' [1966] *Flowers for Algernon.* I try to work students into doing this, and it is hard and embarrassing for so many of them. Part of what's come through so clearly here is that background may have something to do with that. If they don't have these experiences, and most don't today, I need to work more slowly in giving them those experiences. I need to talk over this idea of performing literature more with Joe. I hadn't realized the dimension it adds until I read his section on this. I've used some performances but with less dedication. I wonder, however, if perhaps we're partially talking about the same thing—ways of seeing meaning, relationship between self and a text—in this case through the hearing and the experiencing of the language.

The responses to one another's accounts were extensive, but I hope what Beth has to say illustrates how these teachers began finding explicit patterns in their own teaching as a result of examining other teachers' stories. A second example of this from the same study was Jane's reaction to Beth's description of her grandfather's coaching her in literature:

I was interested in Beth's appreciation of the questioning tactics of her grandfather. I want that in my classroom, too, because I think that it heightens student awareness, but I don't want to lose the genuine enthusiasm my kids have for reading. Somehow there is a difference in the way her grandfather questioned and the way my mother presented stuff. I think it may be that her grandfather, even when questioning, was sharing an enthusiasm for literature. Golly, I make Mom out to sound like a real tyrant, and it is just that she didn't know how to share it, and I think that is going to be an important thing for more teachers to think about.

I really did appreciate a comment Joe made. "And the teacher gets out of their way." It is a hard thing for some teachers to do. They see that as giving up control and, indeed, to some extent it is. But you have to trust what you have given to your students, and you have to trust the students too. I think that is important. Sometimes when you get out of the way they bounce off the walls, and you have to pull it back together, but more often they will come up with remarkable insights and create avenues for their own learning. When Beth tells how her students value her valuing of them, I thought about how I've had my much younger students say the same thing. Not so much about the literature but about the classroom atmosphere. Students of all ages like to know that their opinions are valued. Joe speaks to the humane classroom. What in our background gave this to us? I think that those people from our past gave it to us, and we are passing it on.

Joe adds reflections to these same stories:

It's ironic how people our age seem to be grounded in the classics, sometimes pictorial or comic book renditions, but nonetheless have had some exposure to them. We look at the students that we have and many of them have film experiences with these stories, but they haven't heard the language in the same way that reading or telling stories can bring language to us. I was struck that all of us had these very different but certainly common experiences. I felt I knew the worlds of literature in Beth's and Jane's experiences because they were similar to my own. I'm not certain that I'd feel comfortable in the world of literature that would be the stories my students would tell. I made a vow as I read this, and I am going to find out what their stories are. I want to know where they are coming from. I hadn't thought about that until I read through Beth's and Jane's stories. If I had the knowledge of my students that I have of them, I could be a better teacher of literature.

Juxtaposing histories or providing counter histories for examination may have promise to help us uncover meanings behind our practices or to expand our repertoire of practices.

Understand How School Culture Shapes Teachers and Students

It is important to consider how school culture composes us as *students,* focusing on development of skills, transference of content, promotion of competition, and dissemination of valued discourse and convention. School culture too often values teachers who are dispensers of knowledge and consumers of methods. The taken-for-granted ways we have learned to live in schools as students and teachers have been called into question by many English educators during the past thirty years (see Britton, 1987; Mayher, 1990; and Elbow, 1990, particularly). Teachers who inquire into the culture of schools recognize how classroom culture develops. One way of seeing the school culture is through *symbolic interactionism,* the belief that there is meaning associated with objects. As we construct meaning from our experiences in school, objects such as a chalkboard, grade book, or report card or arrangement of classrooms take on symbolic meaning that can be referents of power, class, ability, or conformity. The interaction of such symbols builds an understanding, a conceptualization of what school is for individuals and how they perceive their particularized role within the culture. Interrogations of school culture can lead us to a better understanding of the inequalities in power and knowledge that classrooms reproduce. Peter Woods' (1983) discussion of interactionist work in education draws attention to the inequalities "acted out in everyday life, how they are imprinted on the minds and personalities of pupils and shape their thoughts, values, and attitudes, how they form moral imperatives for action" (p. 177). He emphasizes how teachers' perspectives and frameworks define their beliefs about teaching and recommends that teachers need to make their processes of inquiry conscious and constantly interrogate the culture of classrooms.

As first-year teachers, Avis, Stephen, Sarah, and Ben struggled to conceptualize expanded roles of teachers in classrooms. These first-year teachers' descriptions of their experiences could be likened to a staged performance enacted before spectators (students, teachers, parents, administrators) who expected them to follow certain rituals and talk in particular ways about their teaching. Avis described some initial advice she received:

> I was told before the school year started to show the students that I was in charge. The advice ranged from 'don't smile 'till after Christmas' to telling me I needed as a first year teacher to give homework every day. I received advice about grading, dealing with tardies and absences, and keeping distance from students' personal lives and concerns.

As these first-year teachers began to critique the grandiloquence of schools and their resistance to replicating the rituals within, they began to probe beyond day-to-day events and their reactions to each experience. They became more proactive and began to ask questions about how pedagogy rather than activities guides curriculum. They were moving beyond a monologic view of teaching and were standing on the threshold of a more dialectic one.

Develop a Language of Reflective Inquiry

Language shapes as well as reflects our thinking, as Vygotsky (1986) theorizes in *Thought and Language.* He suggests that tentative or spontaneous conceptualizations can be reflected on consciously, leading to refined thinking wherein words mediate thought into concepts. Vygotsky stresses that words are functional tools and that "learning to direct one's own mental processes with the aid of words or signs is an integral part of the process of concept formation" (p. 108). Language may provoke us to shape or pursue ideas.

I became interested in the language of inquiry as I began to transcribe audiotaped interviews and conversations with Beth, Jane, and Joe, the experienced teachers who participated in a year-long study on their reflective inquiry. Trying to fit the language of their inquiry into compartments that distort is not my intent, but I found the patterns intriguing. I'm not certain what these patterns mean and my understanding of them is partial and tentative. But, they offer a way of inquiring that may have some power.

Beth, Jane, and Joe's inquiry was often *retrospective,* thinking back and recollecting. Each of their transcripts, which included 80 to 130 pages, contained a good deal of retrospective language as demonstrated in the following quote from Beth's transcript: "The Murphy bed fit in the closet, and I would climb up on the top to read. It was quiet there." *Retrospection* was the preferred mode of the narrative, the stories of their experiences. Retrospection frequently turned to *introspection* as Beth, Jane, and Joe looked inward and thought through the meaning of their stories. For example, Beth interrupts a story of her grandfather's early evening reading sessions to describe how he would "stop to talk through or question what I thought was going on." She goes on to say, "Something strikes me now that I think of it." Beth stopped the story to consider how critical questioning supports literature study. Beth continued by adding, "In teaching we don't often enough give those signals that we really care about students' opinions. I mean, my grandfather cared. I learned from him to care about literature. He was a model." This leads Beth into a further *retrospective* account of a particular group of students she had taught several years before: "That reminds me of the dreaded seventh period with Jed Lynch, Randy Rainey. One afternoon they...."

A third pattern can be labeled *prospective* as Beth, Joe, and Jane look toward the future. As Beth finishes the story of the "dreaded seventh period class," she ends that particular sequence by suggesting, "My intent is to let them know I really care and maybe I don't make that explicit enough. *What if* I were to find ways of doing that? I suppose *if I* spent effort finding ways to show I'm really listening and not tell them so often that I'm listening." Beth has moved, with the use of *what if* and *if I* from the *retrospective* through *introspective* to *prospective.*

The following excerpt from Joe's transcript demonstrates the pattern that can be generalized from these teachers' language of inquiry. Joe tells about a particular classroom incident when he was a sixth grader:

> I nearly swallowed my own throat when she called on me. I didn't know what I was supposed to know. Sister Ann Marie stared straight at me, and I felt my skin turning hot. She continued staring and mumbled something about supposing I hadn't read the chapter. As she walked away Bud Reynolds winked that knowing wink that really said, "Oh, who cares what the old bat thinks?" (*retrospective*)

Actually as I think about that now, it makes me mad. Who has the right to treat students like that? It's de-humanizing. Now, I try hard to create a place where students feel free to express opinions or say, "I don't know" or where they can ask their own questions. That's hard to do sometimes. They are suspicious after so many years of being rewarded for being lifeless primates. (*introspective*)

I wonder if it is possible to get that trust earlier? It generally takes me most of the year. (*beginning of prospective*)

I'm thinking if I start with a very intense training session—like the first week or two where I'll work on that pretty much exclusively. (*prospective*)

There is transitional language that represents the bridging of the retrospective, introspective, and prospective. It functions transitionally to generate or elaborate on ideas, but I believe the language itself provokes the shifts among the three. For example, *what if* or *if I* generally indicates a shift to Beth, Jane, or Joe thinking about the possibilities of what they could do in the future. Moving back to retrospection is often provoked by phrases such as *I remember* or any of the *once upon a time* phrases. Introspection is often provoked through phrases similar to *I wonder; It strikes me now; I was thinking.* Understanding Vygotsky's theories may be helpful here. If language shapes thought, then it would seem possible that we can try out frames of language that may guide our thinking or our inquiry.

I have generalized rather complex thinking patterns into a skeletal outline that demonstrates the *generating language* of reflective inquiry. The detailing of this pattern is not intended to capture rules. From these limited cases, it appears that reflective inquiry opens a space where the tension among *what was* (retrospective), the meaning *of was* (introspective), and *what can be* (prospective) is negotiated. In Bakhtin's (1981) conception of language utterances, tension occurs at "a point where centrifugal as well as centripetal forces are brought to bear. The processes of centralization and decentralization, of unification and disunification, intersect" (p. 272). I find that Bakhtin's theory helps explain this pattern of reflective inquiry wherein past, present, and future pull in one direction to meet a counter force that struggles against it to construct new dilemmas and new meaning. The patterns of thinking that are suggested in the language of reflective inquiry may suggest that we can engage in strategic rehearsals of meaning. Possibly what has been suggested in the educational literature about teachers or students in education telling their stories could be enhanced by careful consideration of the language that accompanies such telling.

Perhaps inevitably, we teachers confront multiple and contradictory beliefs about the purposes, curriculum, and pedagogy in our teaching. As I've talked with other teachers around the country, many expressed feelings of confusion with the competing versions of what should be taught and how to teach it. How classroom communities are defined, how they operate, and the explicit and implicit messages that grow out of the work that goes on there may need careful interrogation. Our past experiences influence our present readings of classrooms. Bloland (1983) reveals in her study of four high school English teachers that teacher choice rests "on deeply cherished beliefs and constructs about language and learning" (p. 264), which she defines as "the inner curriculum—what teachers think they ought to be doing" (p. 268). We may be constrained and emancipated by our past experiences as well as challenged by the possibility of moving beyond them.

For the moment, I'll conclude this idea by suggesting that we can investigate what it means to teach and examine the complexities of making choices in content and practice, often within competing and contradictory intentions and means by considering the "texts" of our own lives. For example, studying an incident that took place in my first year of teaching offers a vehicle for recognizing, reconceptualizing, and reexamining my beliefs and practices.

I recall during my first year of teaching a particular moment when the phone rang and Marlene's mother asked me if I'd lost my mind. Teaching *Lord of the Flies* to her daughter was committing myself to do the devil's work. Of course my heart beat in my throat as she raged on. "About tomorrow," she went on, "just tell the kids it was a mistake and have them read Shakespeare or something."

"I'm not sure," I said. As a first year teacher, I'd moved giddily along through the maze of lesson plans on *Lord of the Flies* and what I thought were great discussions about personal freedom, individual responsibility, human nature, and group dynamics. Marlene's mother shared her concerns: "Isn't it destructive to present adolescents with examples of evil? Wasn't Golding an instrument of the devil's work? Wasn't I, after all, only twenty years old?"

I mumbled something about my dismay, about *Lord of the Flies* being on recommended reading lists, and about how the students, including Marlene, seemed to like reading it. That only seemed to get her more riled up: "Whose keeper are you anyway? Don't you work for the parents in this community? Don't we pay you to do what we want?" She gave me a good talking to, and I didn't know of any alternative but to listen. She concluded by suggesting that it would be right and proper to stop teaching that book—to tell the kids that I was wrong in assigning it and that in the name of an ostensibly better future for all of them we'd read, well, something else. Passionately, on the side of right and the moral lives of adolescents, she kept talking, taking her shots at my inexperience, values, and liberal political agenda.

Finally, I asked her to tell me what exactly she objected to in *Lord of the Flies,* besides that I had chosen it and that it was an instrument of the devil. "Exactly what events or characters or issues in the novel seem so troublesome to you?" Silence. "Well I haven't exactly read it." My response, "What does 'haven't exactly' mean? Have you read it or not?" Her voice was barely audible. "I browsed Marlene's copy and that was enough for me."

I said, "Why don't you call me after you read the book and tell me just what in the novel bothers you. Get back to me. Until then, we'll keep reading." I put the receiver in the cradle, feeling proud and clever that I'd had the last word, at least for the moment. For days I expected a note from the principal, Marlene's mother, or, worse yet, a visit from Marlene's mother with a group of other mothers she'd solicited to persuade me back to the right path. But, I didn't hear from Marlene's mother again that year. Marlene sat in class each day as we lumbered through the remaining four chapters of *Lord of The Flies.* She was a dutiful student. She drew a map of the island, wrote character sketches, found passages that were examples of vivid imagery and discussed how savagery can overcome civilization. She must have noticed that I was feeling smug and successful. I know it showed. I wonder how my choice affected Marlene's construction of teachers. I don't think I'd learned how to negotiate effectively. I still don't know at this point whether or not someone could have persuaded me to quit teaching *Lord of The Flies* or if there would ever be a reason that I would do so. What I do know is that I was more interested in pursuing my agenda than in learning the art of negotiation.

Notes

1. Names of the four first-year teachers, students, other teachers, and administrators are pseudonyms.
2. Because of the complexity of indicating the sources for quotes (ie. group meetings, teaching logs, interviews, or classroom discussion), I have embedded quotations from the spoken material into the text and indented written material and narrative reconstructions of classroom sessions from fieldnotes and transcripts.

Chapter Two

The Predicaments
of Learning to Teach

In the summer of 1966, while educators from the United Kingdom and United States met at Dartmouth for the First International Conference on the Teaching of English, I signed a contract to teach high school. I hadn't heard of the "personal growth model" that John Dixon (1967) presented as the pedagogical position of the UK participants who attended. Drawing heavily on the work of the UK's James Britton and Douglas Barnes, the growth model encouraged teachers to shift their attention away from literary criticism and focus concern on the development of readerly pleasure and meaning-making. Instead, I was one of many soon-to-be first-year English teachers steeped in the "cultural heritage model" in which canonical texts and literary criticism subsumed any personal connections I'd made with literature. That summer I read and re-read piles of literary criticism for every book that was on the list of required reading for the sophomore and senior courses that I would teach in the fall.

In the summer of 1966, without knowing it at the time, I stood at a meeting place of ideas—a site where British and American educators exchanged theoretical and pedagogical positions, a place where my experience as a student informed who I would become as a teacher, and a moment when my love of literature vied for position with my beliefs about how I should teach literature to high school students. Because of the importance of these meetings to my future teaching life, I sometimes engage in a metaphorical imagining that goes like this: At the precise moment when D. W. Harding (1977) told those gathered at Dartmouth that, "It is literature, not literary criticism, that is the subject" (p. 379), I was writing a lecture filled with explanations from the critics on just how in the world to make sense of Gabriel Conroy's commitment to galoshes in James Joyce's "The Dead." When Harding warned the conference participants that "many students arrive at and leave universities with an unprofitable distrust of their personal response to literature" (p. 392), I was compiling a list of critics' responses to Henry James' *Turn of the Screw* to share with my students. These two very different ways of thinking about literature teaching remind me how much I've learned in subsequent years through teaching, collaborating, reading, and writing. Little did I know in 1966 that the ideas about teaching and learning presented at Dartmouth would become central to my beliefs about the purposes of and practices in literature education.

As I study the evolution of my teaching history, I recognize how twenty-nine years and 4,195 students later I've come to trust the constant state of becoming. I understand that neither Dartmouth nor any single incident or belief shaped my life as a teacher. As I suggested in Chapter One, autobiographical and reflective inquiry are meant to further teachers' understandings about their beliefs and practices. Just as surely, such inquiry has additional value as a means for teachers to situate their predicaments of teaching in the setting of the schools and classrooms in which they work. In doing so, they are in a position to examine how knowledge about teaching is acquired and developed in its contextual fullness. Documentation of such inquiry becomes a way for teachers and researchers to examine the processes and substance of teachers' critical questions and issues as they begin teaching.

In this chapter, then, I describe and analyze what I learned from two groups of English teachers who allowed me to document their inquiry as they were learning to teach. The first group of first-year teachers—Avis, Stephen, Sarah, and Ben—offer insights about the types of adjustments they made as they began their work in schools and what they learned from this initial year. The second group of four student teachers—Beverly, Jennifer, John, and Regina—found competing demands for time, values, and authority that provoked tensions and created dilemmas and uncertainty. For both groups of beginning teachers, forming an identity as teacher meant coming to terms with the self in the context of the schools and with the people therein.

During two separate academic years, these teachers were in certification programs in which I taught. As the teachers are introduced in subsequent sections, I will provide background information on each person. One point is worthy of particular note for both sets of teachers. The programs in which they were enrolled incorporated curriculum that emphasizes the examination of "education-related life histories" (Goodson, 1991; Vinz, 1993) including images of teachers as described in Chapter One. Such examination was a tool we used in these programs to encourage prospective students to illustrate and analyze how their experiences inform their beliefs about teachers and schools as well as to encourage habits of reflection.

As Dona Kagan (1992) pointed out in her study of beginning teachers, "One finds no systematic efforts to encourage novices to make their personal beliefs and images explicit; . . . or to reconstruct the image of self-as-teacher" (p. 150). These first-year and student teachers were challenged to confront their conceptions of teachers, teaching, schools, curriculum, and pedagogy in systematic ways throughout their preparation programs. All of these teachers illuminate what informs and shapes their beliefs and role conceptions as well as how entering the school culture introduces anticipated dilemmas.

Mediating Knowledge, Power, and Authority: The First-Year Experience

How would Avis, Stephen, Sarah, and Ben cope with what had the potential of being a disarticulation between what they learned through their preparation program and what they might find is expected of them by administrators, other teachers, parents, and students? How would these first-year teachers who read Jimmy Britton, John Dewey, Paulo Freire, John Mayher, and John Willinsky in their teacher education courses come to terms with the official curriculum and teaching practices in the schools where they would teach? After all, these authors present compelling critiques of teacher-centered and presentational instruction and propose various alternatives in their stead. Mostly, I wondered how they would make sense of teaching as they began to teach and how they would come to question and understand their own processes of learning to teach.

So it was with an intent to illuminate how Avis Johnston, Stephen Lyon, Sarah Martin, and Ben Silverman[1] framed and interpreted their daily concerns that we designed a research agenda and data collection procedures. Since my aim was not to direct their collaborations or inquiries, we agreed: I would have access to their teaching logs, attend group meetings, observe in their classrooms four times during the year, and conduct individual interviews after each observation. I collected their logs after each group meeting and made photocopies of each entry as well as audiotaped and transcribed group meetings, individual interviews, and classroom sessions. Taken together, these sources of data provided me with several key pieces of information: (1) the themes of their inquiry; (2) analysis of changing beliefs and concerns about teaching during the first year; and (3) conceptions of curriculum and how they were enacted in their daily practices. I undertook analysis inductively following a method that allowed me to compare across types of data: (1) textual analysis to clarify themes and patterns grounded in the data as they were being collected (Miles and Huberman, 1994; Strauss, 1987); (2) analysis of developmental and contextual aspects of beliefs and concerns throughout the year (Vondracek, 1990); and (3) analytical categories across types of data to determine points of congruence and incongruence among group discussions, individual logs, and actual classroom practices (Brewer and Hunter, 1989; Denzin, 1967).

Background Information on the First-Year Teachers

Avis, Stephen, Sarah, and Ben developed a friendship as a result of their work together in a four-year undergraduate teacher education program. In that program they took three courses that focused on teaching literature. They examined literature education through the various perspectives of Rosenblatt (1978), Bleich (1978), Eagleton (1983), Probst (1988), Corcoran and Evans (1987), and Atwell (1987). Ben described the format of the courses: "We read some literature that we might be teaching. We kept reading journals, practiced conferencing with each other, led discussions, and designed activities that would encourage kids to get involved in the reading, and considered the aims and purposes of a literature curriculum."[2] Their content literature classes included survey courses in American, British, and World literature as well as several upper division courses that specialized in periods, themes, or genre approaches. Stephen indicated that "the person in front of the room did most of the talking and questioning. A few students would get into it and everybody else would take a rest." Stephen's comments reminded Avis that there was a noticeable "discrepancy between what the English department was doing when they taught literature, and what the methods professors advocated and modeled for secondary school teachers. I didn't realize until I had methods that there were alternative ways to teach."

These prospective teachers participated in two semesters of writing workshops. They read Kirby, Liner, and Vinz (1988), Romano (1987), Murray (1985), Stillman (1984), and Mayher, Lester, and Pradl (1983). Sarah described the workshops as "a place where I actually wrote about my life. I learned about the recursive process of drafting, revising, thinking, drafting, revising, celebrating. I learned to trust myself as a writer." Additionally, they had a course in grammar for teachers. As Avis suggested, "I began to see that it isn't naming parts of speech or doing workbook exercises that count. What happened in this course is that we discovered how to use and develop our knowledge of language to serve us in writing. This was a model for our classrooms." They chose four additional methods courses from a list of offerings that provided more in-depth study of literature, writing, integrated approaches, or linguistics.

At the time of this study, the four teachers were in their early to mid-twenties. In their first group meeting, each described some background information about themselves. Avis began by explaining that she "always wanted to be a teacher. I lined up my little sisters in a row to teach them the alphabet and read to them. My favorite Christmas present was one of those little blackboards that you can roll around. My sisters were in for it then. I had them all reading before kindergarten." Avis' family were owners of a gas station and convenience store. "We didn't have much money, but everyone worked hard and by high school I worked thirty hours a week in the store. I learned to use every minute of my time. I was basically a non-person in school because I didn't have time for extracurricular activities, and at lunch time I'd go to the library to get homework done."

Stephen described the one-room schoolhouse where he attended grades 1 through 6. "It was limited in the subjects we studied because of the number of demands on Mrs. Anderson's time. She helped each grade level individually with the work she'd decided we should learn. The almost necessary result of this structure was that the three or four of us who were in the same grade worked together as we prepared assignments or, as we got to the upper grades, we helped Mrs. Anderson get around to the younger students. Perhaps my first impression of school was that everybody in the room had something to teach and to learn, but the socializing that went on centered on the learning rather than on what would happen after school. Most of us went home to chores after a bus ride of more than an hour or two."

Sarah's parents were both teachers. "Stories of students, of the principal, or of how the year was going provided dinner table conversation. It's almost like I didn't know there were other things that parents talked about. Of course, they took an interest in what we were doing. They'd interrogate each of us, their five children, in turn from youngest to oldest about assignments, grades, how we were feeling about school. They had a great passion for teaching, and somehow I associated my learning life with their love of learning and teaching. I've always felt their presence around me when I'm in school. They died in a bus accident when I was in high school while they were chaperoning the basketball team on an out-of-town trip. Somehow it seemed important to keep their love of teaching alive."

Ben lived in "a typically middle-class suburb. My mother stayed home and my father worked in an advertising agency. My father read constantly and fancied that someday he'd write a great novel. I think he got me hooked on literature, and it seemed natural to go into teaching. I loved English classes, tearing apart literature, and writing some of my own stuff." Ben suggested that he was "mostly detached from school subjects. I was social. I loved sports, but I loved books. I think I'd be a gym teacher if I hadn't torn my knee apart. I still like the idea of coaching, but I have to do it from the sidelines. I can't model. Somehow I always wanted to teach and this just sort of happened."

Avis accepted a teaching position in a small rural high school approximately thirty miles from a population center. The school has ninety students with seven teachers. Avis teaches all ninth- through twelfth-grade English classes as well as two social studies classes. "I find myself getting frustrated with just keeping the material straight. I resort to rest days where students have time to read, or I give them busy work. I need to catch my breath before I can catch my thoughts. I'm constantly behind in reading, preparing, and grading. I just can't get ahead. It's a day by day affair." Several times throughout the first group meeting Avis mentioned how guilty she felt about her strategies for self-preservation. "I feel like we waste time, but then, Stephen has helped me remember that I'm so time driven. I think back about how much pressure there was on me from my parents."

Stephen teaches eleventh-grade English classes in a suburban high school with approximately 1,500 students. "Yuppie city. Most of the kids have cars, leather bomber jackets, and belong to workout gyms. In my building all eleventh graders take American literature. We have an anthology, a few novels, and a curriculum guide that sets everything up chronologically. Just follow the book. I'm trying to figure out what the other teachers are doing, but everybody's too busy to give much help or advice. I'm beginning to suspect they don't want to." Stephen indicated that teaching the same class five times each day "gets old unless I find different ways of getting at the same issues. Of course, the kids are different and their discussions take different twists, but it's still the same. I get behind on grading and lesson preparation. It's still tiring and overwhelming." Avis told him that she "could use a little sameness for my sanity." But, as Stephen reminded her, "One of the main frustrations is the students' resistance to a new way of thinking about classrooms because they are so middle class and are comfortable being mall rats." Stephen, who lived in rural farm country, believed "these students don't know much about work. I had to find moments, nearly sneak minutes between chores, for reading. These kids have the time but no motivation to read."

Sarah signed a contract to teach in a middle school of 300 students in the same district where Stephen teaches. "I have a team partner who teaches American History, and I teach American literature. We work together some, but there isn't time to really talk about what each of us does. It's mostly like we are covering the same period of time, so I move chronologically through the book because that's the way it's been done. There's no passion." Sarah described her own feelings about learning: "Now for me, I got so involved in reading as a kid, even what I was required to read for school. Here, there's no passion, not with kids or teachers that I can see. Being new here, I can't say too much yet." Sarah found it difficult to ignore this lack of passion, likening it to "apathy for everything. I think it's laziness really and an unwillingness to get involved."

Ben teaches ninth and tenth graders in a small four-year high school in a "ranch and farming community. Most people have lived here for generations, but Chicano families come in for temporary work in the fields or orchards. The kids pretty much expect to stay here except the migrants. Those who have grown up here aren't ambitious to leave or go to college. They're satisfied to coast along and see what happens." Ben found that his two preparations keep him busy. He coaches girls' basketball and boys' track. "I never get home before 7:00 p.m. Then I think about what I'll do tomorrow. I need to get ahead of tomorrow, but right now I feel like I'll never catch up." Stephen asked about whether the Chicano influence is of major importance in the school community. Ben responded, "I don't even know yet. I'm just starting to figure things out, and I don't have time to talk to the other teachers. I know they are busy, but unless they need something or have a complaint, they seem to ignore my presence." Sarah added, "I feel like an outsider in this place where I'm supposed to become a professional." Ben expressed his feelings of isolation and suggested that even his students like to keep their thoughts to themselves. "In my family, we shared everything. I remember my dad stopping to share a paragraph from a book he was reading. At times I get so excited I want to share with students or faculty. No way. I know there isn't a conspiracy against me, but I feel so alone."

Avis, Stephen, Sarah, and Ben's teaching jobs were in various communities adjacent to the university where they received their degrees. This made it possible for them to meet bi-monthly. During those meetings, they shared artifacts from their classrooms (lesson plans, tests, unit plans, student products, activities, curriculum guides), talked about the day-to-day events of teaching, and raised broader issues and questions about their developing knowledge and beliefs. Clearly, it is impossible to recreate their first year of teaching or their shared inquiry in all its richness and variety. One artifact of that year can be represented through the nearly 1,000 pages of teaching logs and 300 pages of transcribed interviews, class sessions, and group conversations that are stacked by my desk. Another way of representing that year is through the tentative yet rich themes of their inquiry as well as the classroom episodes that demonstrate how their knowledge is tested and used. What became obvious was how active, value-laden, demanding, and complex were Avis, Stephen, Sarah, and Ben's first steps through the threshold of the door that led into the classrooms where they were becoming teachers.

Roots of Anxiety: From Beliefs to Decision Making

As they began planning during the summer, the school year spread before them like a chasm. There were decisions to be made: the content and strategies that would be taught, the structural and instructional events that would support this teaching, and the evaluation procedures that would be put in place. As Avis lamented, "Now that I have all this time and freedom I'm not sure what to do. It scares me to death. What if I blow it?" These teachers described in detail what English teachers face anew each fall, whether in their first or their thirtieth year—new faces, a new bulletin board, clean chalk boards and erasers, occasionally new books, and always the hope that it will be a productive year.

Ben, Avis, Sarah, and Stephen decided to work on their initial planning together and invited me to join them. As Avis said early in the summer, "In student teaching I could plan for a lesson or unit, for a day or a few weeks. Now I look at all this time spread out before me and I'm not sure what to do with all of it." Making concrete what they believed became difficult. They discussed how they wanted their classrooms to be different and what structures or practices supported that. Stephen lamented several times, "There aren't any guides for the type of program I want. I'm not certain of the components that I need. I can only think of read, discuss, and test. I can't think of workshop approaches. I can't imagine how to combine all this." Often they diverted attention from overall planning to discussions of activities or what activities they might use for certain texts. They began to see this pattern as a way of avoiding what they didn't feel capable of resolving, but felt they made the most progress on planning the year when they dealt with the concrete activities.

The freedom was exciting and frightening. With their district curriculum guides, required reading lists, methods texts, literature selections and anthologies, and materials from student teaching piled high around them, they began a four-day marathon planning session in late June. For these first-year teachers, two issues received central focus: (1) issues of content and sequence (what to teach and when to teach it) and (2) issues of structure and instruction (organization of classroom in time blocks, considerations of teacher and student roles, and determination of activities or experiences that best support the objectives in content and sequence).

One example where their deliberations were clearly delineated was in their discussions of the literature curriculum for their English classes. Each was given a reading list that represented the required content in the literature facet of their programs. This sparked an analysis of the continuities and discontinuities between the authorized versions of curriculum and pedagogy and their developing beliefs. As Ben's department chair told him, "This is about all the reading you'll get done. There is little need to supplement." Sarah and Stephen confirmed this attitude from their department chairs as well. As Sarah's chair indicated, "It's best not to get involved with reading that hasn't been approved. We have censorship issues here. Talk to one of the old timers and they can give you a feeling for this community. It isn't worth challenging that." Avis, the only English teacher in her school, learned from her Assistant Principal, a math teacher, what books were required. They shared their lists with one another:

Avis

9th Grade
The Catcher in the Rye
Flowers for Algernon
Romeo and Juliet
The Old Man and the Sea
Of Mice and Men
Antigone
A Tale of Two Cities
Poe: Eighteen Stories
Myth and Meaning
Animal Farm
The Contender

10th Grade
The Lord of the Flies
Demian
Nectar in a Sieve
Across Five Aprils
The Crucible
Ethan Frome
Our Town
Frankenstein
Short Story Collection
Macbeth
David Copperfield
Oedipus Rex
A Separate Peace

11th Grade
The Odyssey
The Adventures of
   Huckleberry Finn
The Taming of the Shrew
The Glass Menagerie
As I Lay Dying
Billy Budd
Sister Carrie
Death of a Salesman
Cry, the Beloved Country
Secret Sharer
The Tempest
The Grapes of Wrath
Siddhartha
The Cherry Orchard

12th Grade
Black Boy
The Turn of the Screw
A Farewell to Arms
Giants in the Earth
The Great Gatsby
House of Seven Gables
My Antonia
Hamlet
Great Expectations
Richard III
Mayor of Casterbridge
No Exit
Tennessee Williams Plays
1984
Beowulf

Stephen

11th Grade
The Grapes of Wrath
A Farewell to Arms
The Autobiography
   of Miss Jane Pitman
Native Son
Ethan Frome
The Night Thoreau Spent in Jail
The Glass Menagerie
Adventures in American
   Literature (anthology)

The Great Gatsby
Walden
The Adventures of
   Huckleberry Finn
Death of A Salesman
Giants in the Earth
A Separate Peace
MacBeth

Sarah

8th Grade

The Crucible

The Catcher in the Rye

Flowers for Algernon

Of Mice and Men

Hiroshima

True Grit

West Side Story

The Red Badge of Courage

Poe: Great Tales and Poems

Tom Sawyer

Main Street

Babylon Revisited

Pigman

The Old Man and the Sea

Ben

9th Grade

Animal Farm

The Diary of Anne Frank

The Old Man and the Sea

Romeo and Juliet

David Copperfield

The Lord of the Flies

The Witch of Blackbird Pond

Raisin in the Sun

Our Town

High Wind to Jamaica

Mutiny on the Bounty

Flowers for Algernon

10th Grade

Night

The Red Badge of Courage

All My Sons

Julius Caesar

A Separate Peace

Antigone

The Hobbit

Across Five Aprils

View from the Bridge

Hiroshima

Something Wicked This Way
    Comes

The Glass Menagerie

The Adventures of
    Huckleberry Finn

I Know Why the Caged Bird
    Sings

The Grapes of Wrath

A Farewell to Arms

Many questions come to mind: Why is content (the emphasis on text) the central consideration in some literature curriculums? What assumptions about learning literature are posited by such a long and often internally unrelated list of texts? What principle is operating in lists that get longer as the students get older? How can any teacher (Avis' situation particularly) plan to teach over fifty literary selections in any school year? What assumptions underlie the practice of selecting literature prior to knowing the students who will read it? And finally: Who decides what literature to include and exclude on required lists? There were no final answers to these questions, but there was lively expression of opinion and a thoughtful discussion about various ways to incorporate the required lists into curriculum planning.

Avis, Stephen, Sarah, and Ben began this facet of their inquiry by describing their initial reactions to required lists. Avis indicated that she was "overwhelmed, so last summer I just started thinking about what I'd wanted students to get out of any of the reading they might do." Avis hoped her students would learn to "question what they read. I think my planning involved something going on behind any piece of literature. I wanted them to develop strategies for reading." Avis described how she made a list of possible strategies that would encourage questioning: "I decided they'd keep double-entry logs that they would share with a partner and the job would be for each pair to come up with questions from the reading. I also decided I'd focus on how literature reflects who we are as human beings. Then I just went back and chose one of the books for each class to get started. I didn't see any order or particular way of ordering the books, so I started with the ones I knew and liked."

Stephen saw his task as trying to figure out how to organize the texts. "I knew I could figure out either a chronological or thematic approach. I started with that. I did make a chart of the possible reading strategies that I might emphasize—mostly rereading, finding key ideas, and helping students get interested in what they read. I also thought about how to tie each piece to the American History class because that is the basic idea behind what goes on in the school. In some ways the lists made it easy in my situation because I decided to have groups cover particular topics and time periods. I think of all the literature that could be used to teach certain issues or values in the United States, and the list I was given, well, some are better than others. I wonder why these were the ones chosen. Would they be my choices if I could have a dream list and select? Probably not. The big thing was to figure how to structure all this. I worked on that the most."

Sarah expressed her belief in the need "to help students focus on certain parts of the text or to make personal connections with what they read. I spent the summer trying to figure out how to structure discussions that would help students do that. When I was given the list, my heart sort of fell into my shoes. Some of the pieces I like, and others don't do anything for me. I wondered how something like *The Red Badge of Courage* or what I feel is racist in *Tom Sawyer* would sit with my kids. It's scary to teach books you don't understand or believe in. Partly to compensate, I decided that a thematic approach to issues in American life might work. I figured I could supplement with photocopied pieces. I can play some themes off the major works to keep the kids interested. I did worry about how to structure and conduct discussions on books that I don't necessarily love. Somehow I was disheartened with the lack of choice, but I rationalized by thinking that it's just me or just the way it is in school."

Ben raised the question of whether or not all students need to "read all of this literature. I was thinking about the idea of individual preference. Some of the pieces on my required list are great for me, and I've grown to love others. Some are still beyond me, not interesting or maybe I can't make sense of them or don't want to. I want my students to enjoy literature. That's the bottom line, so I tried to think about how to make these pieces enjoyable. I must admit that I started out thinking about what activities might be fun, hoping my students would get into the reading in this way. I don't think all literature applies to their lives, but I'm trying to think of ways that may help them latch onto ideas or find personal meaning in what they read. I'd like to balance shared and independent reading."

As their reflections indicate, Avis, Stephen, Sarah, and Ben created a balance between teaching the required literary texts and determining how to help students engage with the literature. In addition, they consistently focused on ways to structure the required readings and still meet the multiple goals of their intended curriculum. In spite of initial frustrations with not having more choice in the literature for their classrooms, these teachers recognized that they could integrate their purposes and the requirements. Such knowledge gave them a new sense of power. Sarah reported realizing that "mostly I am in control of what I do. Sometimes it's exhilarating to work within all the demands—like manipulating puzzle pieces until they fit. I'm not as intimidated by the planning as I thought I would be. I can fit the requirements from outside into my own goals. I know that now." The elaborateness of such negotiations is evident in three of Stephen's log entries from his summer planning:

> from 7/2—One of the hardest things is to accept that I'm expected to teach all of the works on the list. It's like I don't have any choices in content. Some of the pieces I like better than others but I'd like more reading that adolescents can relate to. I'd like a multicultural approach, but most of what's included (except *Autobiography of Miss Jane Pittman*) would be considered traditional. I started by thinking—ok. How can I supplement? Then I started calculating—four nine week periods. Assuming at least one week out of that for getting started, one for ending and two for semester tests, I have thirty-two weeks to cover thirteen major pieces and an anthology. That is two and a half weeks per piece not counting the anthology. It seems too fast and overwhelming. I have some decisions to make about how to get that under control.

> from 7/15—I'm trying to figure out ways of structuring. I'm not panicked by all the pieces, although it seems unrealistic that everyone would read all of them. I'm taking *The Crucible* and *Ethan*

Frome in a package. Students will select one of these but share readings with the rest of class. We'll also cover those periods in the anthology by selecting one or two pieces or authors to read with a small group (Hawthorne, Edwards, etc.). Then, I'll have each student select an historical novel or other contemporary book set in that time. They'll give book talks on those for their small groups. I think that creating blocks of options may help me organize, but it's also a way to have students know about some pieces they might want to read at another time.

from 7/25—I'm relieved to have the structure for covering the literature selections in place. Now I'm thinking how I'll weave these with the reading strategies we've talked about. I'll choose to emphasize one or two strategies with each block of reading. I'm feeling better about this now that I can see some ways to structure units. I'm trying out possible ways of creating successive experiences and I'm not worrying about the day to day work, just how to organize the blocks.

Stephen planned a structure around the required reading lists that allowed him to meet his personal goals for developing strategic readers as well as to provide supplemental readings that he believed were necessary and important. He maneuvered a compromise solution by organizing the class readings in such a way that both his and the required agendas could be met. Stephen hypothesized possibilities and from these set out a plan of action. He created a structure from which he could continue to flesh out his curriculum plans. In general terms, Stephen demonstrated that he could balance his purposes and beliefs with those of his department. Intrigued by the challenge of bringing the various facets of purpose together, Stephen expressed wonder at what he accomplished: "I take the challenges and enjoy figuring out ways to meet what I think is important and what others think is important. I like contingency planning—thinking through the multiple possibilities. I guess I'm proud of myself when I can do that."

Several issues emerged from Avis, Stephen, Sarah, and Ben's planning of curriculum that illustrate their methods of negotiating between their intentions and those of their departments. The first was that they had to articulate their purposes and beliefs before they could determine how the required demands could or would be met. Second, they created structures within which they could work both requirements and what they cared about and believed should happen in the classroom. From a critical perspective, much could be said about how mandates *negate* the opportunity for teachers to struggle with what and how to teach in specific contexts with particular students. Yet, it was particularly impressive that Avis, Stephen, Sarah, and Ben demonstrated their skills as negotiators and arbitrators. Their processes of planning highlight their praxes, the informed actions that result from critical reflection, and demonstrate how they create curriculum out of a series of required literary selections. In spite of their abilities to engage in such a negotiating process, all four of these teachers acknowledged that they still faced constant uncertainty and frustration as they planned.

At one point Sarah expressed concern about her lack of knowledge: "I need to understand more about the big picture of curriculum. I am beginning to see how it is a framework to which I attach all of the activities and content that I think are important to my students. I'm also trying to figure out how to get my students—I mean this particular group—accounted for in what we do during the year. I'm learning, and I do think that I'll get better over the course of this year." Avis, Stephen, Sarah, and Ben developed a heightened awareness of how routines and rituals subsume as well as challenge the complexities of curriculum construction. Their discussions emphasized their need to re-imagine other possibilities and to find ways of connecting the disparate threads of their intentions with the demands of their particular teaching situation and outside requirements.

For Avis, this became particularly important given the context of the rural, farm community in which she taught. "My students can't find much about their way of life, values, or aspirations in the selections included in the reading lists—Dickens, Orwell, Hemingway, Hawthorne. Can you imagine? What do these have to do with them? I mean, we can find connections but in terms of time, place, age of characters—nothing connects. I take in YA stories occasionally but there is no support for xeroxing, and I wonder how all this fits together anyway? It's just reacting again. It isn't a layer within a well conceived plan. We've got few library resources. I'm at a loss right now, but I'm not giving up." In response, Stephen suggested: "There's a whole history of complacency to overcome. The anomalies and blind spots need to be discovered and that's what I hear you doing. I guess there is the drive to fix situations, to feel at a loss if it can't be fixed quickly, but first we need to elaborate. We can't just find a method or an activity or a story that will take care of this. It's reorganizing and reprioritizing and letting the curriculum and methods grow out of that." In making sense of the planning of curriculum, these teachers were aware and able to articulate the dilemmas in teaching choices. Although they could discuss possible curriculum alternatives and options with some ease, they found it harder to describe how their particular teaching contexts affect their curriculum design.

Becoming more cognizant about the complex relationship among beliefs, school culture, and experience, these first-year teachers provide us with detailed stories of their enculturation that illuminate much about how school and personal agendas influenced them as they entered the profession. As Avis, Stephen, Sarah, and Ben examined the issue of curriculum, I was reminded of what John Mayher (1990) suggests in *Uncommon Sense.* He urges that we must look behind the planning and the practice "to reconceptualize who we are and what we do as teachers" (p. 2). I believe Stephen set a similar goal when he stated, "It's reorganizing and reprioritizing and letting the curriculum and methods grow out of that."

Avis, Stephen, Sarah, and Ben's discussions constantly reminded me that they were learning to negotiate between expectations, both external and internal. Their inquiries document how they gained access to different ways of analyzing the multiple factors that must be put into context as they planned the fabric of their curriculum. Sometimes they resisted openly; sometimes they shrugged their shoulders and compromised; often their explanations or logs demonstrated their ability to negotiate between desire and demand. Avis, Stephen, Sarah, and Ben recognized how multiple intentions and agendas formed part of the interactive context in which they work. Their beliefs and priorities as well as those of others are inextricably interwoven. Attention to one must by implication relate to the other. They engaged in an open and questioning form of inquiry through which they reflected upon the elements that influenced their decision making and recognized seeming contradictions as mutually constitutive rather than mutually exclusive.

Forging the Self as Teacher

Once they got into their classrooms, Avis, Stephen, Sarah, and Ben were overwhelmed by all the tasks required of them—planning, grading, teaching five classes a day, working with up to 150 students daily, and dealing with spontaneously occurring demands during each school day. Frustrated at their lack of skillfulness in juggling and managing all of their responsibilities, they called into question their own capabilities. Sarah expressed her doubts: "I hope I didn't make a mistake. I'm not sure I have the patience to deal with all the demands." Stephen picked up on Sarah's remark by suggesting that "It seems early to think that lack of patience is failure. It's easy to say that, but I do try to convince myself each day that I want to be a teacher and that I'll get better at knowing how to deal with all the demands." Such feelings of inadequacy became an internally persuasive discourse that caused them to examine the sources of tensions between themselves and the environments in which they were working. As Avis, Stephen, Sarah, and Ben began this examination, they looked at their relationships with students and colleagues as well as the conditions that strengthened or weakened their ability to work effectively in the school environment.

Despite their desire to become a part of the school, these new teachers felt that they had not proven themselves to other faculty, administrators, or students. Intercollegial relationships and perceived expectations from students occupied much of their attention early in the school year. During their first meeting, they expressed concerns about their relationships with others. Avis described "feeling alone. I get the feeling that other teachers just tolerate me and hope I won't ask for help. They certainly don't find the need to ask for my opinion." They felt like outsiders with no vested interest in the curricular decisions that were made by others. Ben stressed how perplexed he was by the need to "make demands on the students to do Monday vocabulary tests, and I'm not sure why we're doing these. It's hard to convince students when I'm not convinced myself." I examined their September log entries and found that many of the incidents they recorded were related in one way or another to how they were perceived by students, other teachers, or administrators. Stephen wrote:

> I'm trying to sort through why one of the girls in my first period class is so angry with me. I must be letting her down in some way, but I ask her, try to get a conversation going about her work, or just make eye contact with her. I'm not certain what I do wrong. Jewel is sullen and removed in class. I see her in the halls with friends and she's happy and alive. In class she's always sulking. I talked to her teacher from last year who told me that Jewel was great—motivated and spectacular. I got the feeling my colleague thought I was doing something wrong. I can't for the life of me figure out what or how to get through to Jewel.

In a total of forty entries that represent Avis, Stephen, Sarah, and Ben's combined logs for September, a substantial number focused on their interaction with administrators, students, and other teachers. Certainly these first-year teachers constructed images of themselves in relationship to how they thought others perceived them, and, as their inquiry continued, they began to examine conditions in the schools that they believed caused some of those perceptions.

Avis described how odd it struck her that many of the teachers in her building were not motivated to excel in their chosen profession. "Their attitudes rub off on the kids, and I know my students think I'm sort of an aberration. They tell me to 'chill out,' that I demand too much, and that I'll 'get over it,' after I've taught a few years." She explained how her beliefs were often in conflict with what seemed the pervasive attitude by other teachers. "So much of what I believe about working hard to get a good education, being rewarded for trying, and about fair play just don't seem to be major concerns in my school. 'Getting by' is the motto." Avis, Stephen, Sarah, and Ben expressed their belief that new teachers are expected to assimilate into school structures and an ideology of curriculum and pedagogy that may not accommodate their individual values and beliefs about education. Many mandated and purportedly most "effective" or "expedient" rituals, structures, and methods in the school system are not synchronized with what these new teachers desire or have been educated to presume or imagine. They lacked ownership in much of what went on in the school day. Ben realized the connection between his own need to have a voice and his students' desire to have a say in what they were doing. "In some ways it must be what the students feel if they don't have any say in what goes on. Do this for ten minutes, then do this, don't forget to do thus and so. Each day I have all these things to do—take attendance within the first ten minutes, mark tardies, work within a time limit set by a bell, stand in the hall between classes, get in the xeroxing three days early. I sometimes feel like there's no place for me, Ben." Despite efforts to involve teachers more in decision making, collaborative projects, or restructuring efforts, these teachers' concerns suggest that there is still a need for a greater responsiveness to new teachers' voices and their place in the professional community.

The move from student and student teacher to full-time teacher was a difficult transition. These four teachers' impulse was to search out a stable identity within what were the ever-changing dynamics of the school environment. They came to teaching with the belief that they could and should find themselves as teachers rather than with an understanding that they would create themselves continuously. Avis, Stephen, Sarah, and Ben's struggle exemplifies how difficult it is to balance aspects of their old identities with their identities-in-formation. Further, they were just beginning to understand that the contexts in which they were working would have a formidable influence on just how they would define and construct themselves.

These teachers' sense of self-worth and identity was, at least temporarily, shaken. As Stephen told the group during their second meeting in September, "I remember reading Plato's 'Allegory of the Cave.' It's just that way, this teaching. It's the abruptness, even after student teaching, of being thrown into the light without sunglasses." Avis, Stephen, Sarah, and Ben, in turn, characterized their move from being students at the university to teachers in the classroom as "being dumped from the nest," "a cocoon opening in the dead of winter," "culture shock," and "a free fall." Stephen's comment reminded me of how Plato depicted learning as a journey out of the shadowy netherworld of the cave into a world of enlightenment. Early on, these teachers articulated how the actual teaching changed their conception of teachers' work and how difficult it was to remain confident when they felt alienated. They expressed their desires to make that work meaningful which, in turn, would make them feel meaningful to the enterprise of teaching.

Avis, Stephen, Sarah and Ben's concerns about their developing identities as teachers are embedded in larger issues related to the question of whose knowledge is valued in schools and what authority ultimately controls the structure, curriculum, and environment of the school and the classrooms in it. They expressed ambivalence between wanting to do things for themselves and letting others guide them. Sarah suggested that some of these feelings were caused by "some of the people in my department who act as watchdogs of a curriculum they have created. They keep asking if I've emphasized this thing or the other or when I'm going to teach some particular book. They'll pull out the file folders and all the plans and activities for a novel, and I'm sort of relieved when that happens because I need a break. The only problem is that sometimes I get the feeling I should do it exactly the way that person did, like there aren't any other options." Not surprisingly, as they discussed their feelings, these first-year teachers agreed that external pressures caused tension between their purposes and those of the larger school community.

Avis, Stephen, Sarah, and Ben constantly negotiated this gap between their beliefs about teaching and the constraints imposed on their pedagogy and curriculum construction from the outside. As they examined the issues related to this, they began to question the regulatory practices in schools: Whose knowledge is valued? Who has power? What are the consequences of deviation from the predominant beliefs? Who constructs and disseminates knowledge about teaching and how? Are contradictory expectations mediated? In fact, mediation became the central issue within their examination of power, knowledge, and authority. Three themes of mediation characterized the nature of Avis, Stephen, Sarah, and Ben's inquiry on the issues of power, knowledge, and authority.

Competition. Interpersonal relationships among faculty members were characterized by these first-year teachers as "unsettling," "consistently tense," "strained," and "civil but cool." As Stephen described it, "There is protection of the few resources that are available for faculty. This isn't necessarily related to providing better instruction in classrooms. I'm talking about people who want more than the teacher next door because it's a way of showing you're important." These first-year teachers read a message into the behaviors and attitudes they observed—there aren't enough gold stars or trophies of favor to go around in schools. Avis noted how "even the smallest praise by an administrator for something as insignificant as standing in the hall during passing period will elicit some sarcastic remark from another teacher. It's like they'll lose a power base, and I'm not talking about power related to teaching." Ben believed that in his school "the competition between newer faculty and the fossils was strong. Faculty who have taught in the school for a long time think we bring in too many newfangled ideas and as one of the new faculty I feel resentment that I'm not taken seriously."

This competitive spirit placed these new teachers in a particularly precarious situation. With only a few positions of privilege, it stands to reason that those with power are intent on keeping it. As Sarah suggested, "In my school there is the rhetoric of collaboration and collegiality. But when it gets right down to it, people protect themselves first. Maybe that's natural, but it doesn't make sense when we should be interested in making the school a community. It's obvious to me that we don't know how to do that yet." Competition, then, can be seen as a detractor from establishing a collaborative spirit among colleagues. These first-year teachers did not feel comfortable asking for help, sharing their fears, or getting advice from colleagues because of the competitive and protective attitudes of others. They noticed how readily they themselves began to compete for attention, prestige, popularity, and reputation. Ben told about a moment when he saw himself "groveling for attention. I wanted the principal to know that my students had written some great poems so I sent copies to him. What I realized was that I was doing it to say how great a teacher I was. That, I'm embarrassed to say, was the primary motivation."

It is possible to suggest that teachers seek reinforcement from a system that does not always mediate effectively between the individual's needs and the school's resources or power structures. To the extent that these first-year teachers recognized the dynamic interaction between group and individual needs, they began to frame the larger questions of what a school community means and how it does or does not support teachers' career development. They came to recognize that their conflicting desires to further self, along with their desire to advance the school community, required open and careful mediation. As Sarah speculated, "If there were just one thing that could be changed to improve the sense of community in my school, I suspect it would be the elimination of hierarchies—tenured from untenured, first year from fifth year teacher, administrators from teachers, and students from teachers. At least that would begin to diffuse the central assumption that individuals with more experience or expertise in one area are somehow better." It might eliminate the feeling that some teachers deserve more than others or that administrators have the right to dole out favors. Indeed, the very fact that Avis, Stephen, Sarah, and Ben recognized the many dimensions of competition illustrates the importance of their inquiry. Recognition was their first step in overcoming the feelings of anxiety caused by the competitive atmosphere.

Resistance. Although the competitive context created disillusionment, the second theme of mediation, resistance, affected more directly how Avis, Stephen, Sarah, and Ben chose to teach. Resistance from students, colleagues, parents, or administrators impinged on their practices and curriculum decisions. Ben questioned, "Why do I get resistance from students, other teachers, and my principal? I think sometimes I can't do it right, but then I come here and find we're all feeling this way." Sarah brought up a point that was raised many times throughout the school year. "My students aren't prepared for freedom. They have images of classrooms and they expect me to be a teacher with directions, questions, and answers. I feel uncertain, especially right at first, giving them too much control. I get the feeling they don't think I know what I'm doing. It's a slow process to get them thinking and acting that way."

These teachers had read about, seen, and participated in response approaches, but they had not discussed or worked through the difficulties of student resistance, power relationships, or ambivalence and hostility from colleagues, students, or administrators. As Ben explained, "I never imagined students would object and groan when they are given the freedom to select their own reading or determine the format for their discussion." Stephen added, "I couldn't believe that kids wouldn't want to express their opinions. Sometimes they just sit and stare at me until I decide somebody, even if it's me, needs to talk." Avis gives an example. "Get this—a mother told me that her son wondered if I'd read any of what they read before class. He thought that because I don't tell them what the books are about that I don't know them well enough."

As the year progressed, these new teachers expressed, in both their discussions and interviews, that one of their primary tasks was coping with resistance. The most identity-threatening form of resistance came from their students. However, student resistance did not have entirely negative consequences. It created dissonance which caused these teachers to reconsider some of their choices. As Sarah suggested, "When they [students] resist the most I need to stop and think about how *they* perceive what I'm doing. I've come to see that sometimes they resist because they think I want them to become just like me. I don't know an adolescent who would think that an advantage!" Sarah's comment forecasts how she, along with her fellow inquirers, began to consider the *causes* of resistance rather than the *acts* of resistance as the year progressed. They learned to distinguish between act and cause as they examined why resistance occurred and tried to determine ways to diminish its presence. Mediation became a social process involving negotiations and trade-offs among its perpetrators. It served as a catalyst to move the four teachers' inquiries forward.

Incongruence between ideal and real. A third theme that the teachers recognized as requiring mediation resulted from the incongruence between what they learned in their teacher preparation program and what occurred in their classrooms. Ways of mediating the differences, while desirable, proved nonetheless difficult. As Ben pointed out, "I know what I want to happen; I see it like a dream . . . but in the class it doesn't ever match the images in my head. I know that, but I'm not certain what to do about it." They became disillusioned with formulaic approaches. Ben indicated that after teaching he found what "some books have to say is nearly evangelical." Avis concurred, "I get the feeling that some of these authors have labeled everything into neat packages. Take the idea of everybody reading their own books. First of all, it sounds too common sense, too simple. But, we don't have a library in the school or the town. I can start to build a collection but it will take years, and I need to motivate students to read." Ben added, "It isn't a dinner table conversation in the classroom. It just isn't. It's school and there are twenty or thirty other adolescents in a hot, stuffy room, and they distract each other. They know that the bell is going to ring in ten minutes." As Neil Postman (1988) suggested, "The major problem with sloganeering, whether it is shouted from a picket line or a convention hall, or displayed on a bumper is that it is a substitute for thought" (p. 1). The sloganeering in some of the professional literature may be symptomatic of the zeal to change current teaching practices or the need for closure and "knowing." For that, any of us might be forgiven. Yet, it is possible to suggest that such evangelical rhetoric counteracts the quieter and subtler forms of inquiry that we have begun to value in education.

Avis, Stephen, Sarah, and Ben are in the process of mediating between some official version of knowledge and their search for personal meaning in teaching. They are in the process of mediating between their present situation and some dreamed about, hoped for future situation. They are mediating between their feelings of outsider and their desire to be insiders. They are learning through their shared inquiries that certainty/uncertainty and impossibility/possibility exist within the same space of becoming.

Recognizing the Conventional Gestures of Teaching

When they began teaching, Avis, Stephen, Sarah, and Ben made the assumption that they understood the role of teachers in schools. After all, they spent some sixteen years as students before entering the classroom as teachers. What they discovered, however, was that immersing themselves in the school environment as teachers added dimensions of awareness that they had not seen or understood before. They found many contradictory rules, rituals, and structures as they took on this new role of teacher. Their ability to recognize and examine these conditions as well as to determine how they would deal with them became a central part of their interrogation.

Sarah explained in her log dated December 13th:

> Sometimes I don't seem to be myself. I stand back (in my head) and watch myself teaching, and it's like I see someone else. I don't know who this person is and I am almost amazed. I hear my voice and it sounds like a 'teacher' voice rather than my Sarah voice and the person standing there isn't me. I'm not sure this is making sense as I write it, or that it makes sense to me yet, but I'm trying to figure out why I'm not fitting comfortably into my own skin.

"Not fitting comfortably into my own skin" expressed so powerfully what these first-year teachers identified as their struggle to develop their voice and locate a comfortable position between their private self and their public teaching self. As they described their feelings, I was reminded of Ryan's (1970) account of first-year teacher Gary Cornog who suggested that: "I learned over a period of months that in order to survive in the classroom I had to take on the *persona* of someone acting as a teacher. That is, I had to shut down spontaneity

and candidness on my part and in their place put on a calculated facade of coolness and patience" (p. 14). Avis, Stephen, Sarah, and Ben
described similar circumstances that caused their discomfort.

They saw that teaching sometimes took the form of a staged performance enacted before spectators (students, other teachers, parents,
administrators) who were often detached from the performance but
interested in monitoring the conventional gestures that teachers are
expected to perpetrate. Stephen described one such situation in a log
entry dated January 20th:

> When the principal walked into the room the first thing I did
> was check around the room to see that every student had a book
> open. What if someone didn't? Couldn't a person be listening and
> participating in the discussion? I wanted every eye on me. I moved
> quickly to the front of the room and positioned myself. I used my
> hands more and wrote everything anyone said on the board. I
> nearly died when Jason shouted out an idea rather than raising his
> hand. Yet, I've been discouraging them from raising hands. I want
> them to talk to each other. I didn't even notice what his idea was.
> Tiffany walked out to get a drink of water without permission. I'll
> hear about that. Why do these little routines and accepted man-
> ners determine whether or not learning is taking place in the class?
> It seems like I'm supposed to be a robot who does everything per-
> fectly. Just let the "powers" come in the room and I revert to a
> jumble of nerves and insecurities.

During January, these first-year teachers engaged in intensive
discussions about the relationship between self-determination and
what Maxine Greene (1978a) described as "functionaries in the system" (pp. 42–52). As they examined their roles in the schools, they
questioned the purposes behind routines and conventional gestures. Avis asked, "Why do you suppose we're assuming these conventional aspects stand in our way of reaching our goals? It's
probably more complicated than that. Recognizing that they exist
has helped me think about my view of teachers and what I value in
good teachers, but I don't know what to do about it or if it is really
a bad thing. What difference ultimately does it make if we follow
these little routines?" Stephen described why he believes the rituals make a difference: "It's a way of silencing individuality in teachers, and I've come to know how subversive it is to have a strong
voice in school." Sarah wrote in her log on February 15th:

> I still have the image in my mind that there is a code of behav-
> ior and belief that I must adopt once students started calling me
> teacher and that doesn't always fit with the person I am. How do
> we begin to interrogate such disparity?

Noticing how these rituals encourage a particular conception of teacher, Ben suggested that "when everyone expects certain ways of being in schools, and I mean teachers, students, administrators, everyone—then, it's hard to change things because a complacency sets in. It's comfortable and normal. You know what I mean? Things move along." Avis took the idea in a different direction by suggesting that "even the books we read or the modeling that went on in our college experience encouraged some version of teacher behavior. I'm beginning to see that now. Not that it's all bad, but we should be aware. I guess that's natural because it's hard to start from nothing, but I do think that it isn't just in the schools but in the whole profession that we are looking for some version of the gestures, the way a teacher and classroom are supposed to be." They agreed that the sum of these enacted spectacles took away some of the creative work and potential for wrestling ideas into action that they hoped could be a part of their teaching lives.

Avis, Stephen, Sarah, and Ben's discussion reveals that some of their stress and confusion resulted from the unitary vision of teachers' roles and behaviors that they believed were valued in their schools. As they talked, I was reminded of what Paulo Freire (1970) said about education as a form of domestication, a transfer of knowledge with the purpose of preserving the culture and knowledge that exist (p. 469). These first-year teachers felt that the system was replete not only with explicit controls and mandates but also with implicit rituals and conventions that they were expected to replicate rather than create. Their discussions show a heightened sense of awareness that there are contrary pulls between the authorized conventions and their need to figure out who they are.

Entering the Lived World of Schools: The Student Teaching Experience

The four preservice teachers who allowed me to document their first semester student teaching experience were focused on whether they could relate to the students, manage a classroom, and "fit" into the school. Yet, Beverly Crandall, Jennifer Martin, John Norton, and Regina Riggs did express interest in the study I proposed and during the Fall of 1993 they agreed to participate, after I shared a draft of the research agenda and data collection procedures with them. Since my aim was not to direct their inquiry but to document it, I examined the logs they kept but did not respond to these, accompanied them to the student teaching site once each week where we engaged in informal conversations, observed their teaching, conducted individual interviews after each observation, and held a weekly seminar in which they set the agenda for discussion. I photocopied their teaching logs and audiotaped and transcribed the weekly seminar as well as classroom observations and individual interviews. The data provided me with the following information: (1) their concerns and dilemmas; (2) their conception of curriculum as enacted in practice; (3) contextual factors that influenced their decision making (Vondracek, 1990); and (4) analytical categories across types of data to determine points of congruence and incongruence among group discussions, individual logs, and actual classroom practices (Brewer and Hunter, 1989; Denzin, 1978).

Introducing the Student Teachers

Beverly, Jennifer, John, and Regina faced more than the challenges they'd anticipated in their student teaching site in a Bronx middle school. The irony is that they are part of a generation of college students who flee toward social challenges and social changes, believing that the inner city is where they can make a difference. Of course, their aspirations are compelling. They came to their first student teaching experiences with the intention of entering the students' lives and firing up their imaginations about writing and literature. Instead, they found themselves in the midst of situations that compelled them to engage in a continuing search for coherence and meaning in their teaching.

Beverly Crandall returned to New York City the day before her first day of student teaching. She'd been in South Carolina for her grandmother's funeral. "Crisis follows me," she said. "It never lets up." Beverly has learned to bend and adapt and give up on predictability. She exhibits a toughness in her expectations of herself as a teacher. Early in the semester, Beverly shared a piece of writing from her log with Jennifer, John, and Regina. In it, she described her hopes. "Caring is where I start," she says. "I think there are some kids out there who need me." She wrote:

> Mr. Williams was an old man with big ears, little hair, and thinning patience. It was painful to watch him snap, as we Honors English students called it. I remember the typical cloudy October day well. I remember his arms flapping frantically as he spun around the room, knocking into a poster of Shakespeare and spitting out insults at us. He called us *parrots*. We were horrified and embarrassed. Now, I understand his frustration. He was right about us. We hungered for crackers; we mimicked his words. He wanted

us to fly. But his anger was misguided—we had not clipped our own wings.

Mr. Williams' accusations smacked of far too much truth for me to forgive. Mr. Williams' storm illuminated one of my first moments of real consciousness of myself as learner. I realized then that I wasn't really a learner at all. I was, for the most part, a trained performer, a winner of marks, a collector of crackers. I hope to negotiate space to allow not only for individual voices, but also for the connection of those voices. I hope that no one, neither male nor female, will feel threatened by each other or by their strength and individuality. I hope to repair those wings that have been clipped. I hope for flight.

Beverly is always vigilant to be a model of her African-American heritage as she works with these young people in the Bronx who are African-American and Latino. As she describes it, they need to learn resistance, not to be submissive. "That's the worst thing that could happen to them."

Jennifer Martin had aspirations of her own as expressed in a log entry she'd written in September:

I have no memories of warm laps or soothing voices when I think about literature. What comes to mind are adventures, the lives of characters in the books I loved: Stuart Little, Huck Finn, Holden Caulfield, and Hester Prynne. These characters live in me and I am richer for them. Maybe it was my need to escape into someone else's youth that made my eyes thirst for words. In trying to quench that thirst, I discovered that words could swallow me up and carry me away from myself. I didn't have the ability to run away from the awkward person I was or the strength to fight for the woman I was becoming, but with books as my tools, I built a safe and secret place within me. That's my overall aim for students— to help them through the uncertainty of growing up by putting them in touch with literature.

Jennifer came to the Bronx thinking: "I'm learning to recognize the outward face and the inward eye. I understand that often what lies beneath the surface can betray the facade. But a good teacher can help students to protect themselves without facades, by respecting the uniqueness of each student's experience." Jennifer goes on to say that a teacher can help her students find voice and themselves. "As an eighth grader, after reading *The Adventures of Huckleberry Finn,* I wrote new lyrics to the tune of *Hey Jude*: 'Hey, Huck, I know it's rough . . .' I cried out to this freckle-faced character to be strong, to look to the future, and to revel in his freedom. I want to help my students find themselves."

John Norton spent summers as a camp counselor in a program for troubled boys throughout his high school and college years. He's carrying dreams of closely knit groups of kids to the Bronx this morning where "even Jimmy Aarons, the nerd, the outcast, the kid everybody made fun of was cheered the day he could finally swim across the lake." For John, building a community means "putting in more than you'll take out. That's what I learned those summers, and I want to help kids who are working against great odds." The adolescents who perceive themselves as outcasts hold a special place in John's plans:

> I distanced myself from my fellow students in high school. What I saw as their petty cruelty and general stupidity is epitomized in an episode from my freshman year which I'll never forget. When I switched from my local public middle school to a private high school in a town miles away, there was a lot to get used to. One of the most confusing things was the schedule. It changed every day, and it often sent the students sprinting from one end of the building to the other. When I asked a fellow student for help on whether seventh period was English or History, he told me the exact opposite of what was the case. I ended up running full blast into my History classroom to discover that I was supposed to be on the other side of the building in English. My feelings of betrayal were quickly heightened to utter embarrassment when I walked into English well after the bell had rung to discover my friend had told the entire class and every kid was now "in" on the joke. I was the focus of a barrage of laughter. I gradually drifted apart from the mainstream students at school. My feelings of resentment and my petty adolescent insecurities all come slithering back to the surface when I'm faced with concrete reminders of adolescents who are outside the mainstream. I want to set about helping those students as individuals; the one thing no teacher of mine ever did for me.

Regina Riggs doesn't remember exactly when she became smitten with the idea of teaching. "I think I always wanted to order people around. I remember playing school with my little sister. Each day I would set up a desk for her along with my special blue chalkboard. Of course, I got frustrated with her inability to do exactly as I commanded. I was teacher and she had to do what I said. When Lana ran to my parents with complaints, they put a temporary end to my English teaching career. My obsession may have been a character flaw that I'm trying to legitimate." It would be hard to miss Regina's enthusiasm. "I've located my studies in popular culture and literature and adolescent girls' psychology. I want to share all that with students. I want school to be a safe place for them to learn and to speak their minds. I hope to learn along with the class and have my students teach me just as much as I teach them. I want them to leave my classroom yearning to learn more." She wrote:

I want to provide my students with opportunities to discuss—to defend their beliefs, to debate, to question, to doubt, to speculate. In thinking about my middle school English class experiences, I realize that I never really knew what any of my peers thought about what we were reading. Personal response was not a part of working with a book—you were supposed to take it apart and find the meaning, not to create your own. I went to college with a collection of semi-formed opinions and beliefs, without the ability or equipment to defend them. I think that discussion not only gives students the opportunity to learn to speak and listen effectively, but it also promotes a kind of classroom community that I will strive to create.

References were often made in these student teachers' preliminary life history accounts that acknowledged the reasons they came to teaching and what they hoped to contribute. Often, as all their accounts highlight, personal experiences in school leave deep impressions that appear to influence subsequent actions and beliefs about personal goals as a teacher.

The First Days in an Unfamiliar Position

It's 6:30 A.M. when we catch the No. 1 train and head uptown into the Bronx. Today, a gauze of humidity hangs over the housing projects as we come out from underground at 7:05. Then, a walk over heaving concrete and through the litter of bags torn open by those who spend the dark hours retrieving aluminum cans, plastic, or glass bottles. One skeleton of a car, windows shattered, interior burned to chars, reminds us how the middle school students from this environment live. We stop long enough to consult the hand drawn map to get our bearings. Regina's finger traces the penned X's. I feel the sweat trickle from my hairline across my shoulder blades. This day isn't breathing any coolness our way. Beverly shifts from one foot to the other, impatient to keep moving forward. Jennifer leans over Regina's arm, helping her interpret the scratchings.

We pull open the door, walk up ten stairs to face a guard sitting behind an oak table. He asks our names, checks the list, then glides the clipboard our way with a flick of his wrist and a brusque, "Sign in and mark the appropriate boxes." Jennifer is first. She looks toward me for help. There is a choice for "Visitors Status." Four boxes—Student, Teacher, Parent, Other. "What should I do?"

"Teacher," I say firmly. "All of you mark teacher."

And so their student teaching experiences begin. The hours tick away that first day and through the first week and into the rhythm of day after day of the school week. Beverly, Jennifer, John, and Regina's teaching journals and plan books begin to fatten. During the third week their moods match the October weather, taunted by squalls and occasional crackles of lightning. "There's not much I could have done to prepare for the emotional highs and lows," said Jennifer. "I'm learning to take things as they come."

As Regina states:

> The most significant obstacle in my way of becoming a teacher is that I haven't yet figured how to own my voice. I see myself commanding, "Sit down!" with a voice that says, "You don't really have to sit down." I am afraid. I am not confident enough to see myself in the role of teacher or authority. I hear students' voices who distract me rather than the ones who want to help me. I leave the school each day with many mixed feelings about what is happening and how things are going. I'm certainly not having fun; I'm quickly losing my enthusiasm for *To Kill a Mockingbird*, and I'm not happy. I enjoy the students when they allow me to. Sometimes the class just looks at me and I wonder at my indecision and confusion. I lose my fragile momentum.

Regina said in the student teaching seminar, "You know, I just began to realize that I am teaching students. I had been so concerned with myself, I forgot about them." Regina was surprised how much time she'd spent thinking about herself and not thinking about the students' perspective. She suggested that even the smallest of class routines must involve the students:

> I have to press hard with the chalk or the students can't read what I write on the board; if I don't slow my reading down to half my speed the kids can't understand what I'm saying; sometimes I need to shout or show I'm angry so they know I mean business; if I praise the unconfident student often, maybe she'll begin to gain that missing confidence; when I ask something of the students, I need to see it through or else I lose credibility; a student is more likely to listen to me if we develop a relationship.

This list goes on, but it illustrates that Regina began to see herself in relationship with students rather than viewing them as adversaries or hindrances to her goals, identity, or motivation. Regina indicated that she'd thought "little about the isolation of a teacher from students. I thought I could demand their trust and tolerance because I was a teacher. But, it's a shared experience and I need to learn how I, Regina, can be part of that and take some responsibility for it, but help students learn to take responsibility as well."

Jennifer indicated that a student teacher is "caught between roles and often feels the insecurities and confusion of someone who is responsible for the class but not in complete control of it." Jennifer identified that strange territory that she must traverse. "Having a cooperating teacher is not like having a mentor. I find myself feeling dependent at times. The cooperating teacher has his agenda, which doesn't always coincide with mine. I have learned when to ask for advice and when to fend for myself." Jennifer considered how the shock of taking on the role of teacher required some adjustment. "I think that I am fairly knowledgeable in what students of their age deem cool or interesting, but this group is often beyond me. Perhaps I should not expect to please everyone all of the time, but it is a little demoralizing when lesson plans that I have high hopes for fall flat. I can't figure out whether they will always grumble when I give them assignments. The attitudes shake my confidence."

The everyday experiences of working as teachers revealed the dilemmas that coincide with conflicts in roles, perceptions, competing intentions, and organizational considerations. As Beverly stated:

> I seem so intense and upset about everything. I guess that's a natural transition that many student teachers make from academia to the field. At first, we expect all the 'wonder' of Nancie Atwell's classroom or the 'magic' of Ralph Peterson's. We want all the kids to like us and grow up to be famous writers who will come back and sign books for the new library that we've built with money raised from cupcake sales. Then, we realize that sometimes the kids detest us, and they run away from us when they see us on the street or in the store. They don't laugh at all our jokes, and early on find at least one thing to mock in our clothes, our bodies, or our voices.

Specifically, Beverly confronted expectations different from her own or those she has imagined to exist. What does this suggest vis-à-vis Beverly's conception of herself as teacher? For one, she articulated a recognition that students don't see her as she'd hoped. Perhaps even her dreams for what these students will want to become don't match their intentions for themselves. I suspect all of us who have worked with students have felt the promise of opportunity to positively affect other's lives. The potential to facilitate learning is poignant if we don't co-opt or thwart opportunities for students to find their own ways. Beverly learned about herself and clarified her purposes as she challenged her own romanticized view.

> What I've discovered is that I work hard. First, I want my students to think of me as a partner in their learning, not a giver of grades. Second, I hope to create an environment of trust and respect where students create their own tapestries of meaning. Third, I'm committed to being a PUBLIC LEARNER, not a keeper of a magical canon. Most of all, I hope they are committed to a life of inquiry.

Once Beverly articulated these purposes, she felt that she could begin to create an environment in which all of her actions and attitudes emphasize her beliefs. "It's hard to do this in someone else's class where the agenda and beliefs are the cooperating teacher's. I feel like an interloper." This was a perpetual theme in developing confidence—this feeling that the classroom wasn't theirs.

As John stated:

> This class is *trained* as a lecture class where the students sit back and the teacher lectures. I have been told that since this is an Honors class, I have to teach them the literature. I have many fears. I'm quite aware that I have no power. I've been attending classes for two weeks and nobody knows who I am. Last week one student asked, "Who are you? Why are you here?" To which I responded quickly, "I'm a student/a teacher." Is that both or neither? I'm concerned about my place in this room. I talked with my cooperating teacher and he is willing to "*surrender his room*" (his words), if I play by his rules and follow his directives. He listened to what I hoped to do for approximately forty minutes, nodded, then offered me his teaching guides, painfully dependent as these are on reading quizzes, vocabulary worksheets, and questions to answer.

These four student teachers had difficulty adjusting to a teacher's role, rather than a student's role, in the classroom. Regina said, "I feel so entirely different about teaching—*me* teaching, that is,—I now visualize myself doing it. First, I had no image of myself in the classroom. Then, a vision of me—teacher, a little voice inside my head would hear the words that came out of my mouth, and I stepped back and caught brief images of me as a teacher." This was a beginning of sorts and as the confidence grew, even the leave taking with students at the end of the semester was another first step in understanding. As Regina wrote in her log, "The one thing I'll always remember about today is when all these twelve-year-old girls were hugging me. One said, 'Don't go—we love you.' I said, 'Come on you guys; I love you too.' 'Yeah,' she said, very seriously, 'but we love you *harder*.'"

Beverly, Jennifer, John, and Regina came to teaching with different purposes and beliefs about what they wanted to accomplish as teachers. Locating themselves as individuals in their generalized conception of those roles helped them begin to connect themselves to the particular contexts of the teaching environment. Individual identity as a teacher cannot develop wholly when a student teacher feels like an interloper or does not have a clearly defined sense of self in the particular situation. Beverly, Jennifer, John, and Regina long for self-expression and self-understanding. They cannot achieve this alone. Students and full-time faculty will have some role in whether or not these student teachers are accepted into the school environment.

The process of socialization is restricted in part by the unfortunate status accorded student teachers in some schools and classrooms. Deborah Britzman's (1991) study of the student teacher Jamie Owl deals in far greater depth than I will detail here with the dilemmas of identity and socialization. Britzman's book, *Practice Makes Practice,* has been important reading for the student teachers with whom I work as they begin to recognize that teaching needs to be "reconceptualized as a struggle for voice and discursive practices amid a cacophony of past and present voices, lived experiences, and available practices. The tensions among what has preceded, what is confronted, and what one desires shape the contradictory realities of learning to teach" (p. 8). Beverly, Jennifer, John, and Regina's struggles in student teaching clearly highlight the tensions.

Through an examination of three areas that presented the most concern for the student teachers, it is possible not only to determine what experiences were most significant, but also to see an example of the preliminary ways these four student teachers were socialized into the teaching profession. This study elicited very different findings than Tabachnick and Zeichner's (1984) study of four student teachers. Tabachnick and Zeichner determined that the student teachers retained the same perspectives about teaching at the beginning and end of their experiences. Further, the experience did not alter their perspectives and they were resilient to the encroachment of new perspectives (p. 17). I found that Beverly, Jennifer, John, and Regina's reflections led them to a broader and deeper understanding of how they are composing their teaching lives, and how their perspectives changed as a result.

Facing the Unanticipated

It is interesting how the unanticipated, the surprises, remind us what is peculiar and particular to the job of teaching. Beverly, Jennifer, John, and Regina learned a great deal from situations they did not anticipate. As they shared some of these experiences with each other, they began to weave a continuous conversation about the powerful and very real forces that undermine their idealized images. There was incongruence between what they imagined as possible and the daily issues of students, structural and time constraints, and unforeseen circumstances that they would discover as reality. Let me propose through the following examples how these student teachers remind me of how particular and alive with distinctness is every group of students in every class in each school setting. The following examples illustrate the particular students and environmental demands that caused these teachers to reflect on the meaning of their work in schools.

Jennifer was shocked at how the neighborhood violence encroached not only on the physical but also on the emotional wellbeing of students.

> Last week there was an incident in which one student stabbed and killed another student in a school not far from the one where I am student teaching. Many of the students from my class are from that area and know both the adolescent who died and the one accused of murder. So the incident hit home with my students and there was a strange dynamic in the school. Most kids were scared; some were upset because they were friends with one or both of those involved. I wasn't sure how to deal with it. As a student teacher, I didn't know what my cooperating teacher's attitude was or if there was a school policy. I didn't want to overstep my boundaries. I didn't do anything. On Sunday I was reading one girl's log entries. She was the girlfriend of the kid who was killed, and she picked a sentence from the book (*Annie John*) that reads, "I used to think only people I didn't know died." Joy writes, "I picked this sentence because I used to think this too, but now I know better because my boyfriend is dead and it really hurts." I didn't know how to respond. It caught me off guard. What can you say to a thirteen-year-old girl who just had her boyfriend killed? I asked my cooperating teacher what to say. She said, "just write something supportive." So, I ended up writing something like "I know it hurts a lot to lose someone you care about. I'm here if you want to talk." I felt awkward about writing that, like what right do I have to give this girl advice, but how can I not?
>
> We had a town meeting that the principal convened the week after the incident. The issue of the growing weapons threat was raised. Many students said they carried weapons because they live on a crack block. They are afraid to walk in the neighborhood without protection. One boy said, "I don't bring a weapon to school to have it in school but to have it coming back from or going to school." These are seventh graders.
>
> The culmination of incidents really shook me up. I wondered about living in this environment. What are the chances they will live to finish high school? And how can I, a white, suburban upper-middle-class teacher, relate to these kids? One kid said today, "It's not my fault I live here. I'd love to live in Beverly Hills in a mansion, but unfortunately my mom's not a millionaire." I'm scared for them; I'm scared for myself.

Jennifer's recounting of this series of events led me to think about how these situations affect the actual work of teachers in schools. Social ills are no longer "out there" or simply ignored when the bell rings and the school day starts. A murder had taken place inside a school, a site associated with youth, growth, and safety. As Jennifer suggested, lurking behind such an incident are questions about the impotence of her as a teacher or the schools in general to educate students in a safe environment. Jennifer realized she couldn't control everything in the environment that affected her students. She addressed an issue she grappled with throughout her student teaching experience: "I am responsible for the class but not in complete control of it. How do I reconcile the paradox?" That knowledge led her to question what effect she might actually have on student lives. She came to the student teaching experience believing her teaching would make a difference. She came with the understanding that she could make books the tools to build a safe and secret place within. This incident forced her to realize that escape within may not be the answer. Her larger goal shifted as a result. She determined that her teaching needed to emphasize how to obtain a quality of life through social action.

When Beverly's expectations were somehow thwarted in the classroom, she came face to face with uncertainty about how to take appropriate action. An incident that occurred early in her student teaching experience led her to question the relationship between her expectations for students and the reality of their situations. Beverly recounted this event in her log:

> Yesterday, I tried an assignment out on the second class I teach. Usually this group is my experimental run through the lesson, then I have the night to reflect, adjust, refine, and I do the same lesson again with the first class the next day. Until today, the lesson *always* works better the second time around (Is there a song in that?). I planned about five minutes for presenting some role play I had asked the students to do in pairs. They are reading *The Bluest Eye*. I felt I was very clear about *why* we were doing this and what I hoped to come out of the role play—basically to further explore several scenes in the novel and what they revealed about Pecola. The kids seemed enthusiastic and focused as they worked with their partner. And as I circulated they had some interesting ideas. It appeared they were incorporating these ideas into their presentations. It appeared to be going well. The preparations, of course, took a few minutes longer than I had hoped for, but at that point I felt okay with that.
>
> The first group went and simply read from the book, verbatim, which was boring and time consuming. They didn't offer any new insights, didn't read into and explore possible meanings beyond the dialogue. I knew I was in trouble when the first group's scene took about seven minutes. Hope was still alive though. But,

the next group did the same bloody thing. At this point I began to panic. There were two more groups. I decided not to stop and discuss. I had planned to do that after each group had presented. The next groups did the same thing. Even I was falling asleep. The presentations had taken twenty minutes, not five. The class just felt empty and seemed rather like a wilted flower.

Beverly felt that she had trapped herself by her expectations. She assumed that students would produce effective scenes, but found they did not have a repertoire to create a fine production. She had not anticipated how *teachers' expectations* and clarity of *teachers' explanation* might be incongruent. Neither the students nor Beverly owned this experience. Each allowed the moment to unfold as an exercise that appeared satisfying to no one. Beverly suggested that what she learned from this incident was how she would need to plan ways to teach toward her expectations. That was an important lesson and one that made a difference in her strategies for lesson planning.

Sometimes the unanticipated is not classroom centered as it was in Beverly's case. Regina found that the endemic problem of student absence that pervaded the entire school encroached on the type of planning she could do in her classroom:

Yesterday the class read a short story aloud. Today, I thought it would be nice to discuss the story in small groups. I made a list of "instructions" for each group: assign a moderator, secretary, and spokesperson, and as you discuss the two questions written below, think about how you want to present what you talked about to the class. The small groups were to talk for twenty minutes, and then we would spend the last half hour in a large discussion with a few minutes at the end for writing time.

Well, ten out of twenty-nine students were absent. Most of those ten showed up the next day, clueless about the story. Also, most of the students attending yesterday did not come today. What this meant for me, after a show of hands, was that only four students in attendance today had read the story and were ready to discuss it.

I decided to let that one group of four do the small group activity as planned, while the remaining students read the story. I worked with the small group. Since the students read at different paces, response time was staggered. That means that some students had a good deal of time to write in their notebooks while others had only a few minutes. The latter group of students felt frustrated because they wanted more time. Also, some students weren't sure what to do once they had finished the story. There was no clear end to the class, people just kind of got up and left when there was no time left (we do not have bells). Needless to say, it all got too confusing for all of us. Attendance is a huge concern. In fact, it is probably the biggest problem at the school: getting students to "wake up and show up." This is a first period class and that doesn't help. But, I need to learn to work around that. I think I'll need to make stations accordingly. Activities for students who show up regularly. Alternative assignments for those who don't. For example, tomorrow I'll have the small group who did work today lead our discussion, since they are "experts." Once they have presented their findings, the discussion will open up to other students who have read. It gets more complicated than I'd ever imagined.

This is not an easy situation in which to work. Regina felt trapped in the spaces between her expectations and the reality of student absences. At the end of her log entry she suggested why even her plan to deal with the issue was troublesome: "I don't think I can change students' abilities about the importance of being in class, but I don't want to create structures that suggest I condone what students are doing." Regina considered what kinds of practices were possible within this situation and thus planned stations where students could work individually and activities that would not extend over more than one day. In doing so, she questioned whether the approach was a means of protecting herself and the students from dealing with the problem head-on or was a necessary adaptation to a difficult situation. Regina had her doubts either way, but through the examination of these issues she confronted another of the predicaments of learning to teach.

Regina's uncertainty about how to deal with absences does not illuminate the underlying and more central issue of the reasons for such a high absence rate. Her situation was one that I have experienced and have seen often in the various research projects in which I have engaged. Despite teachers' best efforts, they inherit school structures, curriculum, and the endemic problems of student indifference or alienation. These issues must be confronted on a daily basis and Regina, in her student teaching experience, began to recognize the cycles of contradiction rooted in the institution of school itself. She learned in this first teaching experience that she will need to make decisions based on how much she chooses to legitimize or resist the dominant structures.

Articulating the tensions involved in the unanticipated led John to examine the complications of teacher agency. He found that so much of what happens in a school day is a negotiation of situational and social constraints. For John, what he thought he knew about himself as teacher was challenged continuously by unforeseen circumstances. He clearly recognized that the boundaries between perceived success and failure as a teacher are more fragile than he had assumed:

It was the last day we were going to cover *To Kill a Mockingbird* and I planned on showing the last forty-five minutes of the film. Things had been going very well up to then. I felt I had a nice rapport with the class. I thought I was reaching out personally to each student—talking to each student, meeting them at lunch, inviting cutters warmly back into class, writing letters about each student to their parents or caretakers. I felt very humorous and good natured, engaging, interesting, thoughtful. Basically, I imagined myself in the right career—a super teacher.

We had been working in small groups. We call them "families" or "communities" since they represent characters or points of view from what we read. We often act out parts dramatically, which has been the most exciting structure we've tried yet. Whether we read aloud, act, write reader's responses or create projects, I do encourage their talent. "High-Fives, Jamal—excellent paper." I really thought things were working.

Then, this last day, Friday, my cooperating teacher called in sick and asked me if I'd like to go in anyway. "*No* problem," I said. They are so well-behaved and we have such a great rapport (I was thinking). "I'd love to solo," I told him. I went in that day to find that another teacher had taken the VCR I signed out, but no one in administration knew where it was. I spent an hour and a half going room to room on four floors, introducing myself and hunting down the VCR. I never found it. I later found out that some visiting VIP took it. Politics. My class mutinied when I told them about cancelling the film, and I don't blame them. Any more small group work would be too much. They'd worn it out. It was Friday, the last period of the day, the last day of the marking period, gorgeous and sixty-five degrees.

I gave them the option of going over the mid-semester work, reading aloud, or doing a dramatization of the end of the book. No consensus. The next few minutes went like this:

Rumblings, murmuring
Me, trying to quiet everyone
Yelling, throwing things at each other
Me, angrier, trying to quiet everyone
Mean comments made about me and the cooperating teacher
Making fun of me
People walking around in and out of class
Fighting, throwing
Me yelling
Me making note of who is engaged in work or who is not
Me giving detention
Me being totally ignored

Students begging me to ask them to leave the room
Much, much more...Me, trying to stay calm
Me, who felt so great as a teacher.

Again, the unanticipated—John's example concretizes how his reading of students' attitudes about him and what was going on in class may have misrepresented the reality of the student experience. But, a relationship with students does not have a self-evident or monolithic meaning. In the context of this particular day, students reacted to a change in plans. They expressed their frustrations as did John, causing a near chain reaction of power plays on both sides. John expected the students to react to a change of plans in a particular way. When they didn't, John resorted to one form of what Linda McNeil (1986) identifies as defensive teaching. Sometimes it is easy to forget just how difficult it is to work with and through the unexpected. John's image of who he was becoming as a teacher was challenged through the series of events that took place. At the same time we must recognize that such adverse circumstances produce constricting versions of who John was, both to himself and his students.

These unanticipated moments helped Beverly, Jennifer, John, and Regina further realize the complexities of teaching. Much of their conversation, writing, and reflection throughout the semester was characterized by their frustration or shock at events and situations that thwarted their understandings or sense of control. Their insights are limited because they situate themselves within rather narrow definitions of how to meet their intentions. Yet, I was impressed with how thoughtfully they considered their deep uncertainties. How these student teachers come to terms with the issues is integrally related to their image of themselves as teachers, and how that role is constantly being refined and redefined in the dynamic of the school environment.

Who I'll Become as a Teacher

I can still see Beverly standing on the subway platform at the end of the first day of her student teaching experience. She's had her hair cut short, cropped close to her ears. "My new teacher-do," she laughed as she flipped her fingers through the tangle of curls. She asked a simple question: "How will I become the teacher I want to be?" I knew the question couldn't be answered finally or finely. The answer would keep shifting and changing with each group of students and each year. What kind of teacher am I? What kind of teacher do I want to become? What kind of teacher am I with this group of students? A careful examination of such questions keeps us searching for and articulating a coherence of self that is difficult to maintain in the culture of schools. Yet, these student teachers yearned to find themselves. Becoming a teacher is a continuous process and one through which a teaching identity is produced and reproduced through the social interactions and particular contexts that exist within schools and classrooms. Beverly, Jennifer, John, and Regina had mostly decontextualized conceptions.

What Beverly, Jennifer, John, and Regina discovered was that they could not create a final form of themselves. I've often thought that teachers are skilled schizophrenics. Student teachers are doubly that. They work in an environment where they can seldom revise or reinvent the situation to suit themselves. It's a bit like being in the driver's seat but without access to the accelerator or the brake. Without that control it is difficult to create purposeful coherence and congruence between belief, action, and self-identity.

For example, Regina discovered in December, during the final days of this first teaching experience, that about the time she had defined something of who she was for these middle school students, it was necessary to move into the high school for her second student teaching experience. "As teacher I'm growing more powerful as me." Regina suggested that she had a presence in the classroom that she did not feel early on. Now, it was time to end and begin again in a new classroom.

> Dear Ms. Riggs,
>
> I would just like to say thank you. You taught me how to read better. You gave me a lot of advice on reading. I hope you become a successful teacher. Good luck. I hope other students treat you as good as we did.
>
> > Sincerely,
> > Lillie

> Dear Lillie,
>
> I hope my future students will be as wonderful as you have been. I'm not certain where I'll teach next, but in a high school for sure. I hope students will be as nice as you have been to me. Thank you for your smile and always trying hard.
>
> > Sincerely,
> > Ms. Riggs

Regina initially focused on whether the students in her next teaching assignment would be like those she'd met in the Bronx. She'd grown comfortable working with them. Yet, another part of the story began to surface. Regina admitted that her relationship with students also revealed their very different levels of understanding and success. Lillie was a case in point. Lillie scored a 10+

on her DRP reading test. A classmate, Rabbiyah, scored a 99+. Regina felt both had been labeled by test results over the years. "Why all this fuss in testing? I'm not certain I want to buy into such a narrow assessment measure." Yet, Regina found herself comparing students. "I wonder if they live up to the labels. They certainly are affected by their experiences. When we discussed *Animal Farm,* Rabbiyah talked about Trotsky and Lenin; Lillie talked about pigs and dogs. I went crazy trying to keep both of them talking. I still don't know how to challenge the individual and make each feel worthwhile. I want to become a better teacher." Regina began to recognize the uneasy distinctions between successful and not so successful student performance. Doing so led her to think about who she would become as a teacher and how she would care for the different levels of achievement in her classroom.

Jennifer questioned her role as a teacher in the first days while she began observing in the class where she would soon teach. As she watched the cooperating teacher, Jennifer's ongoing struggle to define herself took concrete form. Jennifer's puzzlement at what she observed provoked her to ask the cooperating teacher about her intentions:

> On this particular day students were given a quiz on *The Contenders* and for the rest of the class my cooperating teacher lectured and led a discussion on the third chapter. It was quiet. Only the teacher read. Students answered questions when asked. Occasionally they would ask for clarification of a point. Later, I asked my teacher why she didn't encourage their reading aloud as well. She responded that they would only spoil it so why let them. She feels it is better when she reads because it will go faster. I want, no, I need more from my students than an occasional sigh or a question to clarify a point. I placed myself in their shoes. One student I questioned about this said, "It's okay by me. I mean, it's easy. I take quizzes, write for a test, and get my grade. It works for me." I'm tempted to say that as a student I never thought like this, but the truth is, I did. There were only a few teachers who could draw me out; most did not try. I hope to become a teacher who helps my students find their voices.

The cooperating teacher's response helped Jennifer determine her goals. It's important that Jennifer sought out student opinion on this issue. What she learned will help her navigate the complex classroom culture. Jennifer derived knowledge about her beliefs as well as about the complexity of the classroom through situated knowledge that developed as she struggled to make sense of the classroom events she observed. Note, for example, how Jennifer tied her own need for sense-making to student reaction as a way to understand the role of teacher.

Beverly decided to try a structure for adopting literature discussions that had been modeled in her methods class. Although this was a successful practice, Beverly began to question small group and whole class endeavors:

> When I started reading clubs, I hadn't realized how difficult it would be to plan the class session. Students handed in journal letters throughout the unit which served as checkpoints for their reading. The letters were intended to help students ask questions and receive feedback. In class, students worked in their groups on character illustrations, advertisement posters, and writing assignments. I wasn't certain how to help students deal specifically with each of the books chosen by the group.
>
> What I decided to do was spend some class time discussing gender roles in each of the books the groups were reading. My timing was off and I rushed to do in one day what should have been done over a longer period. I didn't see a necessary part of what was going on and felt I was more a hindrance to the flow of group work. Part of the problem seemed that the class was really disjointed because everyone was working on a different assignment or at a different pace. It didn't seem much like a class but many small groups. I understand why that can be good but the structure avoids the issue of forming a larger community. I just didn't have a role. From all this I began to question how to work in the classroom. I hope I have made a step in learning more about who I am as a teacher as I try to define my role in this.

With regard to Beverly's concern about how the teacher fits into group work, she conveyed a recognition of her inability to determine her role in the the classroom. As she began to clarify her intended purposes, Beverly reasoned that the possibility of redefining her traditional role as a teacher would prove helpful. "I guess what's made me uncomfortable is my basic belief that teachers take a central role when teaching." Beverly attended to individual students and small group's needs. She continued throughout the semester to question her different roles as a teacher in both small and whole group instruction.

By his own reports, John measures his successes in the classroom by student involvement. "I'd rather study literature that isn't particularly challenging to me at first. Once students are involved, I can bring them along slowly." John expressed his desire to work with students who want to learn. "If I can get them thinking that way, I can help them overcome the problems with feeling inside or outside the group." John described how his sense of purpose conflicted with his cooperating teacher's:

I tried to find ways to get the students involved. In the beginning of class, we read a poem. We started off with Frost's "Fire and Ice." Then worked on Langston Hughes' "Dream Deferred." Much to my surprise my students were not that interested in the Hughes poem and asked if they could bring in poems. I said absolutely, but no one brought one in right away so we began studying "The Sea-Turtle and the Shark" by Melvin Tolson.

Soon thereafter, Andre brought in the lyrics of a rap song. It is not what I'd call a poem but perhaps the students might like it. He suggested I just read it to the class. It seemed funny. Me, white and Waspy, reading it to the class. Also the cooperating teacher doesn't find merit in the lyrics as a poem. I did not take offense to it at all, but my cooperating teacher didn't feel comfortable spending time on it like we did the other poems.

My conflict does not actually have to do with my teacher's opinion. It has more to do with offending the students. If I don't give the lyrics the same treatment as other poems, how can I validate the interest? I do not want to exert too much opposition to my cooperating teacher's opinion but I do not want to seem like a hypocrite to my students. I need to figure out the balance.

John came to understand that this event was not only about the conflicting beliefs between a student teacher and a cooperating teacher. More centrally, he characterized the tensions between wanting to validate student input and his own judgments about what constitutes valuable experiences or materials. John began to examine this tension as a way of more fully understanding his role as a teacher. John found this disjuncture with the cooperating teacher to be a fleeting moment, but the dilemma about defining self and purpose as a teacher was much more integral to his search to explain himself as a teacher.

Learning to teach obviously involves coming to grips with identity as a teacher. I'm not suggesting this is a steady progression of coming to "Know Thyself." Rather, constant examination of one's identity is triggered by various classroom events, students, or colleagues who challenge teachers to consider or monitor their own actions and reactions. Ultimately, these student teachers' identities are always in the making—an identity derived through the flux of experience in continual dialogue with a face-to-face encounter with self.

Living with Uncertainty

How did these student teachers discover or assuage their concerns with composing a teaching identity? The student teaching experience taught them that in the life of a teacher not everything can be controlled. Beverly, Jennifer, John, and Regina found that they had to live daily with uncertainty and some burning regrets for what they couldn't manage to do. Some things about student teaching need to be improved: student teachers should not remain anonymous in the classrooms in which they will teach (i.e., explaining only when a student asks); student teachers should be given responsibility for planning and implementing extensive blocks of time (not by the cooperating teacher changing plans at the last minute or giving the knowing "I told you so" look); student teachers should become part of a community in the school (not treated as second class citizens who get in line last for photocopy machines or the VCR), and should team with cooperating teachers rather than be evaluated by them; student teachers should have opportunities to reflect on their experiences with openness and without fear that their uncertainties and apprehensiveness will cost them the appearance of competence. They need space that allows them to grow into teaching.

Reflective inquiry allowed these student teachers to trace experience wherein something inadequately understood was confronted again. They came to terms with uncertainty through their reflection. Their log entries demonstrate remarkable thoughtfulness and resourcefulness and give us concrete examples of how they came to recognize the issues that will become central to their future teaching lives.

Beverly wrote:

> I have spent a great deal of time reflecting upon myself as student, student teacher, and peer/colleague. Sometimes I've been paralyzed with guilt. These emotions simply compound the angst I feel every morning when I go to school. I am responsible for these kids' lives. I go to school armed with my developing knowledge and my commitment to African American kids. I learned, however, than I cannot command respect, I have to earn it. Students learn best through modeling—what they see is what they do—so if you have respect for yourself and them, the students eventually have respect for you and one another. I imagine my future. Having five classes, rather than two. I imagine students well equipped, mentally and emotionally, to do battle with the social world. Some days I question my decision to be a teacher. Perhaps I am not prepared to move from student to teacher. I don't want to grow up. I don't want to have my every movement scrutinized by a total of 150 students a day. I think I'm just scared, but I'm still learning.

Jennifer made a case for the constant adjustments that are a necessary part of teaching:

> I've learned that (in spite of what some say) there's no one right way to teach, that there's no such thing as the all-purpose writing workshop, that I have to figure out for myself how to make these

ideas that I've heard batted about work for me, personally, with the specific students in my class. There's no magic formula, and although I think I knew that deep down all along, it took attempting to cram someone else's formula into my classroom and seeing it not work very well before I realized just how true that is. I've learned that having a philosophy in place is very important, but not if it deafens me to hearing other ones. I've learned that structure, even teacher-imposed structure, is not bad, it's downright necessary sometimes, and that it doesn't have to be put in place in such a way as to be antithetical to student-centered learning. I've learned that I can work within the constraints of someone else's expectations of me and be true to my own beliefs at the same time. I've learned that teaching is incredibly difficult and unbelievably rewarding. That the kids will often make me happy enough to dance a jig. I've learned that planning is vital, being flexible is absolutely necessary, and thinking about everything is the only way to make things work.

John reflects back on his initial impressions of teaching:

It's interesting to note my words from my first week of student teaching. "But sometimes, you have to go with your plan even if it seems not to be working. You cannot change gears too many times in a class or else you are going to lose them." I think I have changed my opinion on this first sentence. If your plan is not working, change it on the spot. As I said earlier, some of my best teaching moments have come out of this improvisational space. To be truthful, probably some of my worst teaching has come out of this space as well. But, the more you know your class the less risky this improvising becomes in my opinion.

Regina noted her tolerance for uncertainty:

Through my log, I see the movement from writing about the practical side of the life of a student teacher—working with the cooperating teacher, getting to know the students, discipline—to the more speculative. At the end of the semester I'm asking "what ifs." I have discovered that I am obsessed with time—How long will this take? I'm constantly thinking about my goals—Why am I doing this? I try to out-guess my students, and I hope that getting to know them will help me in planning. I don't think that, as a teacher, I will ever be able to plan for every situation. Perfect foresight requires nothing less than a crystal ball. But I have learned to rehearse, to work through ideas, to envision a lesson or a discussion before it actually occurs in the classroom. I have learned I like to work with adolescents. It's hard to leave. I want the updates on boyfriends from Lila and Sophie, the sarcastic comments from Nafees about my choice of shoes, even the vocabulary quizzes. I want to watch them sing "Amazing Grace" again. I wonder where I'll be next year at this time.

Beverly, Jennifer, John, and Regina reveal much about teaching. "You know," Jennifer says at the end of the semester, looking back at a school building that is crumbling away brick by brick, "Last night I dreamed that I came to this school as a *real* teacher. I remember feeling that I knew exactly what the day would be like. Suddenly, I was in the hall, running toward my classroom and I must have been late. I was running and I dropped something and as I looked down I realized I had forgotten to wear shoes. I woke up with my heart knocking in my chest. Isn't that an awful dream to celebrate the last day of student teaching?" She shakes her head. "Will there ever be a time when this gets easier?"

John, his hands deep in his blazer pockets, responds, "Sure, Jennifer, oh, sure. When hell freezes over. For some reason, though I can't for the life of me say why, I feel a sense of anticipation and some dread in facing what I'm searching for."

Learning from Teaching

Several underlying principles were revealed through the study of these two groups of teachers. The first principle is that oftentimes teachers are so deeply involved in the planning of day-to-day classroom activities that they don't engage in discussions of their beliefs about teaching. In one sense deliberate reflection helped bridge the gap between this silence and an articulation of belief. The silence is not at odds with the articulation. It is more a matter of bringing unconscious articulation to a conscious level. How many times have I heard colleagues and myself say: "I don't quite know why I do it that way; It's a gut reaction; There's no way to explain that to the principal; It's just a matter of experience"? Such comments aren't productive if teachers are going to change and grow. Through explicit reflection, teachers can refine their self-awareness and more fully articulate the influences on their current teaching beliefs and practices.

Second, teachers can examine the *what* and the *how* in their role as teachers. All of these teachers questioned: Who am I as a teacher and what are my beliefs about teaching literature? Can I articulate what experiences, ideas, or people led me to these views? From these articulations, what can I learn about the way I put my beliefs into practice? Perhaps it is impossible to give definitive answers to these questions, but in raising them and attempting to answer them, the complexity of the participants' understanding of their beliefs became obvious as they negotiated and reconstructed how their personal experiences have influenced their teaching lives. Finding coherence among their beliefs, experiences, and practices allowed them to know more vividly, to tell more clearly, and to associate more strongly their beliefs with their actions.

Third, reflection may be used as a learning tool to facilitate teachers' understanding of the various contexts that influence their motivations and intentions in classrooms. I came to recognize such inquiry as essentially an investigation played out through practice. Out of the action, the desires, the major players, and the major events that are retold, the teller weaves thematic threads that are often contiguous. Tracing those key threads, as was demonstrated in the discussion of the participants' purposes of and role of the teacher in literature education, may lead the teller as well as the listener to make explicit life as it is "divined from the inside" (Bettelheim, 1977, p. 23).

Despite all the memories that I have from my years of teaching, the time I spent with these two groups of teachers reminded me what I'd taken for granted or forgotten. Learning from teaching is not effortless and unproblematic: there are challenging issues related to expectations, the congruence between personal and public identity in the school culture, of differing recommendations about how and what to teach, of differing beliefs about how students learn. All these must be considered in the complexity of circumstances in which teachers compose their teaching lives. Both the first-year teachers and the student teachers demonstrated ways in which they learned to examine their classroom practices. Having learned much from their struggles, I can suggest three approaches that might aid an inquiry into teaching.

Engage in Collaborative Inquiry with Trusted Colleagues

The discussions, interviews, and logs from both groups of teachers documented the year as a near roller coaster ride of ups and downs. Stephen wrote, "Today was great. For the first time the students were excited. I felt like we were creators of our learning. We were shaping the experiences of this class together. Part of this was because they've learned something about valuing their own reading. We've worked hard and long at that." As I read this in Stephen's log, I considered how important it was for these teachers to share their concerns, questions, critiques of school, and personal or public stories with each other.

Through inquiry, these teachers began to see themselves as active creators of their teaching lives. They worked through many of the issues together. Much of what was interpreted as "abrupt initiation" and "a case of whiplash," was viewed later as the reaction to their attempts to meet so many demands that needed to be dealt with simultaneously. The collaboration through inquiry supported these teachers' developing understandings as well as momentary frustrations. Comparing one another's experiences and assumptions provided a way of thinking beyond particularized content, students, or practices and toward implications from which they could compose their future work. Responding to the importance of shared inquiry, the Coordinators of Field Experiences in our program and I have begun to place prospective teachers in pairs or triads with a cooperating teacher, or more ideally with a team of cooperating teachers, for their year of student teaching. Part of the motivation behind this is to encourage collaborative inquiry at the sites. As a result, our prospective teachers have shared experiences that they can interrogate together, and they have one another to advise and support within the particular context of the shared classroom environment. We intend this structure to avoid the "sink-or-swim" mentality. It's too early to report anything other than preliminary hunches.

Cooperating teachers who have supported us in this effort for two years have described the experience as a good one. One of the teachers said that she found herself "right in the middle of the inquiry with the student teachers. I don't want to be left out. All of us are seeing things differently. I've started studying the critical incidents with them. I'm feeling a spirit of collaboration that I haven't had in my five years of teaching." Student teachers appreciate the support but express a worry that has been stated by cooperating teachers as well. The concern goes something like this: "But what happens when teachers who have had this collaborative experience enter the 'real' world of teaching next year?" I cannot answer the question. I want the 'real' world of teaching to change.

The first group of our prospective teachers who participated in this program are now in their first year of teaching. We are collecting data systematically in hopes of understanding the effects of our attempts at encouraging collaboration. This plan, of course, may not help them move into the first year of teaching if their school still perpetuates isolation and competition. I hope our prospective teachers take into these sites some habits of collaboration.

Develop a Repertoire of Strategies for Inquiry

Establish the habits of mind through which the work in schools can be defined, examined, and refined. One thing to consider is the ways in which a teacher preparation program might bridge the gap between its program and the realities of the school situation. Both groups of teachers detailed what they found problematic in schools—competition, incongruities, limited resources, and resistance. They provided information about the affective considerations that underlie their work—feelings of inadequacy, fear, frustration, and the search for identity. They revealed ways in which they inquired into these difficult situations.

In response to their methods of inquiry, I suggest that teachers write critical incidents, the particular moments in their teaching or school lives that are interesting or perplexing for one reason or another. In our teacher education program, prospective and in-service teachers write critical incidents regularly. Many critical incidents were included in this chapter—situations with students, any of the stories or parts therein of facing constraints, of temporary successes, or particular moments in any class session. The subject matter for critical incidents is bountiful and the possibilities limitless. Create a narrative reconstruction that is descriptive rather than evaluative and write these in present tense to achieve the immediacy of the situation. These two requirements are essential as ways of inhibiting the overzealous desire to analyze and evaluate incidents before carefully describing. This avoids the hurried jump toward conclusions.

The following critical incident was written by David Montgomery, a prospective teacher in our program this year, who was observing in the middle school reading class where he was student teaching:

"Today," the teacher begins, "we will be discussing 'Millie' on page 203. Please open your books so we can get started." As the class flips through their books and gets settled in, a hand goes up.

"Can I read?" Cory asks. One of the results of the question is that three other hands go up. These students also want a chance to read the story.

"No Cory, Not today." Ms. F. replies.

"Man, you're always reading. We never get a chance!" says Cory. As this confrontation catches the attention of the class, several students shout their agreement.

"Alright," responds Ms. F., "if you want to read, I'll let you take a book home and you can practice tonight. If you practice you can read tomorrow."

This seems to satisfy Cory, but now other hands shoot up. Several students also want to read the next day. Ms. F. tells the others that only two students will be allowed to read the next day and the others will have to wait their turn. Several students mumble expletives and one shouts out, "Why can't them who want to read now! Why we have to practice first?"

Ms. F. replies, "If you read today you'll stumble—you have to

> practice first before you read in front of the class. That way you
> won't make any mistakes." The class begins with the teacher read-
> ing the story.

I ask the teachers to bring three copies of what they have written.
Each week, one class member volunteers to bring copies for everyone so that we can collaborate as a entire class on one incident as a
way to help us build our repertoire of inquiry strategies. After the
whole class inquiry, small groups examine their individual incidents. David's writing demonstrates the richness of incidents for
inquiry that are available to these prospective teachers. I've found
this practice helps teachers develop the habit of mind to notice, describe, and analyze the situations around them that can inform their
teaching lives.

Keep Nudging at the Boundaries of Present Understandings

My responses to what these two groups of teachers taught me are
not meant to suggest that English educators or a program can or
should try to anticipate all the problematic situations that first-year
teachers might face. A program should not be reduced to those
things that will be directly applicable. I still believe in a healthy
dose of idealism in the guise of Maxine Greene, John Mayher, John
Dewey, and James Britton. I believe in critical interrogations in
which students hear the voices of Paulo Freire, bell hooks, Peter
McLaren, and Cameron McCarthy. This list of names may create its
own inquiry and criticism, but I mention a few of the writers and
friends who have nudged at the boundaries of my understandings
and have been important to the teachers with whom I've worked.
There are many other concerns raised through this study of first-
year teachers—conceptions of curriculum, processes of negotiation,
development of personal theories of teaching, and trust in becoming
one's self and the uncertainties that accompany this. I want to find
ways to help teachers deal with these issues and to help them understand that they are active creators in their teaching lives. When
they leave our program, I want them to trust uncertainty and ambiguity and have developed habits of mind that will help them compose and recompose the text of their lives as teachers.

   In my first year of teaching, Tollie Morrison, a serious-minded
teacher who was in her thirty-third year of teaching, forced me to
nudge the boundaries of my rather smug understandings. "I'll tell
you this," she said to me when we first met, "I'm fifty-seven years
old and have spent most of my life in this room." Her thick arm
made a sweep, taking in desks, file cabinets, chalk boards, and post-

ers, the edges curled and faded. "It doesn't get easier. About the time I think I've figured out literature teaching, everything changes. I've followed many trends of teaching literature, and I've jumped on a few bandwagons. For years it was themes, then genres, then elements of literature. What is it now, dearie? I suspect you're coming here with some newfangled notions."

Frankly, I was a product of New Criticism. You bet I had some notions, but I stared at her, thinking smugly that she was suspicious or envious or downright intimidated. I didn't expect that I'd see students throughout that year enter and exit her room smiling. They spoke of her in nearly reverential tones. I wouldn't have imagined that students would be sprawled out in the hall working on projects for her class nor that my own students would say with great pride that they'd been in Ms. Morrison's English class last year. Least of all did I expect that she'd have a stroke in January that left her partially paralyzed or that her students would take over the classes with a bewildered substitute, mostly a voyeur of their learning, who puttered around the room getting in their way. No one expected that Tollie would return to Room 311 in April, dragging one leg, steadied by a cane, her right arm drooping, her eye tearing incessantly. I stood in the doorway of my room watching her students crowd around her, asking how they could help, giving her hugs and assurances that they were happy to have her back. She looked from one to the other. Then, in measured and even tones that slurred together into a new melodious quality, she said, "Let's get to work. Show me what you've been doing. On with it."

Chapter Three

Far More Than Technicians: Provoking Reflections on Teaching Literature

My story of literature education begins with my grandmother reading from *The Arabian Nights*. She would take one of the Burton volumes from the bookcase, the leather cracked from use. Her own ten children had, decades before, slipped nearer sleep, listening to her voice bring stories of far away places, adventures, sadness, intrigue, and sometimes death. Now, it was my turn to be educated into literature. On my grandmother's farm in eastern Idaho, in the late forties, after the war was over, most fathers had come home and were well into the rhythms of their work and daily lives. Not mine. What remained of him was in my mother's memory, and the few remaining trinkets and medals that were wrapped in tissue, in a suit box, on a shelf in a closet next to the bedroom where my mother, brother, and I slept. The rest was in shallow earth of rice fields somewhere between Tokyo and Yokohama.

My memories of that period lie foremost in the context of his absence. My grandmother, attempting to fill the space, shared with me the literature that she loved. It was before and into my early elementary school experience when she read *Tom Sawyer, Huckleberry Finn*, the stories from the Grimm's collection and Hans Christian Andersen. I entered the world of *David Copperfield* and *Oliver Twist*, of *Little Women* and *Alice in Wonderland* not long after. I constructed a world of experience and imagining far beyond where I lived, and located myself within the spirit of the grandmother who led me into a life with literature. In the text of her reading more than in the text of the individual stories, the meaning of what she did and did not do stays with me. She invited and nurtured. Through conversations about what we read, we negotiated our private and shared understandings, many times partial, multiple, and often contradictory. Sometimes she led me to revisit an event, or a character's motivation; other times she nudged me to see myself in what I read or to create a new story. She did not overburden my meanings with her own.

For my grandmother, it was the sharing that gave her pleasure. Her family was grown; the farm had been given piece by small piece to her children. Preparing meals, hanging laundry, and reading to a young child filled her days. For me, it is the first conscious memory of my life of imagining, searching out, and experiencing those worlds beyond the small house where we lived. Reading led me into geographic and spiritual landscapes as words stretched beyond that small plot of land with its one chicken coop, two cows, half-acre garden plot, and a small house where my grandmother and mother did their best to raise a boy and a girl who would find it necessary to step out from that quiet world into a world moving at full speed, one far beyond their imaginings.

The time rushed toward 1966 and my first year of teaching. For at least the first several years, students wrote timed essays, author papers, discussed what they thought I wanted to hear, and waited for the bell. Finally, I realized that I had taken on, like putting on a new coat, a literature teacher's identity. I was reproducing what literature teachers from my school experiences had done or what I assumed they were supposed to do. It wasn't until I began to look at myself as the subject of my own history and read theorists and practitioners' accounts that I questioned this socially constructed image of literature teacher and began to negotiate the image and identity of the literature teacher that I was becoming.

Toward Teacher Reflectivity

Many teachers describe how particular experiences or understandings challenge them to think differently about their teaching practices. One teacher explained that her personal reading life was unlike the reading experiences she designed for her classroom. This realization led her to reconsider how she might better support students' reading lives (Brown, 1987). Another teacher concluded that a collaborative research group helped her reconceptualize literature teaching as more than a series of activities (Reid and VanDeWeghe, 1994). A third teacher recognized the intimate connection between students and teachers' expectations, which led him to examine the variety of roles, motivations, and experiences that must be taken into consideration in literature discussions (Nelms, 1988). In each case, these teachers provoked new ways of thinking about their present conceptions of teaching. Their reconsideration, reconceptualization, and recognition—all forms of thinking back or again ('re-')—illustrate how practice-centered reflection may be applied to teachers' work.

Practice-centered reflection, then, might be conceived as a practical activity with the central aim of informing or improving practice by making problematic the situation under investigation. Such reflection can help teachers identify what happened, analyze why it happened, and speculate on possible changes. However, this is not to suggest that the aim of reflective practitioners is limited to the improvement of particular practices. Teaching practices are situated in contexts shaped by interrelated factors such as personality and philosophy of the teacher as well as intentions of students, other teachers, administrators, parents, and the community. Reflection on contexts can increase teachers' insights about the nature of teaching, create dissonance that enables them to reevaluate purposes, and aid their understanding of the complex social forces underlying teaching practices. Consequently, it is worth asking: What do teachers reflect upon and what forms does that reflection take? What is the relationship between the teachers' verbalized understanding of reflection and their use of reflection in planning and teaching classes? What are the implications of answers to these questions for teachers and teacher educators?

Although there is a long tradition of interest in reflection (Dewey, 1933; Schaefer, 1967; Feiman, 1979; Grimmett, MacKinnon, Erickson, and Riecher, 1990), it took an outsider who wrote of engineers, architects, town planners, and psychologists to rekindle educators' interest in reflection as a way to develop professional knowledge (Schön, 1983, 1987, 1991). Schön recognized that "the multiplicity of conflicting views poses a predicament for the practitioner who must choose among multiple approaches to practice or devise his own ways of combining them" (1983, p. 17), and he suggested that professionals do reflect in and on their practices. The growing number of books, journal articles, and conference presentations on reflectivity exemplify the current interest in teachers as producers rather than consumers of knowledge. These include testimonials of teachers transformed into reflective practitioners, discussions about education programs, accounts of mentoring projects, and studies of teacher socialization that illustrate the use of reflection to interrogate institutional contexts (Clandinin and Connelly, 1988; Clark and Lampert, 1986; Gore, 1987; Korthagen, 1985; Zeichner and Gore, 1990). These accounts emphasize that through teachers' deliberate interaction with a situation or belief they develop new forms of understanding that can lead to changes in practice.

Many discussions emphasize the conditions that promote reflection. Reflection can be encouraged by presenting alternative points of view that help define multiple possibilities for action. For example, Zumwalt (1982) found that teachers reflect when they examine competing versions of knowledge. Teachers reflect on the situational contexts that inform practice when they identify conflicts or misunderstandings (Sanders and McCutcheon, 1986). Discussions about curricular and instructional decisions provide a catalyst for reflection (Zeichner and Liston, 1987; Russell, 1988). Researchers and theorists have concluded that reflection is a learned activity that informs professional knowledge (Holt-Reynolds, 1992; Hunsaker and Johnston, 1992).

The ends achieved through reflection have been examined as well. MacKinnon (1987) suggests that teachers who engage in a process of cyclical reflection and goal setting are more likely to consider new curricular approaches or practices. Some researchers describe the emancipatory possibilities of reflectivity. For example, Bullough and Gitlin (1989) stress that teachers' critical clarification of educational means and ends helps them understand how intentions are explicitly related to practice. In the field of English education, researchers and practitioners recommend an uncommon view of teaching that emphasizes teachers who improvise, frame problems in new ways, and engage in hypothesis testing as they reflect on practice (Mayher, 1990). Knoblauch and Brannon (1988) believe that "the habit of reflection that teachers can derive from their inquiries will make their teaching practices more thoughtful, more responsible to students' needs, more deliberately (as opposed to casually) flexible" (p. 26). It is generally believed that reflection effects the continuous process of knowledge construction.

Studies on how to promote teacher reflectivity and those describing the outcomes of inquiry provide valuable information about teachers' reflection. Much remains to be learned, however. Few studies give accounts of the relationship between teachers' verbalized understanding of reflection and their use of reflection in planning and teaching. For example, James Britton (1987) suggested that "every lesson should be for the teacher an inquiry, some further discovery, a quiet form of research" (p. 15). Yet, comparatively few descriptions exist that portray the teachers' understanding of reflection in a specific discipline or their use of reflection around instantiations of practice.

Provoking Through Contradiction

Perhaps inevitably, literature teachers confront multiple and contradictory beliefs about purposes, curriculum, and pedagogy. "The teaching of literature has from the beginning been under considerable pressure to formulate itself as a body of knowledge" (Applebee, 1974, p. 245). Literature teachers express feelings of powerlessness when confronting competing versions of validated knowledge and practice (Vinz and Kirby, 1991). As outlined by Applebee (1974), it is easy to notice a near melodramatic search for purposes: a literary canon that transmits cultural and ethical values; literature as experience or literature as transaction that engages readers with text; or New Criticism that focuses on the conventions of literature. Practitioners, researchers, and theorists offer a confusing array of purposes. Behind all these, the literature anthology looms larger than life in most classrooms, offering literature teachers an array of activities and questions.

The emphasis on exposure to great authors in the cultural heritage model (Muller, 1967), along with an emphasis on content and close reading of text as espoused by the New Critics, has given way to various reader-response and transactional approaches. Rosenblatt's (1978) theory has been adapted from popularized versions of theory into practice in secondary literature classes (Probst, 1988). As Rosenblatt describes it, reading is a co-creation between text, reader, and the larger community. Not only is the theory a psycholinguistic one, but also sociolinguistic because she emphasizes "the attitudes and social relations fostered by the way literature is taught" (Pradl, 1991, p. 23). The changing emphasis on the authority of readers and texts has caused teachers of literature to confront their own constructions of beliefs and practices as well as their investments in habit or preference. How classroom communities are defined, how they operate, and the explicit and implicit messages that grow out of theories about readers and reading challenge more traditionally legitimated discourses on teaching and learning literature.

Teachers' past experiences have been shown to influence not only their readings but also the readings and practices they validate in classrooms. Zancanella's (1991) study of five teachers leads him to suggest that "pedagogically useful knowledge exists in these five teachers' personal approaches to literature" (p. 5). Bloland (1983) reveals in her study of four high school English teachers that teacher choice rests "on deeply cherished beliefs and constructs about language and learning" (p. 264), which she defines as "the inner curriculum—what teachers think they ought to be doing" (p. 268). Thinking through the ways in which past and present experiences inform the other, no teacher is free of history and context. From this, I assume all teachers are constrained and emancipated by their places of experience as well as the challenge of possibility. Peter Elbow (1990), with an eye to the future, considers:

> In the end I am tempted to say we are a profession both polarized and paralyzed around literature. We see the problems: it unreasonably privileges certain texts and certain kinds of language and certain kinds of reading; it heightens certain destructive political divisions in the profession; it destructively narrows the profession. But in those very problems we cannot help but also see virtues (p. 101).

Recognizing these tensions led me to ask three veteran teachers, each with at least fifteen years experience, to allow me to document and examine their reflections on the teaching of literature.

Faced with questions about what literature study means and to whom, I wanted to understand how these teachers inquire into their purposes and practices. How do they make use of their knowledge and beliefs to determine how and what they teach? What are the processes through which they examine their beliefs about and practices in literature education? As Bruner (1990) notes, "To insist upon explanations in terms of 'causes' simply bars us from trying to understand how human beings interpret their worlds" (p. xiii). Rather, to "be conscious of how we come to our knowledge and as conscious as we can be about the values that lead us to our perspectives" (p. 30) is the goal of inquiry. So it was with an intent to illuminate the nature of reflective inquiry in literature education that Beth Carter, Jane Weston, Joe Conrad, and I began our inquiry into their constructions of teaching literature.

Writing this after spending seven months of intensive study with Beth, Jane, and Joe is my way of considering what they taught me, documenting what they taught themselves, and proposing how their inquiry might be valuable to others. During our last formal session together, Beth said: "Every step we've taken is part of a joint story. I see that now. The multiple versions of teaching and learning that we've relived for ourselves or told each other helped me think about what's behind what I do. I've found new ways to think about who I am as a teacher. There's so much inside of and underneath and around the day-to-day classroom enactment." There is a message in

Beth's statement that can't be glossed over. These teachers helped me consider more carefully how beliefs, experiences, and practices intersect and how centrally important it is for them and for all teachers to understand the complexities of composing a teaching life.

Introducing the Experienced Teachers

Jane Weston has been teaching for fifteen years in elementary classrooms. During the year when we documented the process and content of her inquiry she taught fourth grade. Jane is actively involved in language arts curriculum projects, textbook adoption committees, and a reading group whose members discuss professional literature monthly. Jane earned a master's degree in early childhood education. Her earlier experiences in teacher education were "fairly nondescript and it seemed like we were mostly getting initiated into the language of teaching . . . I did have a few good models of teachers who were really trying to get students thinking and involved in learning." Jane experienced reading and writing workshops in language arts methods classes. "That opened up some possibilities . . . As I think about that now it seems progressive for the early 80s. Going back for the master's degree later also revived my energy and interest." As Jane pointed out, "My own learning is enriched by what my students bring to me through their questions, frustrations, and successes. I've learned so much about literature from listening to them." It is important to her that students love reading and feel satisfaction and success when they pick up a book. "I've often hoped that when they read to their own children—well, you know—that they'll remember with pleasure some of the stories we shared together and pass on a love of those to their children."

Beth Carter has been teaching for eighteen years in middle schools. She taught three seventh grade, one eighth grade, and two ninth grade English classes the year we inquired together. Beth received a master's degree in Curriculum and Instruction. Since that time she has been actively involved in district curriculum revision as a facilitator and writer, served on textbook adoption committees, and is a member of a monthly reading group. Beth recalled that she had little experience in education classes until her master's work. "I came in by alternate routes. I had content area background and the French along with a Fulbright experience that got me through the door and into the contract office. Things were much looser then." Beth believes her teaching experience has been the best teacher. "I've learned a lot along the way, but part of that happens because

I'm teaching at the same time I'm learning. I don't know what it would be like to sit in classrooms and talk about teaching without ever having done it. Teaching literature has always allowed me to find a reason to raise issues that are critical to the survival of decent human beings. We develop sympathy, compassion, and the greatest of all human qualities—empathy for others."

Joe Conrad has been teaching for nineteen years at the high school level. His literature courses have included American Literature, World Humanities, Russian Literature, a genre approach to World Literature, and a chronological approach to British Literature. The year we documented his inquiry, Joe taught senior English. He had a master's degree in Classical Studies as well as a master's in English Literature. He has been actively involved in district curriculum projects, served on textbook adoption committees, and has written numerous district curriculum guides at the high school level. For Joe, "methods classes were really at the tail end of my work. I was in the Jesuit seminary first of all, and I left with this traditional and classical education. I didn't think about teaching." Joe believes that most of his opinions were formed by what he observed in school; most of the classes he took for certification also taught him to replicate what he had seen as a student. "In fact, I did that for years, but sort of grew into my own by having colleagues who enjoyed talking about teaching or questioned teaching. I started playing around with ideas late in my career. I realized I mostly heard my own voice in the classroom. That was like a whack on the side of the head. Just maybe kids needed the same chances to fall in love with pieces of literature."

Developing History as a Teacher

I began this study with an uneasiness caused by the enthusiasm for reflective practice that has led to teacher educators' implementation of models that purport to teach reflection. Much of the professional literature suggests that teachers who reflect are better teachers. But, what does "to reflect" mean and how does that concept get translated into practice? I wanted to understand reflection from teachers' perspectives and determine how they, as Schön (1987) describes it, reflect-on-action as well as reflect-in-action. From this, we may learn how reflection becomes actualized, which in turn may be useful in facilitating the process for other teachers.

Table 1 depicts the data sources and the time frame for collection. Nine *interviews* were semistructured allowing freedom for Beth,

Table 1. Phases of Data Collection

	Phase I October–December	Phase II January–March	Phase III April
Interviews AT	*Baseline* Concepts of Reflection *Autobiographical Profile* (2 per participant)	*Clarification of Artifacts* (2 per participant) *Clarification of Themes* (2 per participant)	*Group Interview* (2 for the group)
*Observations** (Classroom)	6 classes per participant (consecutive 2 days)	8 classes per participant (consecutive 2 days)	
Follow-Up Discussions AT	After 2-day sequence (3 per participant)	After 2-day sequence (4 per participant)	
Artifacts WP	Collected (Chronological Order)	Analyzed	
Transcripts WP	Copies given to participants for feedback	Participants' feedback examined	Participants' feedback examined
Chapter Drafts of Findings WP		Delivered to participants	Delivered to participants (written feedback returned to researcher)

* FN, VT, & WP Planning logs were provided by each participant prior to the observation.
Abbreviations: AT, audiotaped; FN, field notes; VT, videotaped; WP, written product.

Jane, and Joe to develop other lines of inquiry (Goetz and LeCompte, 1984). Interviews lasted approximately one hour each. The *baseline interview* was designed to elicit Beth, Jane, and Joe's descriptions of the purposes and objects of their reflection. In two *autobiographical profile interviews* they described personal experiences with literature that influenced their beliefs about teaching literature. Beth, Jane, and Joe compiled a collection of artifacts from their years of teaching, arranged in chronological order, for the *clarification of artifacts interviews*. Artifacts included representative lesson plans, tests, teaching activities, assignments, and student products. Beth, Jane, and Joe used the artifacts as a vehicle to reflect on changes in their practices. They reviewed transcripts of previous interviews as well as my interpretive drafts before the two *clarification of themes interviews*. During those interviews, Beth, Jane, and Joe clarified issues that were raised in the transcripts or by my interpretations before we met for *two group interviews* that served as the culminating experience. Fourteen *classroom observations* were arranged in blocks of two consecutive days. Beth, Jane, and Joe wrote lesson plans in their *logs* that I read before class sessions. During observations, I scripted what they and the students said as well as noted classroom structures and the general atmosphere. This technique is similar to that used by Goldhammer, Anderson, and Krajewski (1980). All class sessions were videotaped so that I could check the accuracy of my notes and generate transcripts of what was said. In follow-up interviews, Beth, Jane, and Joe described catalysts for reflection during as well as after the class.

I undertook analysis of the data inductively following a method that allowed me to make constant comparisons across sources of data (Goetz and LeCompte, 1984; Lincoln and Guba, 1985; Erickson, 1986). Initial analysis began during Phase I of data collection. From this analysis, data were classified into three categories: (1) the types of reflection; (2) Beth, Jane, and Joe's use of reflection to inform practice; and (3) features of their reflection in planning and teaching particular class sessions. I labeled discrete incidents or statements from all data sources until I could make empirical assertions (i.e., "Beth determines, as a priority in planning, how to connect particular texts with student interest."). This process continued throughout Phase II, but with the added task of writing extended versions of the empirical assertions. For example, the assertion made in Phase I, "Beth determines, as a priority in planning, how to connect particular texts with student interest," was extended into a three-paragraph analysis of how Beth reflects, using examples from the data that illustrate the connection between literary selection and student interest. This elaboration included how Beth studies various literary selections to determine the subject connections with student interests. Existing categories were redefined or refined as empirical assertions were clarified and illustrated. During Phase III, I prepared case descriptions on each teacher as an additional way to refine the interpretation and presentation of their reflection. The separate cases were then brought together for purposes of comparison and contrast. In this chapter, I focus on patterns that emerged from cross-case analysis.

Autobiographical Inquiry

What was suggestive about Beth, Jane, and Joe's reflection into their own histories was how the authority of their early experiences continues to influence their teaching. Through inquiry, they began to challenge the authority of experience and to rethink the relationship between their present work and past beliefs and experiences. The purpose was not to sentimentalize and overgeneralize, nor to be aware when that was happening. In part, this required that they distance themselves and read the text of their retellings and remembrances to unearth the constructions of literature education that have contributed to their self-identity as teachers. When past and present were considered as dimensions of the whole experience, these teachers authored new stories that transgressed particular moments, beliefs, or actions. This did not occur to the exclusion of the subjective, the logical, or the spiritual. Rather, a web of feeling and meaning emerged that took them beyond concreteness and the particularities of any one experience.

Teachers' Purposes in Literature Education

Beth's personal experiences helped her see that literature can open a world of possibilities. "A world of questions that get readers to respond and think about life and make connections with their own lives and others' lives. I think now that all the adults in my family expected me to think about what I read and to make some sense out of it." Joe indicated that his father's acting out of stories was important "to my teaching. I think of how he got inside the literature and lived it through those performances of his. I've been willing to risk doing that in class because he was an important model." Jane recalled that reading was a pleasurable experience and "the joy may come through the beauty of the language or the ideas. I don't wear the overalls with the deep pockets that my father kept books in, but the books are there within easy reach. I make it a point for students to know that." As Beth, Jane, and Joe continued to examine their experiences, they began to interpret in what ways this personal history with literature was formative in shaping their beliefs about literature education.

Beth's high regard for opportunities to think, talk about, and share this record of human thought and imagination is central in the narrative of her recollected experiences. "That's kind of my Southern background, that idea that literature is instructive. Sometimes I may think I'm reading to be entertained, but if I'm being entertained, I'm learning something as well." Beth remembers that the significant adults in her family would say, "Why does this happen? Why can she cut off their tails with a carving knife? Is this really fair?" Beth finds this framework for literature's instructive purposes compelling, perhaps because her initiation into literature's purposes provided her with a strong example. "My grandfather wanted a response. He wanted to know what you liked and why you liked it . . . What was good . . . What struck a chord . . . with him there was always dialogue going on."

Joe finds that "there's a whole aesthetic side to literature." His emphasis on developing the aesthetic sensibilities is a thread that weaves into the fabric of his autobiographical account. Often in discussion, he referred to Orwell's "Shooting an Elephant." "It's a hell of a good piece. It's just beautiful. There's that moment and then the elephant becomes suddenly old and begins to sag slightly." His belief in aesthetic appreciation is informed through his father's deliberate way of focusing attention on the potential of language to evoke images or "recreate a feeling through the sound as much as the idea. My dad got me thinking by asking questions about language and he emphasized the beauty of a passage when he'd read and reread." Joe emphasizes the importance of preserving the oral tradition of literature. "I'd say that my early experiences sort of set that purpose in mind that literature needs to be heard. My father had this beautiful reading voice. I'd like to think that reading from the page can't ever take the place of literature as performance." Connected closely with Joe's concern for the development of an aesthetic sensibility is his belief that part of the purpose of literature education is to provide models for writers. "I learn from other writers. Reading is a way to help readers discover the good three sentences that reach out and grab us in." That in turn, as Joe sees it, translates into readers' understanding of the writer's resources.

Jane sees literature education as a series of experiences with, and exposure to, various kinds of literature that bring readers "to understand more places, emotions, and ideas than they experience from their own life. It's a way of living vicariously." She does believe that literature education rather than reading instruction is the effective and humane way to develop students' reading skills. As modeled by her father, there are multitudinous ways of "talking about what we read—reciting, reading passages to someone else, talking through ideas." Jane believes that doing so opens up new experiences. As Jane sees it, students must carry away the love of literature. "Someday it will be armor for them, this love, that will help them through television and computers."

Their initiation into literature suggests that while each has a unique series of situations, which cannot be reduced into generalization, it is critical to see how vital the home and family experiences were to their formative conceptions of what literature is and means. It is interesting that all three, through the course of seven months of interviews, mentioned at some point how the entrance of television into their lives threatened to take away the literature experiences in each household. All agreed that they perhaps oversentimentalized their early experiences even with distance from the events. As Joe said, "it might be the Golden Age syndrome," but as Beth reminded him, "as long as these experiences provide positive models that influence my teaching, I'll live with that."

Their autobiographical inquiry raises important questions for me about how viewpoints, idealized or not, mediate or structure belief. Kelly (1955) speculates in his personal construct theory that a person's accumulated experiences may build a network of meanings, a construct, that continuously makes sense of, anticipates, or reformulates knowledge. These early experiences become near touchstones that contribute to their understanding of teaching. Recollecting their literature histories offered Beth, Jane, and Joe ways of repossessing the inner meaning from their early experiences. Just as with reading any story, they read their own stories, alert to the signs of character, setting, complexity of feeling, anticipated action, or motif. In the context of their teaching, Beth, Jane, and Joe tend to create narrative representations of past experiences that provide information about their present teaching choices and decisions. It might be argued that their narrative representations endow a kind of legitimacy to what they do, or suggest that these early and positive experiences with literature have made them good teachers. I resist representing the complex intersections and dimensions of actual experiences too simply. On one hand, it could be suggested that there is a normalizing or idealizing impact that results in Beth's expectations that literature should be instructive, Joe's view of the beauty of literature, or Jane's concern that students love the literature. As these recollections may become exaggerated conceptions, part of these teachers' work in inquiry was to begin to demystify their knowledge as some seamless authority. They began to consider the uncertainties and multiple representations.

The inquiry shifted to considerations of their school histories with literature, which were filled with many taken-for-granted constructions—basal readers, recitation, anthologies, exams about literature, literary criticism, essays, and questions at the end of reading selections. Unlike the contemporary, yet provisional, challenges asserted by transactional and reader-response approaches, literature study was predominantly exposure to classics, authority of text, and the apparatuses of textual criticism.

Beth's early school years were nearly tortuous. She was not allowed to attend kindergarten because she was already reading. It was well known that a reader was a behavior problem. The next year, in first grade, Beth was told that she read wrong because she couldn't sound out the words. "It was a bad start. I remember the precursors of dittos and workbooks. Then, the family made a series of moves practically every year." As Beth describes her remembrances of herself in school, "I was always the new person, the kid in a corner with books, spending time in the school library reading." Beth began acting up in school by pulling fire alarms and plugging toilets. "Schools don't know how to deal with bad girls. They beat boys. They don't know what to do with girls." At ten, Beth was sent to live with her grandfather in the back hills of Tennessee. "He was wonderful. I lived with literature again. It was a central part of his life. When he deemed me civilized, at twelve, I went back home." As she describes it, her school experiences were routine after that. She has one or two memories of literature teachers who made a difference in her life. In eighth grade, in North Carolina, Beth had a teacher who completed a master's study on *Marshes of Glynn* by Sidney Lanier. "She loved it so much and we were at the marshes. Right outside the door. Yet, it was still her love. We went along. She would read a section and we'd go look." In one or two other classes Beth felt connected to literature. As a senior in high school, Beth had a teacher who turned the class over to the students. "I thought it was brave of him. We made a film of *Beowulf*. We pooled our money and bought a 16mm film and rented a gorilla suit. Beowulf arrived in a canoe with a hole cut in the bottom. It was a wonderful film and he wouldn't let anyone outside our group see it. He decided it was irreverent to *Beowulf*. He chickened out." Most of Beth's school experiences with literature were reading, explicating, and critiquing. There was no mystery, no connection to life and other human beings. "I knew when I started teaching I didn't want to be like that."

Joe attended Catholic schools and mostly remembers the stress placed on oral reading. As he suggested, "I have a few mean nun stories, and so I just think of the angst I went through. I try to have a reasonably humane classroom. Kids are sometimes fearful about literature." From Joe's perspective, school literature was not the same as reading literature at home. "We had, if not reading circles, at least class oral reading all the way through high school. I'm not

talking about reading performances, just getting the reading done."
Most of Joe's education in literature was "very traditional—reading
literature, analyzing it, hearing the official interpretation, finding
out the background, and learning terminology." Joe doesn't have
strong images of what his teachers did or didn't do. "A monotony.
That's what I remember—read, discuss, pop quizzes, tests, essays. A
lack of passion."

Jane remembers much the same pattern in studying literature. A
few memorable experiences are included. Her sixth grade teacher
loved poetry. "We took the poems apart and dissected them and
looked into them. I found that exhilarating. We memorized poems.
Each student bought a paperback, *101 Best Poems,* for fifty-two
cents. Frost was one of my favorites. I've never lost my appetite for
poems. I'd read with a kind of perusal and a selfish way of reading
just for enjoyment." A few teachers gave her "the tools and the confidence, both of them, to feel good about myself as a reader, but we
glossed over the enjoyment."

To what extent can these school experiences provide examina-
tions for critique and possibility? The role of power and authority
that enables or denies young readers from making a personal connection with literature is very much in teachers' hands. The place
of self-identity in and through the literature was nearly absent from
the sanctioned work of literature study for these teachers. My point
is that the disclosure of these experiences even in narrative demonstrate how Beth, Jane, and Joe felt that the pedagogy of their literature education was contextless, androgynous, disembodied, and
dispassionate even with an occasional particularized remembrance.
With few exceptions, school did not provide images or experiences
of engagements with literature or the emancipation of readers to
mobilize their interests, strategies, and agendas when reading literature. Whether or how Beth, Jane, and Joe's school experiences can
be said to determine their beliefs and practices is not easily gener-
alizable. Precisely for this reason, Beth, Jane, and Joe began to probe
more deeply into the role of teacher of literature that each of them
has constructed and continues to construct.

The Role of Teacher in Literature Education

Although Beth, Jane, and Joe each stated that their personal histories shaped much of their vision of the role of literature teacher,
they acknowledge that their images of what teachers could do in
classrooms was limited. Additionally, constraints—institutional,
temporal, and societal—affected the ways in which they could

imagine how to teach literature differently. Many competing forces contest for a place in the composing of teachers' identity.

For Beth, the teacher's role is to open the dialogue with and about a piece of literature and help students find the importance for themselves. She believes that the role of the teacher is "to ask the questions and to really listen to what [students] get from the literature." The teacher is an enabler who facilitates students' readings. For Beth, a good teacher models this open and questioning attitude. "I listen to the students and expect from that model they will listen to one another." The models from her early life stay with her. "I mean the best teaching times are when we are talking about a piece of literature, and everybody is throwing out ideas. My grandfather was the model of a questioner and prodder in nearly Socratic ways."

Beth's focus on student involvement is resisted by some students, parents, and administrators. Demands by students "for more clarity in assignments, more focused discussion, and knowing the teacher's opinion" often challenge her view of a unitary self. During the inquiry, Beth began to question if there was a way to meet everyone's agendas. "I keep thinking that I know what they need. Now I'm beginning to question why I think my agenda is better. I rationalize by saying they don't know and school has always been this other way for them, but am I just imposing something else that isn't any better?"

As Joe tells it, the teacher facilitates entrances through which students can make the bridge between what they know and do not know. "Making connections helps them feel like insiders, not always like novices." Too many teachers, in Joe's belief, make literature a passive thing. "We don't do anything with literature except tell kids to read this or that story, and we'll discuss it. We need to find ways to get them into conversations with what they're reading." Joe often turned his reflection on the teacher's role back to his personal experience. "Now my father made literature accessible and pleasurable. He'd dramatize scenes, laugh, question, and really pay attention to what I thought and what I liked. Why should it be different in schools?" The teacher needs to connect reading to writing. Joe emphasizes that the literature teacher should nurture the student as a writer. "The question isn't whether you're a literature teacher or a writing teacher. Study of literature is a starting point for writing and writing is a starting point for understanding literature."

Joe began to recognize through continued inquiry that in many ways his role was oppressive. "As free and open as I've thought I am, I've misled myself. It's my agenda, my ways of learning literature, what I think that's important that gets put into place as rituals." As Joe continued to grapple with how he was coming to view himself, he began to see how recognizing contradictions opened spaces for the possibility of refining his understanding of the teachers' role. "I keep thinking that the students will get into my routines. Now, I'm wondering why I don't help them find their own ways in. Does it need to be drama, oral reading, and writing? I don't know. I can't quite imagine how to do that. That's the tricky part."

Jane sees the role of a teacher of literature tied integrally with developing student interests as lifelong readers. Jane believes reading and literature are intertwined. She rejects the notions of reading groups or basal programs. As Jane describes her belief in the teacher's role, nurturing students is central. Launching them. A teacher must have faith that students will develop interests in literature. "Constant immersion into literature. That's what worked for me. Always having literature around and central in my life and the lives of people I'd admired." As Jane tells it, "Readers are more excited in learning from one another, and they build on each other's ideas and reading experiences. When it is going well, we hear them saying, 'I read something by him, too, and isn't he great, and you have to read this one if you liked that one. You're going to love this.'"

Jane examined the implications of her guidance. Some of her most compelling arguments for her classroom practice had underlying assumptions that she began to challenge. "For me, constant immersion was important. I love literature and while I blame myself when all my students don't, I think underneath I blame them. I value the students who are most like me." Jane expects students to share, to be excited, and to learn from one another. She has structures in place that can help make that happen. In her final autobiographical interview, Jane stated: "It isn't that I can make them me. I think underneath much of my nurturing, I'm trying to get them to be more like me. I need to question my strategies and priorities and how to help bring out who they are."

Through the inquiry, Beth, Jane, and Joe articulated a developing consciousness of the multiple positions, desires, and identities they negotiate. Confirming what Belsey (1977) has argued, individuals are "not a unity, not autonomous, but a process, perpetually in construction, perpetually contradictory, perpetually open to change" (p. 132). Teaching identity is influenced by a wide variety of factors. Working through multiple and contradictory facets of identity, Beth, Jane, and Joe's inquiry was a complicated one. They began to recognize the continuous reforming of identity. The dissonance this created led them to defensive reactions at times. Joe said, "I can't do everything. I don't have the imagination or energy." At others times, they interpreted their experiences as contingent understandings. As Jane expressed it, "What I try at any given moment is the best that I can do then. I know that I'm open to change, that I invite it. I won't think or act in exactly the same way next year or the next. The changes are sometimes subtle."

The autobiographical inquiry was a way of keeping Beth, Jane, and Joe's thinking about teaching in process. They were able to distance themselves through narrative, not only to retell and recollect but also to reconceptualize ways in which they interpret their underlying assumptions and practices. This inquiry encouraged them to view their teaching lives as dynamic, ever changing, always responsive to contexts, events, and other people. These teachers, who have spent the better part of two decades in classrooms, have had many opportunities to formulate, reformulate, and test the consequences and implications of their beliefs and practices. Through this facet of their inquiry, they found an explicit medium to traverse the complex landscape of their multiple realities. They used their autobiographical accounts as *purposive agents* for learning how they view the constraints as well as the possibilities for planning their future practices.

Teacher as Model. Jane, Joe, and Beth read to their students, share their own reading interests, describe current reading projects, and give students various degrees of responsibility for their own learning. Joe shows students how to "open conversations with the text," and Jane demonstrates her lifelong passion for literature of diverse types. Beth models curiosity and a questioning attitude. Joe demonstrates how language sees and sounds differently. Beth makes her reading processes explicit, and Jane discusses with students how she chooses a book. The participants utilize various ways to model and apply the idea of models in diverse ways, but for all, modeling enables the teacher to assist learning. As Joe stated, "I hadn't thought consciously about how often I model for students. It's more important than I realized in my teaching." But just how interactive is the modeling?

The very claim of purpose—to empower students—becomes something to be questioned by the teacher, as if liberation by the White Knight were necessary. At one level, Beth, Jane, and Joe began to see this as they studied the language of their discussion. Joe noted, "I hear 'teacher' and 'I' as if we are the only models of learners." Jane questioned whether or not modeling gives students a monotone way to approach literature. "Students might think of more if I weren't so strong in showing them, in setting the structures." Beth noted that this would require "rethinking, I'm just not sure. I see the benefits of being a model of a learner, but I have new questions." The three of them were stunned that they had begun to question something they believed in so completely. This is one example that underscores the importance of reading teaching histories as a text.

Teacher as Writer. Jane began writing stories as she walked the woods outside Truckee. Beth was writing letters of apology and a family newspaper to "keep the extended family up on the gossip." Joe found fiction writing as a way to bridge "noticing and applying." The three believe that literature teachers need to be practicing writers, and each continues to explore the making of literature through their writing. The poems that Jane writes for her granddaughters and students, the short stories that Joe shares with his writing group and classes, and the poems and personal narratives that Beth uses in class illustrate the importance of writing in their teaching lives.

Long before the research and practitioner literature was filled with dicta about the role of English teacher as writer, these teachers had established writing as a central part of their lives and their students' lives with literature. It is not difficult to state that the teacher of literature should be a practicing writer. To see three teachers acting in and through this belief is a very different thing. These teachers are reconceptualizing their histories with literature into classroom practices. As Carl Rogers (1969) notes, the experiences of learners are often "self-discovered, self-appropriated" (p. 277). These teachers believe in the importance of using the strategies of their own learning with that of their students. Writing happens to be one that the three share in common.

The difficulty is always one of creating the possibility for engaging in literature through writing, but leaving the door open to other opportunities. Their inquiry on teacher as writer foregrounded the issue of whether or not emphasizing the strategies from their own learning might appropriate strategies that students learn for themselves. Problematizing the issues of students' sense-making, these teachers began to ask whose interests they were serving. "Not all students want to do this writing. I've downplayed their concerns, thinking if they just hang in there and get some experience they'll love this," Joe stated. But students are multiple and positional. Joe, Beth, and Jane began to explore the complexities of their basic assumptions about writing and the reductiveness that may result from emphasizing one method that they believe in so firmly. Those students who like to write and write well are in a privileged position. They can work in ways that their teachers validate and value. The inquiry did not lead to answers, but it certainly raised questions about how to reconceptualize the importance of writing in the literature curriculum.

Teacher as Facilitator. Beth, Jane, and Joe articulated the essential role of literature teacher in ways very different from more common conceptions of literature teachers, as those who transmit knowledge about specific texts, provide background information, give tests, or ask students to answer questions at the end of selections. They each value the teacher's role and believe it is "to provide entrances and bridges between what they know and don't know," "nudge, nurture, and prod," "make students active through questioning, thinking, connecting," and "connect their interests and lives with what they choose to read." The teacher facilitates students' "initiation into experiences with literature," "finds where students feel most comfortable and confident," and teaches them to think critically by "looking into literature." Given the differences in grade levels that they teach, Beth, Jane, and Joe express relatively consistent views on how learners learn literature. The teacher can't teach literature to students, but can support and guide. This idea is echoed in Jane's statement, "I'm not sure we ever really teach literature." Joe's query, "Don't they (students) find it for themselves? It's like the teacher guides and throws a few bones until they find one they like to chew." Beth asks a similar question. "Isn't there always a temptation to rush the process and just tell them? Is that learning? Or teaching?" Beth asks students "why," Joe says "listen," and Jane guides them "through choices." All agree more learning takes place when students are personally engaged and encouraged to take a journey of discovery for themselves.

Finding ways to make literature relevant to students' lives and to help them understand the connectedness between their lives and what they read are cornerstones of Beth, Jane, and Joe's conceptual understanding of what it means to teach literature. Stepping back to analyze these statements, they began to see the profound challenge of mediating their beliefs and practices with students' agendas. For all the ways in which their statements ring true for what they might hope for their students, these teachers, in language and conception, were functioning as chief agents to the learning. Not that they were forgetting students entirely, but they began to recognize how strong their own agendas were. They had to deal for themselves with Britzman's (1991) question: "What kinds of power and authority are taken up and not admitted?" (p. 17). By questioning their beliefs and practices, they struggled through another reexamination of their texts as teachers.

A Few Questions

Does autobiographical inquiry affect Beth, Jane, and Joe's long-term conceptualizations and the sense they have of their multiple identities as teachers? How does their autobiographical inquiry make explicit what might not have been articulated before? Perhaps it is impossible to answer these questions, but in raising them, the complexity of Beth, Jane, and Joe's attempts to understand more about their teaching lives became obvious. They negotiated, questioned, and reconstructed how their practices may be constraining or exclusionary. They looked at themselves, their motivations, and actions carefully. Perhaps autobiographical inquiry provided a way for them to articulate in propositional form what had been tacit. Finding dissonance among their beliefs, experiences, and practices allowed Beth, Jane, and Joe to know more vividly, to tell more clearly, and to associate more strongly with the dynamics of their teaching lives.

In this way, autobiographical inquiry may be used as a learning tool to facilitate teachers' understanding of the various contexts that influence their motivations and intentions in classrooms. We came to recognize such inquiry as essentially a method through which these teachers could map the terrain of their teaching histories. I have detailed a few of the issues that seemed both interesting and problematic. Each will require further inquiry and analysis by Beth, Jane, and Joe as they continue to compose their teaching lives. Certainly their inquiry demonstrates how many long-running practices in the teaching of literature must be questioned, if not contested, and how even admirable intentions and goals must be unpacked for critique as well as possibility.

Planning and Practice

Beth, Jane, and Joe's discussions and examples of reflection suggest that they gained knowledge about their teaching through the circumstances in which they work and through their long-term study of the debates about theory and pedagogy in literature education. They rely on specific examples from their teaching to situate present events in the context of classroom rituals, student reaction, teacher/student interaction, or a myriad of other events that illustrate the store of situational knowledge they possess. The objects of reflection were often connected to a critical incident, a moment in time when something occurred that caused them to question their beliefs or actions, as described at the end of Chapter Two. The objects of such reflection were unexpected outcomes in lessons, challenges from colleagues, paradoxes in beliefs and practices, or school-wide mandates. A second factor that caused extensive reflection was the changing conceptions of English teaching, both theoretically and pedagogically. Beth, Jane, and Joe's knowledge of the debates in the discipline creates dissonance that keeps them from complacency in their teaching. To better understand how their reflections caused them to rethink their teaching, we'll examine three aspects: (1)*purposes of reflection*, (2) *types of reflection*, and (3) *examples of reflection in planning and teaching episodes*.

The Purposes of Reflection

Reflection on purpose takes many forms but here it is motivated by Beth, Jane, and Joe's need to understand themselves. They generate the agenda for themselves and so such reflection is not localized in the day-to-day events of the classroom. Rather, reflection on purpose centers on questions of meaning. Through such reflection, they consider themselves in relationship to their work, struggle with the implicit messages in their curricula, or explore how competing educational beliefs about teaching literature have informed their work.

The search for self-understanding. Teaching is an act of interpretation and reflection is a vehicle for its production. One purpose of reflection is a search for self-understanding. A working analogy of the mirror-image-as-reflection helped me understand this purpose. In a mirror we have the unusual capability of seeing ourselves seeing. Beth, Jane, and Joe expressed this sense of "seeing themselves seeing" in a variety of ways. Beth described her "dual vision" in the classroom: "teaching and watching students' reactions but watching myself teaching at the same time. I am participating in the events and often directing them, but I'm also standing back and watching myself teaching." Joe captured this same idea in his suggestion that "Reflection is peripheral vision. I'm in my head thinking about the next move, but outside of myself watching my every move." Jane revealed how "narcissistic teaching is. I do watch myself teaching. I watch the children's reactions, too, but usually related to how I'm seeing the image of myself in action." Reflection, taking the form of a mirror image, captures the quality of seeing one's self seeing. Importantly, the directed gaze captures the object in a moment of stasis for closer examination. One of the purposes of reflection for Beth, Jane, and Joe was to better understand themselves as teachers, not only by studying the situations of practice, but also by examining their own methods of observation.

Examples of these teachers' reflection most often occurred when they considered moments from their biography of teaching, an inward gaze that produced a double reflection of past and present. From recollections of particular interactions with students, images of teachers from their own literature education, memories of particularly exhilarating or perplexing moments, Beth, Jane, and Joe studied themselves. During Jane's artifact interview, she told the following story about an incident with her fourth graders:

> One of them had treated another one pretty shabbily. "Listen, I want to recite this poem to you. I want you to hear this poem." And then I did "The Quality of Mercy." I thought, "I'll give it to them." You know they weren't being very merciful. I said, "You know, Shakespeare decided that the quality of mercy was pretty important. There are a few people in here who don't understand mercy. But he's talking about it being enthroned in the hearts of kings, and an attribute to God himself." And the class asked for it a second time at a later date. They said, "Remember that poem you recited about mercy? Do that again for us."

In telling the incident, Jane brought that moment into her gaze again, held the image as a point of reflection to consider what she believed were important aspects of her role as a teacher of literature. Jane elaborated on her double vision. "I thought about this incident when I reread this poem by Sadie Dawn (the poem was in the artifact collection). She was in the class that year, and she was the brunt of the teasing that led me to recite Shakespeare. I could see myself reciting that poem to the students, and I know now where that impulse came from. As I've told you, my father often recited poetry to inform me on how to live life. He challenged me to learn from and hear the literature from the adult world and here I was reciting Shakespeare to fourth graders. In this collection of student work, I found Sadie's poem and the line: 'It's teasing that brings the rain from my eyes.' It brings the situation back." Jane continued, "I'm not sure we ever really teach literature. I want to model for my students that there are meaningful pieces of literature that I embrace and use to inform my life and that there is so much to learn from one little passage." Jane's philosophy, her practices, the way she interacts with her students, and her values and beliefs about literature education are mirrored in this one story of her teaching. Reflecting on the story informs Jane's self-understanding about her beliefs and purpose in literature education and her role as a teacher.

Beth, Jane, and Joe's reflections toward self-understanding demonstrate how the genesis for teaching beliefs grows out of fundamental experiences with and exposure to literature. Their early literature histories inform the fundamental outlooks behind their present practices. What became increasingly apparent throughout the interviews was the close connection between their personal experiences, the kinds of phenomena and knowledge they deem as centrally important in literature studies, and their interest in the consequences of their beliefs, planning, and practices in shaping students' experiences with literature.

Reconceptualizing curriculum. Curricula may reflect traditional assumptions about literature as a program with prescribed texts from the canon, literary criticism, and understanding of conventions as focal points for study. Another version is experiential, conveying key principles from Dixon's (1967) personal growth model. Or, literature curriculum might be based on reader-response or related theories that place emphasis on the development of students' strategies in reading literature. The variations are fluid and hybrid, and the reality of any approach probably lurks somewhere between the extreme ends of the spectrum of possibilities, which require that the participants reflect on the explicit and implicit messages they present through curriculum.

Beth's description of curriculum planning illustrates her constant reconceptualization. Whether she designs a year's curriculum, a unit, or a lesson, Beth tries to imagine what experiences students will take away from her class that inform them as readers of literature. She sees a design that includes "purposes, experiences, activities, and ways to evaluate." Take a specific example. Beth is required to teach *Flowers for Algernon*. This novel is one in a series of texts—some are chosen by Beth, others mandated, and a few selected by students. Beth must consider how *Flowers* or any other single selection will fit into her overall curriculum plan for the year. Beth must determine "some coherent whole. I know that a literary selection doesn't make a curriculum, but I'm still struggling to create a framework around individual works. It's easy to move from book to book and not worry much about the whole plan." Beth negotiates among the component parts within her framework and gives each varying emphasis as she plans how a sequence and individual lessons will unfold.

Reconceptualizing curriculum has been a constant task for Beth, Jane, and Joe and has led to diverse representations through their long teaching careers. They have learned that any construct of curriculum comes down to deciding how to combine the purposes for educating into literature. Then, they determine how to facilitate those conceptions with scope, sequence, and practice.

Considering the relationship between theory and practice. Tensions exist within an array of possibilities. These three teachers find themselves surrounded by competing versions of purpose, process, and pedagogy in literature education. Beth, Jane, and Joe keep informed through the professional literature in the field, attend conferences, and collaborate with colleagues. Joe finds "how much has changed in the field since the mid-1970s when I began teaching. I just get a handle on a new way of thinking about teaching or about how readers construct meaning and then I read or hear additional information." All three reported feeling exhilarated by all the information in the field but overwhelmed at the same time. Jane indicated that "about the time I find a place of comfort, say, for example, in conferencing with children about what they are reading, something else comes along for new concern." The pedagogical tradition in literature education has changed in response to theories that articulate reader-response related approaches. Joe catalogued the "various instructional techniques, activities, supporting rituals, and new evaluation plans that seem to be associated with responses to Iser, Fish, Rosenblatt, and all the others." The changing face of pedagogical approaches prompts Beth, Jane, and Joe to determine the practices that adhere to their current and ever-changing conceptions. This does not mean that their articulated purposes are always congruent with what actually takes place in the classroom. At times, their stated intentions are changed by particular events that take place during class. Or their reflection may lead them to new discoveries. They do, however, reflect on their practices by juxtaposing their beliefs with what actually transpires.

Types of Reflection

Beth, Jane, and Joe acquire professional knowledge by deliberately thinking back on their actions and beliefs. Additionally, knowledge is produced during practice through a form of spontaneous reflection. These two ways of describing the processes of reflection are much in keeping with Schön's (1983) distinction between "reflection-on-action" and "reflection-in-action," respectively. When thought of in this way, reflection is both a response to puzzlements and an act of creation. Reflection urges episodic, spontaneous, and digressive thoughts and often triggers various responses to particular situations, actions, or ideas.

Reflection-on-action. Beth, Jane, and Joe "think back" on their actions and interrogate aspects of critical incidents to characterize what they have done and what they might want to do in the future. The views they use to inform their decisions are multiple. For example, Joe reflects on his conscious effort to use theory to design or evaluate lessons he has taught. "I'm tinkering with new approaches now. More often than ever before I try to take what I'm learning from various reading theories (Iser, Rosenblatt, and Holland are interesting to me) and create a lesson that shows readers' strategies. For example, I had students create a poem from a short story they read. For me it was a concrete way to put Rosenblatt's idea of the reader creating the 'poem' into practice. The next time I collected reading logs, I noticed that several students had created poems from other stories we'd read. So, in hindsight, I think the idea was valid." What Joe suggests here is that his reflection is recursive, influencing both the shaping of his practice and his evaluation of its effectiveness. He has developed propositional knowledge through his implementation of theoretical principles in practice, and his reflection consolidates his understanding of the connections.

Beth relies on her long history with middle school students to inform her beliefs and practices in teaching literature to adolescents. "I've learned students relate to the literature when I create assignments that ask them to make connections with their lives. I have a list of 'dos' and 'don'ts' in my head that are generalizations but still important. For example, seventh graders are closed-mouthed about their own experiences so in discussions it's better to ask them to make connections with other characters, friends, or film idols. They need distance. By ninth grade, the students like to talk about themselves again." Beth employs her insights about students to implement appropriate and successful approaches and uses her previous interactions with students to inform her present ones. With this conception of knowledge to guide her, Beth derives practical principles from her reflection.

Jane's philosophical view about the role of a literature teacher frames how she reflects on the success of the structured activities, rituals, and evaluation measures incorporated into her classroom routines. "I decided a long time ago that I needed to get out of the students' way. I believe they need to develop their own interests in reading, but I have to balance that by giving them the tools so they can do that. I'm constantly thinking about classroom rituals and structures that will support their independence and yet they are young and very dependent. It's a constant negotiation between what I believe and what the children seem to need." Jane's strong philosophy-based orientation extends into most of the reflection she engages in. It is the data she uses to evaluate the effectiveness of her teaching. This aspect of reflection is tied to how well the individual teacher understands the content of her philosophy.

Beth, Jane, and Joe's use of reflection-on-action illustrates that they are articulate about debates in the field, have learned how to read the cues given them by students, and have articulated philosophies that inform their practices. These are the data that they use to constantly reevaluate and reframe issues in teaching literature that are important to them. Crucially, their reflection-on-action shapes their ability to respond inventively and leads to the construction of new curriculum designs, practices, routines, and evaluation plans. Even more importantly, however, the reflection demonstrates that they are always working from some base, an articulated critical stance or point of focus, from which they engage in reflection.

Reflection-in-action. Much more will o' the wisp is reflection that occurs suddenly as a reaction to the immediacy of the situation. Beth, Jane, and Joe's reflection-in-action is embedded in the contextual meaning of the classroom in action. As Mead (1934) suggested, "All reflective thought arises out of real problems present in immediate experience" (p. 7). This form of reflection illustrates a spontaneous process with multiple levels of interaction occurring simultaneously. These teachers described how they have developed expertise in this type of reflection through years of experience, but it is important to note that their reflection is not serendipitous. Rather, reflection-in-action is still a form of principled reasoning, connected theoretically and practically to the participants' experiences in and beliefs about teaching and learning literature.

Joe invokes the immediacy of reflection-in-action: "In the classroom there isn't much time to think through a dozen alternatives in detail. I get flashes of alternatives in my mind, and I guess I've built a repertoire for making instantaneous decisions. This isn't armchair reflection. I'd call it 'in the trenches' reflection." Joe goes on to point out that the alternatives have roots in his beliefs about teaching literature. "When I find myself in a position where I must choose a direction quickly I usually trust the things I believe work best. If there is a good deal of confusion about a passage or a stanza students are reading, I wouldn't ask them to write about it. I'd read it aloud so they hear the living language. I've found that they need to hear the language to make sense." For Joe, it is developing a sensitivity to the resources of language that guide his spontaneous decisions and "often lead me to stop and read a passage aloud when students don't understand, or I get them to act out scenes. I still hear my father reading to me, and I believe it makes a difference to hear language." This sequence of Joe's reflection-in-action reveals that he has a framework of beliefs through which he simultaneously assesses the viability of alternatives. Joe relies on his propositional knowledge to inform decisions. Thus his reflection-in-action helps him translate beliefs into action.

Teaching dilemmas don't always lend themselves to an immediate course of action, yet in certain circumstances a decision must be made. As Beth reveals, a teacher sometimes must carry on a personal argument with self before determining how to interact with the students: "One boy in third period asked whether Holden (in *Catcher*, you know?) was bisexual or gay. The other boys started to laugh, mostly out of embarrassment. The girls shrank into their desks. I was watching the reactions and was angry with the question, knowing his question wasn't sincere but thinking if I get angry then the students will think I'm sensitive to homosexuality. At the same time I was speculating on whether or not there were gay students in the class and how they were feeling. Finally, I had to take action and all that went through my head in a few seconds. It was up to me to keep trust between the kids in this classroom or they wouldn't be able to share questions or ideas honestly, so I took it as a serious question to set a model. I waited a few moments and then asked: Why would it matter? What more would you know about Holden if you had that answer? Would it make a difference in whether or not you care about his story?" Armed as she is with a highly attuned focus on the students, Beth made a decision based on what she might teach students through her example. Beth draws from previous interactions with students to inform the present situation, assuming, for example, that the question was not genuine. She must have some basis for this belief. Additionally, she conjectures that the question could jeopardize the trust she is trying to build in the classroom. Again, Beth has a long history of experience with students that leads her to this consideration. In response, then, Beth interprets the present through the past and constructs a response based on that reflection.

Jane describes the act of teaching: "When a class starts, it's like the floodgate opens and all this stimuli comes rushing toward me and some days I tread water, others I do leisurely laps, or sometimes I swim furiously just to keep from drowning, but I'm confident that whatever my overt style there is within me a core of beliefs." If the events of a day are ill connected with Jane's instructional and structural beliefs about teaching literature, she focuses on the incongruity as the class session unfolds and determines how to make adjustments. Jane does not work through an analytical description of what is troublesome, but "comprehends it . . . a gut reaction" that triggers her reflection-in-action. Jane's is a kind of reflection carved out of and shaped by her beliefs, a knowledge constructed and reconstructed through her experiences with the children. "I have a holistic way of seeing what takes place during an hour in class. I know when Mary doesn't want a conference or Gloria had a fight with her brother and can't settle into reading or all the children are anxious about recess. That's when I take an opportunity to just stop everything and read aloud to the children. It's just a form of knowing what to do." Thus Jane's reflection-in-action is a form of living in the children's minds, a vicarious experience that leads her to action in accordance with her beliefs about the experiences she hopes to create with them.

Access to teachers' reflection-in-action is seldom direct. Beth, Jane, and Joe capture moments of reflection and elaborate on those experiences. The substance of their inquiry is drawn out and rendered incomplete, but always involves an encounter with themselves in ways that broaden their understanding of how they act or react and what motivates them to do so. Through reflection they have made some knowledge of themselves explicit.

Examples of Reflection in Planning and Practice

Through Beth, Jane, and Joe's planning logs, observations of actual teaching episodes, and follow-up discussions, I examined the features of their reflection both on and in action for fourteen class sessions each. Their use of reflection in the more localized acts of planning or teaching a particular class session emphasized how they synthesize knowledge from reflection into design and action for particular moments. The explicit features of their reflection are easily recognized: explications of purpose, questions, structural considerations, and typified responses to recurring dilemmas. Yet, a tacit reflection lurks beneath the surface of overt reflection which helps these teachers use their knowledge of teaching to react to very particular moments of practice. Paradoxically, they found it harder to articulate their reflection in planning or teaching particular lessons because they felt the complexities were much greater in these localized circumstances than in the more generalized conversations of their uses and understanding of reflection. In what follows I attempt to capture their reflection, but with the understanding that the web of explicit and implicit is intricate and richly interwoven with complexity.

**Planning of class sessions: Clarifying, predicting, and imple-
menting.** *Rehearsal* seems an accurate word to describe how Beth,
Jane, and Joe plan their class sessions. It is through rehearsing the
possibilities that they bring theoretical and practical knowledge to
bear upon the scripting of prospective classroom events. Beth emphasized how she "imagines what will happen. It's like I'm in a film
of my classroom before it happens." Jane indicated that over the
years she has "become more secure in letting my creativity guide
me. I'm free to write the play as I want. Of course, it doesn't always
turn out as I've written it." Beth, Jane, and Joe expressed how comfortable they have become with the rehearsal process. As Joe described it, "There is something spontaneous and stimulating. I feel
like an author who can push the limits of what's happened before
and create something new." As I read and reread their planning
logs, the participants' reflective activities illuminate at least three
aspects of their preparation for class sessions: *clarifying, predicting,*
and *implementing.*

Clarifying. Clarifying is a result of effortful rumination. Specifically, clarification could be found in several types of reflective behavior exemplified in Beth, Jane, and Joe's logs. The most common was
their orientation toward specific articulations of the relationship of
purpose to choice in practices. For example, Joe clarifies his purpose for a lesson on Cheever's short story "Torch Song": "I want
them to question what they know about the main character because
she is ambiguously defined in the story. I want them to think
through whether she is actually dangerous or if that is just a perception. If they work collaboratively they can wrestle with the various
complexities of characterizing her. They need to consider why an
author would create an ambiguous character." Specifically, Joe clarified what aspect of characterization he wanted students to study
and how he thought this might be accomplished. Therefore, he
plans to make some desired purpose achievable. Through this rehearsal, Joe links his long-range intentions, "to create their own
complex characters over the next week and learn something from
Cheever about characterization," to the immediate objective, "to
explore the complexity of the character of Joan."

This aspect of planning can be seen in the logs of Beth and Jane
as well. Beth clarifies what she wants to examine with students when
they read *A Tale of Two Cities*: "I want students to understand from
the beginning the antithetical nature of the opening. This is an important theme throughout the novel. I'll need to get them thinking

about the antithetical in their lives." Jane examines the characteristics of particular students' reading progress for individual conferences: "For Jen's conference: *Bridge to Terebithia.* She's ready to learn about character development. Ask her if Jess A. is the same at the beginning of the novel as he is at the end. Also how the death of a friend affected him." Thus, clarifying is a process in which Beth, Jane, and Joe name what they will attend to and define the features of a situation as to its focus and limits. At times, they consider the relationship of the situation compared with larger issues of curriculum, but generally their clarification frames situation-specific plans.

Predicting. Beth, Jane, and Joe's planning often includes some element of prediction that presents how students will react to or learn from particular activities. Their predictions are based on prior experiences and embedded in a contextual understanding of their interactions with students. In some ways they exhibit image-making capabilities similar to the descriptions offered by Connelly and Clandinin (1988) during a study in which the researchers describe how teachers reach into their past understanding to connect meaningfully with what they anticipate in the present situation. Image-making capacities play a vital role in Beth, Jane, and Joe's predictions about students. These teachers "see" their students in action. They predict student behaviors, what students will say, or the specific interaction of two or three students. These images of students become ways through which Beth, Jane, and Joe articulate the basis of their decisions, consider alternative possibilities, or refine their plans.

Joe's log on Cheever's "Torch Song" shows how he uses his knowledge about students to inform his planning: "I want students to explore the complexity of the character of Joan in the story in more than a free floating discussion—not everybody throwing out opinions that don't go anywhere. A few discuss—Stephanie, Jeff, Rita. The rest just hang out and get ideas from those few who contribute. So, I'm thinking I'll have them work in small groups and find quotes about Joan that they have to write out for the rest of class to see." Through his prediction of student behaviors, Joe plans ways to accentuate student involvement that are based on his understanding of their typical behaviors. Beth predicts how the context of a particular day may affect student involvement as they begin reading *A Tale of Two Cities:* "First the students are coming back after a week of spring break so they aren't particularly focused on school. I need to figure out how to tie events from their lives that will locate them where the novel starts. Actually, the antithetical is so strong in the beginning of the novel that it would be a great way to start. These kids can relate to the idea of good and bad things happening simultaneously. . . . like good and bad things that happened over spring break." Beth decided to use the students' immediate experiences as the basis for her lesson. On the other hand, Jane knows each student as a reader because of her use of individual conferences. Her predictions concern individuals: "Gina and Sarah have read enough of *Sarah Plain and Tall* to act out a few scenes for class. This will keep them focused enough to finish reading the book. They are beginning to lose interest. They aren't getting far." As Jane predicts particular students' progress, she creates a plan of action.

The ability to predict makes the thought processes behind the label *reflective inquiry* more accessible, for it captures how teachers prepare for particular events through considerations that involve more than determining specific activities. It is likely, therefore, that experienced teachers can predict beyond the routine planning of what to do in class and in what order because of their ability to focus on the complexities of context that they have learned through experience. The ability to predict may be a precondition for what experts have recognized as "fast and accurate pattern recognition capabilities" (Berliner, 1986, p. 11). These capabilities are useful in instruction because Beth, Jane, and Joe's experience makes them better able to anticipate situations they are likely to encounter in the classroom and to implement contingency plans they have in mind.

Implementing. Joe considered various ways to involve his students in the characterization work on Cheever's story: "What's a way to record so that groups share responses? They could role play scenes but I'm not sure that will *show* the complexity. They could draw a character map that shows graphically how they think she is characterized. I want them to *see it*. A graffiti wall comes to mind. They can write quotes, questions, slogans. I see it like bathroom graffiti. Instead, we could act out scenes. Maybe the graffiti wall or role playing." Joe considered various ways to implement his purposes through a catalogue of alternative ways to get students involved in characterization. He determined various activities and structures that would help him reach his purpose, and he evaluated these for their viability as instruments to reach his intentions: "They could draw a character map . . . A graffiti wall comes to mind . . . we could act out scenes." He sorted through his repertoire of practices in his planning of this lesson.

Unlike Joe's rehearsal of possible structures for each class session, Beth has structures that remain fairly consistent across changing content. Students write in logs, discuss in a large group, take an issue raised in large group to continue discussing in small groups, and often end a class session with a journal entry or small group reports. She plans some workshop time each day "so that students leave while they are involved in the work. That way there is a better chance that they will finish the homework than if I assign it at the end of the period." Beth examined how to accomplish her intent with *A Tale of Two Cities* in this way: "I could get them thinking about what they would be willing to fight for. What actions would they take? So, I'll probably start with the idea of the good and bad things that happened over spring break. I'll have them write a list in their journals. Then, I'll draw a chart of good and bad on the board and from that we will discuss the best and worst of times in their lives. I'll have them share details of an experience in small groups or with a partner and then we'll come back together. I'll lead that into the best and worst of times." The sequence of events that Beth planned was consistent with the routine structures in her classroom. The structures provided the sequence for how she would incorporate themes from the novel into her lesson. She considered alternative ways of doing this—"locations that they know," or "what they're willing to fight for," or "the ideas of good and bad things happening simultaneously."

Jane's fourth graders spend approximately two hours each morning reading books of their choice, peer conferencing on their reading projects, or conferencing with Jane. In Jane's rehearsals for the workshop, she prepares for conferences and plans mini-lessons taught to the whole class or to small groups. For one of the conference days, she wrote: "For Hannah's conference: *Journey to Jo'berg* (half way?). Have her read a few pages to check on difficulty level. Check on whether or not she's figured out an answer to her question: 'Why do the black people tolerate the white people being so mean?' Move Hannah to focus on craft. I want her to pay more attention to detail and begin to think of that in her writing. Maybe it's time for her to share a passage of this book to encourage others in the class to read it." In her log, Jane determined how to help Hannah sustain reading, recognize elements of literature, understand historical context, focus on craft, and share her reading with others.

Supporting Berliner's (1986) belief that experienced teachers have a repertoire of scripts developed through years of practice, Beth, Jane, and Joe demonstrated that prior experiences with students, knowledge of multiple structures and practices, and the clarity of long- and short-range intentions allow them to plan with some sense of confidence. For whatever the differences in emphasis, content, or processes of planning, they each demonstrated a repertoire of strategies in planning, which seems to enhance their ability to be flexible as actual classroom events unfold.

Actualizing intentions through practice. I believe after interviewing Beth, Jane, and Joe and observing in their classrooms that their acts of teaching have a backdrop of reflection behind them in three major areas—beliefs about the purposes of teaching literature; understanding of the debates in literature education, both theoretically and pedagogically; and knowledge about the complex workings of the classroom. Their reflection contributes to the pedagogical moves they make during a given class session. Thus, decisions of practice are informed by the cumulative reflection-on-action that represents their historical understanding of teaching, as well as the immediate reflection-in-action that takes place during a particular lesson. Of course, these occur nearly in concert and one obviously informs the other.

In the transcript and supporting narrative that follows, Beth's opening session on *A Tale of Two Cities* will be used to exemplify the reflection that goes on during a teaching episode. On an evening in late March, the Sunday before school began after spring break, my phone rang. Beth's voice: "One of the ninth graders just committed suicide. I don't know what mood the kids will be in tomorrow. First, they're just coming back and this just happened. Do you want to reschedule or come anyway?" I asked Beth, "What do you think? Would it be hard for the kids with an outsider there?" She hesitated, "I don't think it will matter to them. Why don't you come. It might be tense but interesting."

Beth's Class: 7:40 A.M., April 1

Beth is not in her room when I arrive the next morning. Within minutes she bustles in with a stack of papers and her briefcase. "We just had a quick faculty meeting to talk about how to handle this." Sarah, Harriet, and Stephanie walk through the door. Harriet announces that she finished two novels during break. Beth, visibly preoccupied, arranges the room and gets herself and her things located. I survey the student work on the walls. It has changed since I was here last. The backdrop in this classroom is student generated—artwork, writing, memory maps, and poetry. Books, magazines, and newspapers are organized in clusters around the room. Beth comes over to fill me in on the meeting. Eric shot himself. He was not in one of Beth's classes but was probably a friend of many of her eighth graders. "There's a fine line here between creating hysteria and ignoring something important to them. I'll feel out the mood,"

Beth tells me. The principal begins the morning with an announcement welcoming everyone back and telling students about the death and his sorrow. The class sits quietly, numbed and not quite believing this is real.

"Let's spend some time writing in our journals. That can be our way of just settling in today." Beth writes with them for approximately ten minutes. The students are quiet. "Would anyone like to read what you've written to the class?" No volunteers. "Would anyone like to say anything?" No response. "Maybe you need time to talk with your friends. Let's do that for a few minutes and see where we are." The students relax visibly and the tension eases. Clusters of students begin to converse. Some talk about what they did during break; others speak in whispers. When Beth brings the class back together, she begins by making a statement, followed by a question: "People my age say it's great to be young, that it's carefree and easy. You may have a different perspective. What are some of the things that are really great in your life?" She lists their responses on the board—health, freedom, basketball, a girlfriend. "What in your life isn't so great, the worst things?" Again, Beth lists—parent hassles, grades, school, not old enough to drive, divorce, war. "Well, that's certainly a good start. Now let's each do our own private list. In your journal. It might look like this to keep things straight." She categorizes on the board:

Good Things	Not So Good
Health	Grades
Freedom	School
Basketball	Homework
Girlfriends	Divorce
Money	War

Students spend about fifteen minutes listing and sharing their lists with others. Beth elaborates. "Probably everybody of every time and place in this world has felt the same. Whole books have been written about those feelings. We're going to start reading one today. Anybody familiar with the writer Charles Dickens?"

Craig: Yeah, he wrote *Oliver Twist*. I saw the movie.
Stewart: I read *David Copperfield*. It got pretty boring. It's too long.
Beth: Anyone know what he wrote about?
Rosie: Mostly bad conditions of his times—like orphans and schools and people in poverty and not getting fed.
Beth: Hm, the bad conditions? What do you have on that side of your list?
Harriet: Well mine aren't as tragic. Probably only to me. Like divorce.

Jamie: But isn't divorce larger than just your family? So it is an issue larger than you.

Harriet: Yeah, ok. I guess so.

Beth: So, you see, as Dickens saw, some of the bad stuff going on. What about the good? Did any of those things you read by Dickens show a good side?

Jim: Sure, some of the characters don't give in to the bad and let it ruin their lives. They fight it.

Jeremy: Yeah, like the bad didn't overwhelm like it must have with Eric (first mention to the entire class of the suicide).

Craig: Maybe he just put a list like this together in his mind and the bad was more than the good.

Susan: Or, he didn't think about the good. Sometimes I like to feel sorry for myself.

[This discussion extends about five more minutes].

Beth: So what I hear you all saying is that for the most part seeing the best and worst is a matter of perspective. It depends on where you focus, the mood you're in, and what is going on around you. Well, Dickens sees times like that, too, in the novel we'll read.

Colin: *Tale of Two Cities,* right?

Beth: You got it. What makes you think so?

Colin: Well, it starts, "Best of times, worst of times."

Beth: And what does that mean to you now?

Sarah: Like our charts, like Eric, like ourselves. He must be describing two sides of the same event.

Jen: Wasn't it the French Revolution?

Stephanie: Yeah, I think so. So it's like the novel may be about two sides. We see both sides.

Sarah: Do you think the two cities are one?

Jamie: Could be. I don't know. I haven't read it. But isn't *Les Miserable* the same?

Beth: Well, let's start reading it and find out. For today, let's start with me reading the first paragraph.

[Beth reads]

Brian: Sure it's right there. Like in a revolution it's good because people are excited about change but bad because of war.

Andrew: Like the Persian Gulf. It's best to be protecting but worst to endanger life.

Stephanie: My own life has its best and worst. I lost two pounds over break but I lost my tennis match (laughter).

Jeremy: Pretty self-centered Stephanie!

Beth: Let's end today just thinking about those two sides again—for Dickens and the French Revolution, for Eric, and for ourselves.

[Beth reads once more. The bell rings.]

Beth stated several goals for this lesson in her planning log: to connect Dickens' theme of antithesis with student life experiences; to understand the use of the antithetical by Dickens as a backdrop for the French Revolution and predict why he might do this; and to articulate the tensions between the best and worst of times. Beth hoped that this introduction would lead students to an understanding of how Dickens' use of the antithetical portrayed not only the lives of people during the revolution but also tied to the students' lives.

Beth reconsidered her original plan because of the circumstances of the suicide although what she understood as the importance of Dickens' theme only became stronger in light of the situation. Although Beth's purpose changed in essence, it did not vary in content. In some ways, the events surrounding Eric's death supported what Beth hoped students might find in Dickens—that his themes are relevant to their daily lives. Beth described how she felt as class began: "They were so quiet at first. I had to give them time. I was shaken and didn't know whether to just forget what was planned. But, I tried to think how important it was to tie what they were thinking about with literature. After all, literature teaches us and is a solace. I want them to see the relevance to their lives. But, I felt like I was forcing something on them. Dickens' antithetical opening fits with their concerns. Particularly today."

Improvisation. For all practical purposes, Beth's planned session was disrupted on this particular day. Her understanding of the classroom and students, however, remained intact, reflecting her confidence from years of accomplished teaching. Her beliefs, her understanding of the field, and her experience informed the decisions that she made. No other teacher would have done exactly as she did, but her actions revealed her beliefs about the purposes of literature education. Although she must juggle the intended order and take a slower move forward, Beth still uses the literary selection to promote students' exploration of their own lives, always her overriding purpose.

Beth demonstrates how teaching requires an immediate response to events as they take place. Beth started with a series of interchanges to determine students' mood—journal writing, invitations to share their writing, talk with friends. She made judgments instantaneously with a basic goal in mind to ease the tension. From the beginning of the session until the end, Beth monitored students' emotional state. The students' uncomfortable silence was an injunction for her to move slowly. "I just went with what seemed comfortable for the kids. I spent most of my time reading their cues. They were stunned and their lack of response, well, told me that I needed to give them time." Beth's improvisation while teaching seems to have arisen from her ability to deal with the multifarious signs that demand attention. Experience enables her to recognize and to react with actions that incorporate her purposes and priorities in situations of the moment. Improvisation is the ability to frame the present situation by seeing and acting on alternatives. Her opening question as she begins to introduce the antithetical manifests the improvisation: "People my age say it's great to be young, that it's carefree and easy. You may have a different perspective." Indeed, she suggests, Eric had his perspective. The improvisation that occurred in this lesson seemed the result of Beth's understanding of the complex interactions going on in the classroom in these unusual circumstances.

Analysis. Beth analyzed how she might link her agenda with the particularized needs of her students on this day. Beth described her thinking behind the actions. "I was thinking what I'd said in our first interview about why I teach literature. I remember saying I want an environment where they can learn to actively question and get meaning for themselves. I'm constantly thinking about that while I'm teaching. I wasn't certain what they wanted or needed from this time together." Beth stated that much of her reflection during this lesson focused on whether or not she was creating space for students to say what they needed to say about the suicide. As Beth analyzed the situation, she believed that students were nearly relieved that the work of the class had moved forward. However, it is also evident that Beth prodded students to find out how her intentions and those of her students balanced: "Would anyone like to read? Would anyone like to say anything? Maybe you need time to talk with your friends." She moved forward carefully, constantly monitoring how students were reacting and watching for signs. As a teacher, Beth was skillful in drawing connections in the activities to student experiences and interests, but as with many teachers, she yearns to find ways to do this better. Most of her questions or comments on this lesson were not procedural in nature, but focused on affective questions about student feelings. What Beth did in this lesson illustrates the value of having a repertoire of strategies and inclinations from which to make appropriate responses in difficult situations. Beth appears cognizant of the various options available to her and while she analyzes the choices as she makes them, she does understand the alternatives as she determines an informed choice.

Principled judgment. Beth employed a variety of instructional strategies that were flexible and responsive to cues from students about how the lesson was going. The on-the-spot decisions have behind them a principled judgment, that is, acting on a principle of belief in a way that is congruent with that principle. The ability to make adjustments during a class session based on what information is to be transmitted on a particular day. This is a day when things need to run smoothly, and Beth knows how to make that happen. Beth understands her students' moods and respects the boundaries of what they do and do not want to talk about. She demonstrates a quiet sympathy. She manages to balance the subject matter and even capitalizes on it to aid the students' understanding, and in many ways she responds to their needs.

Returning to the question of what is central to Beth's reflection-in-action: "It depends on the context of a particular day and the particular students." This is most evident in Beth's case where the cloud of an adolescent's death hangs over what she does. Analyzing a single class episode can only suggest what types of reflection-in-action go on in the classroom, and of what assumptions, knowledge, and beliefs about the purposes of literature education are embodied within. But, I do believe that the class session offers a concrete manifestation of how reflection contributes to the action a teacher takes.

Knowing the contexts and working from the situation as it was, Beth's introduction to *A Tale of Two Cities* is a complex series of negotiations within the multiple contexts in which she works daily. I asked her where she thought the class might take all this tomorrow. "Oh, Stephanie gave me an idea. I'll get them started and see where it goes. Come back and you'll see." I did just that. Without describing the processes of the day, I offer two examples of the product:

> It was the best of times it was the worst of times, it was the age of excitement, it was the age of boredom, it was the epoch of belief, it was the epoch of "say what"??? It was the seasoning of oregano, it was the seasoning of basil. It was the spring of innuendoes, it was the winter of frankness, we had New York seltzers before us, we had hamburgers and fries before us, we were all going directly to high school, we were all going directly into the pit of the unknown—in short, adolescence is filled with uncertainty much like drawing from a deck of cards, that the most popular of our breed remember it fondly, for now and for the summer, until next year comes crashing in.
>
> There were students with brilliant yet lazy minds in the first five periods; there were students with slow and lazy minds in the last two periods. There was a moment of chaotic jubilance and brilliance between the two and there was no escaping it until the end of the year.
>
> Carey S., student

It was the best of times, it was the worst of times, it was a quarter with math victory, it was a quarter with a health loss, it was a quarter with jokes, it was a quarter with trouble, it was a quarter of great friends, it was a quarter of powerful enemies, it was a quarter of sun, it was a quarter of snow. I had a soccer season before me. I had a history report before me. We were all going directly to straight As; we were all going directly the other way—in short it was a time we would all remember fondly, yet we dreaded the actual minutes and hours.

There were a young boy with flaming red hair, who committed suicide under the Broadway Bridge; there were a man of 106 in the mountains of Virginia. In both areas it was clearer than icicles to the people of the country, that there is no escaping the quarters of our lives.

Jamie S., student

Dickens' text was, in turn, a text to be read and a context for students to situate themselves in an antithetical framework for a brief moment as a way of seeing their own life experiences. For Beth, this was one of many moments in her life as a teacher where her decisions were based on her beliefs about what is important in the teaching and learning of literature.

Acting on Beliefs

I am convinced that these teachers are thoughtful, outstanding teachers who reflect continuously on their work. But, I have come full circle from where this study began: What does "to reflect" mean? While the overall results of this research are far from surprising, the study nonetheless offers detailed discussions of the specific ways in which these experienced teachers use reflection. These teachers reflect as a way to create or clarify meaning about teaching literature. They build a repertoire of responses to new situations out of their classroom experiences. They continuously act upon their beliefs about the purposes of literature education, the content of literary study, and the pedagogical principles that support their assumptions. They reflect on the day-to-day life in their classrooms and in doing so foster their professional knowledge. Whether or not their reflection takes place in the classroom within all the confusion and activity of interaction or in Beth's den, the faculty room, at Jane's desk, or in Joe's car, I'd suggest that such reflection proceeds because of a critical interest in thinking through problems or plans that will bear on the work of teaching. Like the reflection described in Schön's (1983) work, the deliberative process takes place in "the action present." The value of Beth, Jane, and Joe's reflection is that they have developed explicit knowledge about their own theoretical and pedagogical stances and predominant orientations toward literature. Reflection creates dissonance which triggers more reflection. Moreover, one of the underlying aims of this study was to suggest that we need more images of the possible, demonstrations as it were, of what teachers understand about reflection in their work.

Indeed the accumulation and adaptation of a repertoire of purposes and types of reflection are used to connect teachers' understanding of curriculum construction, self, theory, and pedagogy to their beliefs about teaching literature. This desire for consonance provides the framework through which teachers can deal with the competing versions of knowledge, the situational contexts, and the particular practices they will define and refine as they continue to add to their repertoire. While reflective practitioners integrate their understandings of philosophy of teaching, pedagogy, and subject matter into a whole that makes it nearly impossible to discern the separate parts, they come to know the consonance of a situation by interacting with it.

These experienced teachers describe, analyze, predict, create, compare, illustrate, and clarify. These verbs are important, and I have explained how I think they are used in reflection at the end of Chapter One to show the various ways in which reflection becomes located. Through such language, Beth, Jane, and Joe came to understand the relationship of what they do with how they believe. Their accounts were often retrospective, but such thinking back was used to frame present understandings. When retrospection turned to introspection, Beth, Jane, and Joe connected their explicit and implicit beliefs. In the language of projection, Beth, Jane, and Joe looked toward the future where they would make their beliefs and practices more consonant through their visions of "what if" and "if I." Possibly what has been suggested in the educational literature about teachers or students engaging in reflection by telling their stories is not quite enough. It might be important to encourage various methods of looking by concentrating on the verb form: "to predict," "to refine," or "to illustrate"—any and all of the verbs that force us to think differently about the data we confront. Then we might consider examining the resulting interpretations from various distances by adding the grammar of past, present, and future.

How much did the study itself promote the particular nature of reflection that was exhibited? The methodological framework led both these teachers and me to involve ourselves in examining the role of reflectivity in teaching. Because I was more interested in their reflective potential than in the practical problems of daily life in the classroom, it is not surprising that Beth, Jane, and Joe found themselves concentrating on their reflectivity as well. How can we elicit concepts and processes as slippery as reflection? My hope, then, is that this study continues the dialogue on teacher reflectivity. Perhaps Beth, Jane, and Joe's undaunted desire to keep learning and struggling with the complexities of teaching defy my urge to find a genuine version of how they reflect and what they reflect on.

Can we foster reflection? The examination of Beth, Jane, and Joe's reflection indicates the importance they attach to understanding themselves and their purposes consonant with their instructional and structural practices. Various forms of teacher research, the writing and analysis of case studies on reflection (including their own), and a careful examination of the competing theoretical and pedagogical discourses would be a first step in helping teachers understand and explicate the various dimensions of their work. From this particular study, I learned that it is possible for teachers to articulate the purposes of reflection, to offer examples of such reflection both on and in action, and to describe how reflection supports them in the planning and enactment of particular lessons. In staff development programs we might begin a systematic and long-term education into self-understanding and self-development that is supported by theoretical rationales, instead of demonstrations of the much too often "what works." Possibly a goal of such programs would be to support teachers in "seeing themselves seeing" rather than telling them how to see. Opportunities to experiment with changes in practice would be supported by collaborative reflection and increased opportunities for interaction with colleagues where they could learn from each other the purposes, types, and enactments of reflection.

From these teachers with nearly sixty years of combined experience, I learned how important patience is. Any program, any package, or any model that purports to teach reflection will not be successful if immediate and measurable results are the goal. Beth, Jane, and Joe keep refining and questioning and comparing. I do believe, however, that they demonstrate habits of reflection that they have developed over time, and teachers and teacher educators alike may be able to encourage and support such habits in self and in others.

Beth, Jane, and Joe led me to examine the daily challenges not only in classrooms but also from the competing discourses on learning and teaching literature in the discipline. I believe we can help ourselves and other teachers develop a repertoire of strategies for inquiry that will establish habits of reflection through which we can define, examine, and refine our work in schools. If we can locate what is problematic in teaching literature—required reading lists, censorship issues, student resistance, reading abilities, diverse interests, and limited resources, to name a few—this is the first step in pushing inquiry forward. If we can see incidents from a variety of viewpoints and push our abilities to inquire through retrospective, introspective, and prospective accounts, we might reach toward a more elaborate understanding of our work.

I suspect the future will hold more studies that account for experienced and less-experienced teachers' reflection, the effects of direct instruction or intervention on reflection, and the relationship between reflection and performance. I don't think we are clear on our views of these issues as yet. In calling, then, for a serious exploration of reflective inquiry, I offer what is to be learned from Beth, Jane, and Joe as a starting point. As I write this and you read it, I suspect they will be in their classrooms "thinking on their feet." As Joe said in a way that I am hard-pressed to paraphrase: "Inquiry is a form of literacy all its own. When we abandon possibility, someone else will step in to take control, leaving us with our complacency. Reinventing is hard work and the labor of it may be a form of mind masochism, but to neglect it is to let someone else co-opt the power."

Chapter Four

In Teachers' Hands

As with many other Septembers, past ones and those yet to come, teachers walk through the doors of schools into corridors, in the half dark of early morning, for the first day of a new school year. Before the classroom fills with a sea of new faces, I often find myself ferreting out the ghosts of past years: Netta, shy and awkward in September, found Toni Morrison's novels and by March wrote and performed a series of monologues created out of Morrison's characters; Sam, angry and sullen in October, got hooked on Vietnam war literature and told us in April that his father died in Vietnam; Nathan, lively and talkative when school started, put a shotgun muzzle to the roof of his mouth and pulled the trigger in May. Each year I and many other teachers still wonder what the year will bring. Surrounding us are the laughter, joy, excitement, awkwardness, fear, and smell of adolescence. We arrive with a new grade book, without the proverbial stack of papers to grade, and with the less than haggard look we'll have come June. Many arrive with hopefulness and some uncertainty. Then, the journey begins, and each year I ask: "What is in teachers' hands?"

To be a teacher is to be part of a constructive and shaping enterprise. For me that shaping is most memorable because of Miss Elizabeth Melton, fourth grade, Washington School. She read *Anne of Green Gables, Alice in Wonderland,* and *Black Beauty* to the class after lunch on long spring afternoons. From Miss Melton's class I carried with me her love of language, of books, and the powerful desire to write. I started writing a novel that year. She held in her hands the power to awaken my sensitivity to language and story. She was part of a long tradition of those who have earned the name "teacher."

Take Plato. Plato depicted learning as a journey from the chains of illusion, shadows, and darkness of the cave into a world of enlightenment. Teachers not only help others along that journey, but also have to make a journey of their own. As teachers, we sometimes feel anxious about the roadways we're traveling in our classrooms. We may search for a straight boulevard that will lead us to the Temple of Athena, but oftentimes we don't find such a road on the map of teaching. No one has written the directions for where we must go. Then we take another journey through the more tangled and tortuous labyrinth of uncertainty. The difficulty is not the lack of content knowledge. That can be cured easily. Nor is it knowing how to plan units, lessons, and activities. That skill develops with experience. It is the willingness to live with uncertainty and to understand that learning does not fall neatly into categories, labels, or sequences. Confucius taught tolerance and respect for a variety of opinions. "Truth cannot be monopolized," he said. "Propriety, avoidance of extremes, the educated person does not impose his opinions on others." We hold in our hands the possibility of wandering the labyrinth of intentions and meanings, searching out ourselves only to get lost again. I think that's the way we find out what is in our hands as teachers.

Reading the Text of Our Teaching Lives

Many of us have jumped on or avoided a few educational bandwagons in our day; others of us may have found ourselves asked to teach a curriculum that we had no part in designing. I also suspect that many of us have decried top-down implementation of some bits-and-pieces teaching models, management schemes, or grading and assessment measures. Over the last twenty-odd years, teaching reform advocates, such as Ted Sizer, Chester Finn, Diane Ravitch, Ernest Boyer, John Goodlad, and Madeline Hunter, have raised important questions but have mainly failed to understand the complexities of teachers' work and have taken much of the discussion about teaching away from teachers. Too often the reform literature is technocratic, functionalist, and essentialist, presenting a series of decontextualized principles or procedures that represent what teachers do or should know. It all sounds deceptively and alluringly appealing—these formulaic and reified dictums that prescribe what teachers and teaching ought to be. For example, Linda Darling-Hammond (1994) suggests, "Ensuring that all students have adequate opportunities to learn requires enhancing the capacity of all teachers—their knowledge of students and subjects, and their ability to use that knowledge—by professionalizing teaching. This means that teacher education policies must ensure that *all* teachers have a stronger understanding of how children learn and develop, how assessment can be used to evaluate what they know and how they learn, how a variety of curricular and instructional strategies can address their needs, and how changes in school and classroom organization can support their growth and achievement" (p. 17).

The author's statement sounds responsible and simple, but I want to know who are the teachers of teachers who have the knowledge for "enhancing the capacity of all teachers?" Will the responsibility for "professionalizing" teachers be kept out of their hands? Further, I'm curious as to what professionalizing teaching means even with the elaborations that it "means that teacher education policies must ensure that *all* teachers have a stronger understanding" and so forth. By whose definition of "understanding" and whose measurement of "stronger" will these objectives be achieved for all teachers? By whose criteria is a stronger understanding of children, knowledge of assessment, and some knowledge about school and classroom organization handed down to teachers? More importantly, who decides what understanding of children, what knowledge of assessment, and whose knowledge of school and classroom organization count as validated knowledge? Who decided this is the most important agenda in reform? I'm always suspicious when someone advocates improving teacher capacity as if it could be gained through a healthy dose of cod liver oil or an infusion of knowledge from teacher educators to teachers.

Darling-Hammond goes on to urge that "substantial teacher and student involvement in and control over assessment strategies and uses are critical if assessment is to support the most challenging education possible for every student, taking full account of his or her special talents and ways of knowing" (p. 18). Yet, I don't hear any teacher or student voices in the article except for one teacher who is quoted at the end of the article—one, lone, single voice emphasizing how important it is to have teacher input. I question further who will decide what "challenge," "special talents," and "ways of knowing" mean. Obviously these are terms that get thrown around nearly as often as "empowerment." If such words become codified into assessment schemes, will the clarity of meaning deprive the productivity of indefiniteness?

In short, we need to read articles such as this critically. We owe it to ourselves to ask who is setting the agendas, who benefits from what agendas are set, and who benefits from the publicity garnered by the various research centers that study teachers, tell teachers how to collaborate, judge the effectiveness of teacher knowledge, and make suggestions about how teachers might be professionalized. The serious discussions too often occur without teachers or students present, although they may be invited into the end of the process as window dressing or to make cosmetic changes. What is in teachers' hands in the flurry toward reform?

I don't want to engage in bruising rhetoric, but the point needs to be made that it is important to examine what is said and by whom. In some ways teachers have been amazingly silent about who sets the agenda and who declares the principles of professional performance. A common form of resistance is to go into the classroom and close the door. Despite the proliferation of research on teachers' knowledge and systemics of reform, there doesn't seem to be a ready answer that makes much difference to any given teacher in any given classroom on any particular day. It seems that many teachers aren't likely to resist openly, but are we teachers to be the inventors or the implementors, the writers or the plagiarists, the artists or the forgers? At present we have this situation where much of our current thinking about education isn't, as anthropologist Clifford Geertz would recommend, "grounded" in local knowledge. As Geertz (1983) warns,

> Rather than attempting to place the experience of others within the framework of such a conception (of how a person is set against the whole of what people are), which is what the extolled "empathy" in fact usually comes down to, understanding them demands setting that conception aside and seeing their experiences within the framework of their own idea of what selfhood is (p. 59).

Ironically, teachers have been rendered voiceless in the cacophony of reformers' slogans and recipes for improvement. How is it that we've allowed teachers' work to be portrayed as devoid of life or lust, deadly dull and unimaginative when simplified into "mastery teaching," "4MAT," "democracy in education," and "time-on task"? I'm feeling that we teachers have allowed ourselves to become the objects of someone else's creation of knowledge about teaching and that we've abdicated our knowledgeable and experienced voices in the discussions about the future of education. I do wonder how the dust jacket will read on the History of Education book that will be written on these years around the turn to another century. The question for American education will be whether we made important decisions that enhanced the learning of our children in this ever-changing educational culture. It is important to remember that we are not on a journey to find the Wizard of Oz at the end of the educational yellow brick road. He turned out to be a fraud anyway. For Dorothy and her companions and for us as teachers, the importance is in the journey itself, the constant living with speculation, exhilaration, and uncertainty. It is sharing moments of recognition, of challenges met, and of questions asked with our students and colleagues that seem an important part of the educational enterprise that is seldom described except in the practitioner's professional literature.

By looking at our work carefully, we might find the voice to speak out clearly and strongly, sharing the meanings we've constructed from our experiences in the classroom. The acts of articulating these meanings may help us actualize who we are and what we are about. This is why I suggest that we begin reading our teaching histories in much the same way we read any text—to open a field of inquiry. I am sensitive to the difficulty of doing this. While a journey through our teaching experiences might appear self-absorbed, it may also provide us with insight into the resources of mind and spirit that keep us searching for all those things we yearn for when we get ready to start a new year in September—wisdom, patience, clarity of purpose, insight on adolescents, fairness, and good judgment. Obviously the list could go on for several pages. Our yearning is informed by the wealth of critical incidents that represent our experiences. The narrative text of our teaching lives invites us to make meaning from it.

In earlier chapters, I suggested various ways in which three groups of teachers reflected on their teaching and some of the influences that provoked them to look again at their beliefs, practices, or the situational contexts of their work. I hope this chapter will provide another angle from which you can engage in "reading the text of your teaching life." We have in our hands the potential to use our teaching experiences in a variety of ways that may help us to better understand our current, as well as our future practices. In this chapter, I will describe four different sources of inquiry and the practices that resulted from reading the text of my teaching life.

Reading Silence in the Classroom

The first example illustrates why I believe particular instances from the classroom have importance for us as teachers if we take the time to examine them. Too often in a rush, I skip over and ignore a moment from which I could learn a great deal about my present teaching or that offers within it seeds that suggest future practices or habits of reflection. It seems so simple now, but the following incident had a dramatic effect on the way I subsequently thought about silence in the classroom as well as my deliberate teaching strategies that encouraged students' encounters with silence. In this case, I learned from a student the value of silence.

Laura didn't say much in class discussions, ever. She would bore her eyes through the text or would write in her notebook during class discussions. At times I sensed she wanted to shout, "Stop talking." Of course, she didn't, and I didn't understand her lack of participation. In truth, she irritated me. Here was a group of twenty-five bright twelfth graders sharing their perceptions, frustrations, and questions about literature. Why was Laura detached, preoccupied, seemingly above the talk? She wrote wonderfully reflective essays, short stories, and poems.

During a discussion of *Great Expectations* I called on her. Probably out of spite. Laura looked up, startled. "Just a minute," she said, her voice firm. "I just realized something connects all these hands together, and I don't want to lose my train of thought." She turned back to the text and continued to read, lost in her own thoughts. The whole class turned to look at Laura, then at me. I motioned, "Hold on." We waited an uncomfortable five minutes or more. Laura absorbed herself in her reading and didn't notice. The bell rang.

I did some serious thinking through the next class, through lunch, through the long ride home, and into the night. I was startled by the revelation. How could I have overlooked that the classroom interaction had been set by my questions, my leadership in discussions, and the dominant peer voices who engaged in the continual talk that averted silence? We had conspired together, however unwittingly, to keep silence out of the classroom. We had not allowed individual readers to have the time to find their own ways of working with the text. Laura put me on the track of silence. She led me to reconsider the constraints and restrictions that confine student thinking when powerful voices of teacher and more vocal peers take control. In reflecting back on this situation now, I'm amazed at how a seemingly innocent and simple exchange had the impact that it did on my subsequent actions and behavior in the classroom.

The next morning I gave each student a copy of Jon Anderson's poem "The Blue Animals." The poem's brevity, along with the silences in subject and form, raised the issue of silence again. We had a long talk about silence that day. Laura entered the discussion. "I need more time to think. It takes think time to piece everything together. If I talk about what I'm thinking early on, it's like I've ended the story and closed it off from my mind." Others began to agree. John said,

"I try to show I've done the reading, or that I've had some bright ideas." Susan added, "I always talk right away because I think the teacher likes that. For them it seems to be a way of checking to see if we're prepared." "How," I asked, "can we do this better?"

Respecting silence. The talk we had in that classroom in the late 1970s was the forerunner for what we now think of as "going meta." Metacognition, the explicit inquiry into how we carry out our mental work, helps us come to understand why silence is important. The most potent insight, and possibly the most hopeful, is that the students in that classroom wanted to support other students' ways of working. We began to consider how we might benefit from both sound and silence. Of course, my role had to change as well. I had to overcome my disabling habit of saying too much, too soon. I had to hold myself back from calling out the name of the first person who raised a hand. I learned to wait as a way of protecting the silence wherein students had time and space to think. Students were not always comfortable with my silence nor I with theirs. It took some getting used to. No longer did I take full responsibility for a class discussion. I wasn't the only person in the classroom demonstrating, validating, questioning, or explaining strategies to help others make sense of the text. Of course, this took time. We sometimes stammered and stumbled along, but we worked at getting better during the rest of that year.

Most of the students in this community of readers made progress at becoming reflective and sensitive to the use of silence. Even in whole-group discussion we learned patience. As the students developed an increasingly sophisticated sense of wait time, think-before-speak time, they became more sensitive to each others' need to speak. The overt effects of our newfound understanding of silence were noticeable: students quit raising their hands during group discussions. Each listened, paused, gave peers time to think through ideas, and then, one voice would begin. More silence. One or more students jotted a few notes. The others waited. Students watched each other for signs—a circle of quiet where reflective readers made space for one another's thought time. Although the silence was no guarantee that each reader would obtain insight or make meaning, or use the silence to that end, each had the opportunity to shape and pattern and fine-tune the text toward those ends.

Rehearsals of silence. In the process of implementing silence, its use sometimes took other tangential forms. Students were more tolerant of questions being asked that were not answered and of leaving a literary text with some uncertainties about a definitive interpretation of a particular person, image, or symbol. They became more comfortable with my resistance to clarify their puzzlements with my teacher answers. Many times questions remained unanswered, pregnant with ideas for further exploration. Out of this evolved one organized activity that I have used in classrooms ever since that year: A round-robin question session. Questions are thrown out one after another—with a pause between. None are answered. Questions without answers or accompanying clarification result in a provisional stock of topics and lines of inquiry.

Certainly writing extends the time for reflection. After that year, I encouraged students to spend more class time writing reactions to questions other students asked, responding to passages another student quoted, or reacting to the group discussions. These instantaneous reflections give students time to grapple with their thoughts. Writing to learn has been a strategy celebrated in our professional literature and not new to most of us. In a classroom where tentativeness is nurtured, such writing gives space for the silence that allows time for reflection.

Further deliberations and reading helped me understand other forms of silence through which readers might shape, modify, or represent the text in ways that keep speculation open rather than closing it down. In order to encourage time for reflection and to discourage students' impulses to produce immediate interpretations of literature, I've learned that it is important to:

- encourage open-ended questions, both from the students as well as me;
- promote tentativeness of interpretation;
- introduce "inferential walks, ghost chapters" (Eco, 1979, pp. 214–216) along with dialogue journals (every reader has a partner) that encourage students to see a text in several ways;
- ask students to monitor and to articulate how their reading changes with additional readings and peer input;
- connect present readings with past reading, with personal experiences, or with hypothetical possibilities;
- introduce the writing of literature as a way of studying a text (for example, write a stream-of-consciousness portrait of self while reading Joyce's *Portrait,* or write an amusette when reading James' *Turn of the Screw).*

These encounters with text keep students from forming hypotheses too early. Sensitivity to silence allows student readers time to define a work of literature for themselves. Silence is a strategy that promotes tentativeness, improvisation, and creation.

Refining silences. I remember very well how pleased I was that same year when Jason interrupted a peer response session: "Why don't we give ourselves a chance to think? We just keep talking and Julie (the writer whose personal narrative was being discussed) can't possibly have time to think about what we're saying." Jason brought the strategy of silence to the writing workshop.

Other students kept refining the process as well. "What if the writer doesn't try to explain but just listens?" said Jeff. "Every time we say something, the writer decides to explain. That doesn't mean that's what's in writing. I think the writer needs to stay out of the conversation sometimes." Imposed silence. I borrowed these student adaptations for future years. In naming silence as a strategy for learning, I came to recognize it as a powerful tool used in written text. Students recognized the forms of silence—dashes, paragraphs, stanzas, thin poems, fat poems, white space—as a potent vehicle for contemplation. They recognized the silences a writer creates for the reader. Student writers began to experiment with such silences in their own pieces of writing:

Across Dakota

Late at night
after
moon lights my pillow
I cross the Dakota plains
back
in
Wisconsin
the dark, flat, dry summer
when I lay down in warm dust
waited for the train.

—Tonia Galdos

In this way, silence extends and transforms and becomes a powerful resource for thought.

Silent moments. Some days I crave silence in the classroom—the silence that allows time for students to construct meaning. I do not wish to underscore the power of a community of readers, for we all know students learn through dialogue and discussion. But no matter how fine a class discussion twists and turns around meanings, I still search for the productive space between voice and voicelessness in the classroom. Sound and silence are both acts of interpreting and imagining. Silence has an integral relationship with thought. It opens a space where thinking can shape and reshape through continued contemplation. Time with our developing perceptions keeps us from the stranglehold of too-easy formulations. Silence suggests time for indeterminacy.

Before Laura caused me to rethink silence, I feared it in the classroom. It suggested lack of preparation or engagement. However, silence is not speechlessness. Silence allows us to turn the corner of our imaginings and meet new wonderings. Laura reminded me of something I knew before. I learned about silence through years of musical training. Rests hold equal value with notes or chords. Rests extend or emphasize melody lines, offer delays or obscurities. Rests enhance the aesthetic and technical breathing of musical composition. I find the same operating principles in language when writing and reading poetry or prose. In language, line breaks, stanza breaks, paragraph and chapter breaks, dashes, commas—all are tools of silence. So, silence is the active partner with sound in music, in language, as well as in the classroom. Laura helped me recognize the potential of silence in my teaching, and her influence changed my teaching practices.

Learning from local knowledge. This elaboration on silence is intended to illustrate that we hold in our hands a wealth of classroom experiences that have changed our practices. I'd like to imagine these brought together in a huge mosaic that represents teaching. I wonder what we could learn from this mythic mosaic? What could it tell us about curricular or instructional reform or about the necessity of systemic or ecological change in schools? Consider the multiple principles about teaching embedded in the experience with Laura and the subsequent actions resulting from her response. Though theorists and researchers do not agree on how learning occurs, many describe cognitive and social processes that enhance meaning making. It would be possible to trace various ways in which such information has been used to recommend teaching practices that illustrate what has been learned. Our teaching mosaic would offer a parallel description, using different terminology and more local illustrations, of similar processes on how learning occurs. Unfortunately, teachers, theorists, and researchers rarely or systematically engage in dialogue about our shared knowledge. Mostly, we don't speak the same language or use the same terms and labels to describe the common knowledge we share.

Given all of the above, one of our agendas may be to more actively vocalize the local knowledge we have and be adamant that our professional knowledge is valuable. As I mentioned in the Prologue through the example of Cynthia Linn, who suggested, "It makes me feel funny, talking about my teaching," some of us are uncomfortable in sharing the knowledge we have or consider it of little value to others. "That's just lore and war stories," Cynthia suggested. Such attitudes are conspiratorial in that teachers ruefully accept that their knowledge isn't important. Yet, I think how important the knowledge is that I gained from Laura and her classmates. I learned: silence allows time for productive contemplation; silence can be encouraged through a variety of structures and activities; silence can increase sensitivity to other's voices; silence is a resource of language used to construct meaning. This was learned from one incident—think what the mosaic could teach. The lurking danger is that even with this issue of silence, once it's concretized as a principle, it gets turned into a teaching strategy to list in someone's "principles of good teaching." I worry about that, but don't know how to avoid it. I do know we need to celebrate the intellectual work behind our understanding of practice. I don't want that taken out of our hands.

Negotiating Revisions

A second example of reading the text of my teaching life illustrates how a conference presentation stimulated a new way of thinking about students' revision on writing. This new approach to revision began in a session conducted by John Mayher and Gordon Pradl at an NCTE conference nearly ten years ago. In the session, John demonstrated what he and Gordon labeled as a "cold" reading of text. John explained that he believed in modeling the types of strategies readers use by presenting to students an "out loud" protocol reading of a text that he'd not read before. John demonstrated his point by reading a poem that Gordon presented to him "cold." John began reading the text aloud, stopping to describe as nearly as he could what questions he was asking, what he noted particularly, and what meaning he was making as he continued to read. Through his reading and his protocol, we could easily see how he negotiated meaning between what the poet had written on the page and the meaning John was taking from the poem.

John talked and read his way through the text. He pondered, deliberated, and asked questions. If I'd been the poet, I would have liked to have been in the workshop as John co-created meaning from my images and crafting of ideas. How much, I remember thinking at the time, that poet might have learned. It struck me then. Why not make this strategy a part of peer response procedures when student writers work on revisions? Why not make this a strategy not only for reading literature but also as a part of the revision by helping young peer responders see someone read, question, enjoy, or struggle with the writer's language and ideas?

John's demonstration led me to think that our young writers should hear someone else read their writing aloud. That isn't a particularly novel idea, but an accompanying protocol with the "cold" reading might help student writers understand the congruence between their intended meaning and the perceived meaning elicited by the reader. In this way, a writer could see how a reader was making sense of the work during the first reading. Using this method, students could hear explicitly how a reader responded, what the reader understood, what questions the reader had, and what the reader reacted to particularly. So, from this session at a conference, I took away the seeds of an idea that I needed to tinker with before introducing it to my students.

Turning an idea into a plan of action. As I set about devising a plan, I knew that this particular revision strategy would be especially useful with drafts that have the substance and sequence of the entire piece as the writer envisions it. So, I intended to begin a demonstration of the strategy by asking a student to share with her classmates an early draft of a poem. Lacie agreed to share an early draft of one of her poems:

> The elephants hunker down
> searching for old bones, white
> bones whispering through
> African nights. Death seeps
> from river's thick sand, pulls
> death to life and white tusks
> stand like tall trees exposed.
>
> Old graveyards resurrect in water,
> flowing Northeast past Juba or
> maybe through Renk or Atbara
> where ancient women loom along
> the banks, breasts sag, darker
> than night, suckle their children
> before their bones, too,
> take the Northwest curve
> near Aswan. Before their bones
> grow again when the river dashes
> its relentless fury against
> the bank, longing to rise.
>
> —Lacie Randall

Lacie revised this draft before it was duplicated for her classmates. As she described her intentions: "I worked to make the meaning a little clearer. For example, I added 'gray and listless' to line 2. 'Whispering through' is changed to 'knuckling up in' in lines 3 and 4. I changed 'stand' to 'loom' in line 7 and added 'almost human' to line 8. I determined that I wanted specific locations, so a generic river wasn't good enough. The Blue or White Nile would set a more specific and visual locale. The White Nile seemed right, so I added 'Death seeps from the White Nile's' to line 5, particularly to re-emphasize the bone imagery. That introduced a new meaning that led me to change 'thick sand' in line 5 to 'shears sand away.' I wanted the White Nile to be aggressive."

The following version was handed out in class:

> Elephants hunker down, gray
> and listless, searching for white
> bones knuckling up in African nights.
>
> Loosening death's memory, the White Nile
> shears sand away until tusks loom
> like tall trees exposed.
>
> Old graveyards resurrect in water,
> flowing Northeast past Juba or
> maybe through Renk or Atbara
> where ancient women loom along
> the banks, breasts sag, darker
> than night, suckle their children
> before their bones, too,
> take the Northwest curve
> near Aswan. Before their bones
> grow again when the river dashes
> its relentless fury against
> the bank, longing to rise.

Joe Taylor volunteered to model his "cold" reading of Lacie's poem. Joe read the poem aloud, commenting on what is most nearly coming to mind as he reads. He described his confusions, understandings, and the reactions that take place as he reads. Lacie recorded his comments in the margin of her copy of the poem. A transcript of Joe's protocol follows:

Joe reads: Elephants hunker down, gray
and listless, searching for white
bones knuckling up in African nights.

Joe speaks: I wonder what 'hunker' means? I get an image of slouched, but I don't know for sure. If the elephants are searching, I can't believe they are listless. I wonder why the writer used that word? Is it deliberate? Knuckling reminds me of knuckles. I see someone raising a fist, knuckles first. That gives me an image that bones rise, rigid and solid.

Joe reads: Loosening
Death's memory, the White Nile
Shears sand away until tusks
loom like tall trees exposed

Joe speaks: I'm confused with death's memory but think of bones as the aftermath of death. Death's memory is loosened by these bones that knuckle up. I can almost see it. It's the fault of the White Nile. I don't know why however. When sand shears away, I think the river is too high and carries everything in its path. I get the images of what is left behind after a flood. Tusks. But are they tall? Maybe magnified, but tall doesn't sound like the right word—something like a flood exposes and brings to the surface what's gone before—like old ghosts returning and haunting the new land. The bones are reminders of a more ancient history.

Joe reads: Old graveyards resurrect in water

Joe speaks: Now I'm pretty sure this is a flood. Are these actual burial groups? For people or elephants?

Joe reads: flowing Northeast past Juba or
maybe through Renk or Atbara
where ancient women loom along
the banks, breasts sag, darker
than night, suckle their children

Joe speaks: I wonder how the elephants tie in to this part of the poem. I get a strong visual sensation of the river water moving faster as it rises and then, like around a bend, here are all the women maybe washing clothes in the river. Their presence is a strong contrast to what has gone before. There are images of fertility—breasts, suckle—but I'm not certain how that is associated with the flood.

Joe reads: before their bones, too
take the Northwest curve
near Aswan. Before their bones
grow again when the river dashes
the relentless fury against
the bank, longing to rise.

Joe speaks: Powerful. I get the impression that this forecasts their death, like they'll be swept away by the flood but they will rise again at sometime in the future with possibly another flood. I'm not sure I understand why they "long to rise." I love the images in this poem.

Lacie listened to Joe reading her poem and his thoughts about the poem. She made notes. Lacie indicated that she was particularly struck by Joe's reaction to her use of "listless." He confirmed her choice by suggesting that the knuckle gave an image of rising up. By the time Joe finished the reading, Lacie felt she had a number of reconsiderations about revision possibilities: she'd look carefully at her use of "listless"; determine ways to clarify death's memory; find a better way than tall to describe the bones; try to extend the image of elephant, and examine if the images of fertility were appropriate.

As a class, we discussed what in Joe's comments would be helpful to the writer. They thought the most helpful points Joe made were related to: inconsistencies; lack of clarity; words that lead away rather than toward meaning; repetitions; redundancies; lack of detail to make a point clearer; and issues of sequence of images or ideas.

By the time we had finished the demonstration, twenty-five minutes of class time remained. Students paired and began a similar reading for each other.

Looking Back. Lacie worked on revisions for a few days, then brought another draft back to her classmates. We made copies for the class and compared them with the earlier draft:

> Elephants hunker down, gray
> and patient, searching for white bones
> knuckling up in African nights.
>
> The White Nile shears sand
> away until tusks rise
> like tree roots exposed.
>
> Graveyards resurrect
> in Bentiu and past Malakal
> along the river's course.
>
> Not even elephants bury bones
> deep enough to keep them from
> the grip of rising.
>
> Women of the Sudd deserve one
> line in this story. Standing on banks,
> they beat the river back with spears.
>
> Copper and ivory rattle against
> their skin. Kanga skirts
> tremble at a rumor of floods
>
> on Niobic graveyards. Ancestors
> unearthed. Tribes down the river hear
> the music of grief rise; the Nile
> headed their way.

Lacie described some of the changes to the class, explaining that she tried to emphasize the importance of the bones of ancestors not being disturbed for both elephant and human. She had considered Joe's concern about her images of fertility seriously and decided it was not central to the poem. Thus, the changes in the latter part of the poem reflect Lacie's attempt to clarify her intention. Now, the women were trying to beat back the spirits in the flood, hoping to avert the unearthing of bones that would mean the spirits of ancestors were disturbed and unleashed in the world. "When Joe suggested he didn't understand the 'long to rise' I realized that I was giving the wrong impression," Lacie explained. "What I really wanted to do was the opposite—the fear of rising." When Lacie rewrote the end she decided that it was important to leave the poem with the tension that a great catastrophe had taken place and that it was not over. "I wanted the poem to end with tribes down river hearing the impending doom headed their way."

Rediscovering the text of teaching. As this case of "cold reading" illustrates, I take in my hands the clay of an idea that I can mold and shape in whatever ways the students and I find meaningful. This is no small point. As Montaigne is quoted as saying, "It is good to rub and polish our brain against that of others." This is part of the social value of sharing our ideas with other teachers, whether at conferences or in the faculty room. Other teachers' ideas become a sounding board for our interpretations and purposes. Ideas are the lifeblood of our occupation. The best of ideas leaves plenty of room for individual choice. To make an idea our own, we need to capitalize on the unique interests and strengths that personalize teaching with our unique signatures. That's what I tried to do with John and Gordon's idea. I've seldom learned to do anything worthwhile that is an exact reproduction of someone else's thinking or practices.

As teachers, we act on our developing beliefs and constantly reflect on those actions. It isn't that we never quite get it right, but that no matter how right it is, it can always be done differently. I still teach this revision strategy some ten years after the conference where I first contemplated the potential of the idea. I've tinkered and refined the various explanations or demonstrations to suit particular students and haven't introduced the strategy the same way twice. Perhaps that's why the unremitting flow of events in the classroom is never completely a surprise nor does it meet all expectations. Continuously, as we make one choice after another, the mosaic of our teaching life deepens and take other shapes.

Stalking Vision from the Masters:
A Lesson on the Third Eye

As you've seen so far, I'm suggesting that teaching engages us in explorations that often bring us to imagine new ways of working. We have in our hands the potential to see behind any event, reaction, or action the dim, hardly defined, miniscule seed of an idea. A student led me to refine my understanding of the use of silence in the class-room and in writing. Colleagues led me to consider new strategies for teaching revision. From a workshop that a colleague and I conducted at NCTE in Detroit, I learned about the third eye.

Fran Claggett and I co-chaired a full-day workshop on combining visual and textual representations when studying literature. We brought a mixed bag of ideas to our audience—all founded on the pedagogical notion of doing rather than observing. A final "hands-on" afternoon of watercolor, mandala-making, and poetry writing carried the theme into practice. We wanted to offer teaching techniques that encouraged the fine tuning of perception and observation, hoping to evoke the hidden, the unilluminated potential of what lurks behind the obvious.

After any workshop of this type, I find myself searching for culminating insight gained from the preparation and presentation. After this one, I couldn't make the imaginative leap that would help me explain why this had been a particularly important moment in my teaching life. "Start at the root of vision," I kept thinking. One of the important points we'd made throughout the workshop was that possibly we spend too much time shuffling through the literary text with students, lining up the literature like artifacts in neat rows, which keeps students standing at a distance from a text rather than working within it. I wanted to find ways to encourage students to see some hidden, unguessed potential in the text, to walk around inside the text and find what it has to tell that is more than words on the page.

Shortly after that workshop, I read Margaret Atwood's (1983) "Instructions for the Third Eye." She states: "The eye is the organ of vision, and the third eye is no exception to that. Open it and it sees, close it and it doesn't. Most people have a third eye but they don't trust it" (p. 61). Behind all we'd done during the workshop, the essence of what we were trying to get at was that as teachers we want to help students see within the literary text, to open their eyes differently. Atwood goes on to suggest: "What's the difference between vision and a vision? The former relates to something it's assumed you've seen, the latter to something it's assumed you haven't" (p. 62). Within a literary work we find another's vision, but we co-create the vision as well. That's a slippery notion, but I'm thinking that there is a form of dual vision that combines what the writer has created with what the reader sees.

For example, imagine moving inside Othello and seeing the scene as he sees it rather than standing back and watching his actions, removed and distanced by some intellectual miles. Can we imagine taking a place in one of the drawers in Salvador Dali's

"Composition of Figures of Drawers" and seeing the setting that surrounds the drawer? I'm suggesting that the gaze of imagination can construct that setting. The provocative inner life is given freedom to imagine if we see with our third eye. We will need to educate this eye along with attempts to trigger our students' access to its power. At every turn, active participation is the key. Atwood goes on to say: "If you want to use the third eye you must close the other two. Then breathe evenly; then wait" (p. 61).

After that workshop, I experimented with many ideas to engage students with the third eye concept as I could best understand it. The most obvious way was to encourage students to begin looking outward at the events and happenings in a piece of literature by moving into one character's position and gazing outward. Writing assignments, then, were experiments to test vision from that perspective.

Seeing from the character's point of view. The delineation of characters in Faulkner's *As I Lay Dying*, with the distinctness of the vision and voice of a character, made it an obvious choice for experimenting with point of view and perception. For example, Dewey Dell observes the events that go on around her differently than Cash or Addie do. Dewey Dell creates her own metaphors for the world as she casts her gaze on the field, the river, and her family. The assignment was a simple one. After students read the first two or three chapters and understood the point of view change from character to character, they divided into small groups for reading aloud. Each person in the group chose one character and read the appropriate chapters. My intention for the read-aloud was to help students internalize the language, viewpoint, and cadence of individual characters. We stopped to discuss what and how each character sees. We watched carefully to see the subtle and not so subtle uniqueness of each. Then, students were asked to add sections to either chapters in the novel or to create a separate chapter for a character. The idea was that these student writers would need to see from inside Dewey Dell, Addie, Cash, or Vardaman, observing through the lenses that made the characters unique. This was an experiment on educating the third eye.

Elizabeth, a twelfth grader, experimented with Dewey Dell's vision of things:

> I stand a-side mother wavin' the hot, dead air to cool her sick, sweatin' face. I dont do much. Ma's face is still sick and sweatin'. Darl told me that ma is going to die. Maybe its the dead, hot air. The dead, hot, pale air touches her naked through the pale sheet. Maybe the dead air is making her dead. It cant be helped a-course because the air is everywhere sucking at ma's life. I know that my

fanning her face don't help her not die. The dead air seeps in through her naked body. But this is what I'm supposed to be doin' for ma cause it makes her feel better.

The dead air may be sucking at me too, sucking my life into its guts. But I cant be dying cause if I die, no one can care for pa, and Cash and Jewel and Darl and Vardaman. I am Dewey Dell and they is my brothers except for pa. But that is not all, there is another, and it, which is inside my tub of guts.

Ma twists in the sheets and puts herself to sleep again. Sometimes I want to tell her. But I remember about when Vardaman came along. Ma was sicker than a colicking horse of us kids and would leave Vardaman crying in his box. His cries filled the house and overflowed into the expanse of the land as does water when you fill the tub too long. Ma wouldn't understand about what is in my tub of guts. She is long past understanding.

Darl knows. But being a man, he dont understand neither. I am Dewey Dell. I am a woman, I understand.

Eric chose to experiment with Jewel's way of thinking:

He's always following me around. He says Your mother was a horse what was your father Jewel? You lying son of a horse yourself. He's always following me around and smiling and saying Your mother was a horse as if I didn't know what he means. He used to follow Dewey Dell around. He thinks he can see inside. We're not the same and he don't know what I think.

I saw him though beside the barn. He wanted her out there so he could get rid of the smell. We carried her in because he said he didn't want no buzzards on her at night he was just waiting for me to close my eyes. I did and he sneaked out like a cat scratching earth over its shit, she lying there and not protesting while he was dropping oil on the ground. He should have put such oil on Cash's leg before the cement. I see him drop a match and I scoot off and back to bed and close my eyes again until he comes. Come on, I say and we go to the barn together. I stop in front of her and he says Quick the horses and I see his point. No need to burn up horses and cows when all you planned on was just her.

Lisa opens the door of Cora's house and sees the Bundrens standing there:

There werent no moon that night when they showed upon my doorstep. Three of 'em—Anse, Vardaman, and Darl. Anse all hunched over lookin like someone was fixen to hit him. Bein' a Christian I ask 'em in out of the cold but Anse sayin he werent beholden to no man or woman. We stood there shiverin in the cold and lookin at each other in the cold and Anse shifted his weight and sucked at his gums. The wind was fierce that night and the bare tree branches scraped against each other making it sound like the woods was full of animals though I know no livin' creature was out in this cold. "We come to ask your help in lookin' for Jewel, he ain't home yet." Anse shuffled around and mumbled and sucked his gums again. I went inside to get my jacket, knowin what a neighbor was obliged to do but Jewel, that Jewel and the woods screaming in the cold and he might be froze to death out there and already in the arms of heaven.

As a way of educating the third eye, then, I asked students to look closely at whatever that character might see—the wind, the barn, another person's actions, the sound in the woods—through that character's point of view. I was hoping to educate them and them to educate me into looking more closely—perhaps to see the wisp of hair on Addie's pillow, fine dust around the barn, the scar on Anse's cheek. Together, we were only beginning, however, to educate our third eyes. We continued throughout that school year to become different see-ers.

Seeing from a writer's point of view. I write this section knowing that the idea of modeling and imitation have lost favor as a way of teaching writing. Yet, I do think apprenticeship has some value depending on its use rather than abuse. Frank Smith (1983) argues that writers will "read like a writer," using authors' "nuances of expression," "relevant syntactic devices," and "turn of phrase" (p. 41). Continuing along with the third eye metaphor, I began to experiment with how the third eye becomes educated using immediate and exacting observation accompanied by precision with language. We can learn about observations and crafting from other writers. There are conscious choices to be made in what we see and how we choose to represent what we see. I've found it helpful to exemplify that to students through imitation. We can teach ourselves and our students something about observation by examining what and how other writers record what they have observed or imagined. Seeing what others do can help us exercise the third eye and can extend our capacity to see differently or more fully.

We can learn fundamental principles of imagination by studying the logic of the eye. As Suzanne Langer (1957) suggests, "A model always illustrates a principle of construction or operation" (p. 281). One way to educate the eye is to model someone else's way of seeing and to make explicit what can be seen and how it is seen. I introduced this concept to students one year using Hemingway's opening paragraph in *A Farewell to Arms*. From Frederick Henry, the narrator's viewpoint, we are led to see:

> In the late summer of that year we lived in a house in a village that looked across the river and the plain to the mountains. In the bed of the river there were pebbles and boulders, dry and white in the sun, and the water was clear and swiftly moving and blue in the channels. Troops went by the house and down the road and the dust they raised powdered the leaves of the trees. The trunks of the trees too were dusty and the leaves fell early that year and we saw the troops marching along the road and the dust rising and leaves, stirred by the breeze, falling and the soldiers marching and afterward the road bare and white except for the leaves (p. 3).

To engage the students in an apprenticeship of sorts, I asked them to examine what the narrator observed and how he described what he saw. Students noted the sequence of what was observed, explained the types of sensual details used, suggested that the rhythm of the passage matched the movement of the troops, and identified the movement of the narrator's eye from expansive aspects of the landscape to minutiae. Following this discussion, students were asked to take an observation of a setting they had written earlier in the week and revise it, modeling Hemingway's paragraph.

Eleventh-grader Maria Kelley, following Hemingway's syntax and method of observation, revised her description:

> In the early part of that day I sat on the beach in the sand that looked across the waves and the foam to the sunrise. In air above the ocean there were seagulls and cold mist, white and clean in the light, and the water was blue and barely moving and frothing on the shore. I went by the pier and past the boats and the fish they caught scented the mist of the morning. The nets of the men too were full and the fish lay dying that day and I saw the tails flop up and down and the smell strengthening and nets, stirred by the breeze, flapping and the men working and afterward the fish dead and piled next to the nets.

Maria concentrated on the rhythm and the movement between big objects and small details. Maria said, "It hadn't struck me before that part of observing is the order in which you see the objects in the scene. I didn't think of that as a resource. That forced me to see some small details in the scene that I didn't include in the first draft. I also worked consciously on the rhythm. I didn't realize that the sentences create part of the rhythm."

Robert Hammer, also a high school junior, wrote:

> In the empty cellar of our home we played in the dark in a room that stretched across the tile and the concrete to the stairway. At the end of the room there were boxes and clothes, cool and musty in the dark, and the floor was hard and sharply echoing and slick

in the basement. Ants went through the cracks and along the tile and the mounds they made dotted the seams of the wall. The base of the stairs too was dotted and the ants came early that spring and we saw the bugs creeping along the wall and the mounds rising and cracks, widened by the insects, growing and the bugs working and afterward the room dark and empty except for the ants.

Robert allowed his third eye to take over when the ants swarm and take control in the basement. Robert suggested that "the details began to stand out. I realized how much more there was to see in this scene than I'd seen before. For example, the seams in the wall, the cracks, the smell of the basement, the slickness of the concrete. I stretched to see more and that was very helpful. I need to remember as I write to see what isn't the most obvious. To get the rhythm I wanted the ants everywhere."

This illustration of imitation is meant to point out that we can help educate the third eye. Even Hemingway does that. One of the reasons I introduced this passage of Hemingway's to students was so that I could show them an example of modeling. I read, nearly at the same time I was reading *A Farewell to Arms,* the short story "Sophistication" by Sherwood Anderson. His opening paragraph begins:

> It was early evening of a day in the late fall and the Winesburg County Fair had brought crowds of country people into town. The day had been clear and the night came on warm and pleasant. On the Trunion Pike, where the road after it left town stretched away between berry fields now covered with dry brown leaves, the dust from passing wagons arose in clouds. Children, curled into little balls, slept on the straw scattered on wagon beds. Their hair was full of dust and their fingers black and sticky. The dust rolled away over the fields and the departing sun set it ablaze with color.

I'd suggest that Anderson informed Hemingway's ways of seeing. Hemingway informed Maria and Robert's ways of seeing.

What I've found is that students articulate more precisely what they see another writer doing in a literary text if they try modeling. I'll offer a final example of a student's third eye at work. This happens to be a high school senior's interpretation of *Hamlet.* Harriet decided on a poem as her genre of choice:

The Guts of a Fish Tale

King Hamlet is a fisherman.
He's a shade with gear: fisherman's intuition
He knows the shadows
In which he'll snag young Hamlet.

Young Hamlet is a fish.
Like all the Danish people.
Like Daddy was.
Daddy King Hamlet . . . WAS the granddaddy fish
In the Riverbed Denmark. But, when your life
is yanked without the consecrated oil
of a priestly trout, your fate (who dictates?)
is to troll by night, itch by day.

(You fisherman soul)

Until you set the drag—
     hook your murderer
     and reel him into hell.

But first you need bait,
An accomplice to wriggle that hook
Into that new daddy-by-murder
Now kissing fish lips with your wife
In your incestuous bed
Of pebbles.

It's way past Hamlet's Hamlet's beddy-bye.
Son is snagged.
True to the royal fish family
Hamlet will drag the line
Until he hooks
Murderer Claudius crook-
ed as his king-

Brother.

Drop a line
Ripple, "Swear. Swear."
Verify to remind
Father's got a hold
Of the pole
He'll never let go.

Hamlet's rigged.

Lots of fish in Denmark's dead water.
Perhaps Fisherman knew
He'd have to flip the bail
As Hamlet wanders to Ophelia.
Tourniquet with worms
A soil of love.

Fisherman lets more line
Hamlet hooks Polonius
Fish brain mistake, but never fear

Hamlet has hooks—one, two, a whole slew.

Swim to Hamlet's mother
Fisherman's fish love
Old love knows
Planted deep in her breast
With the slightest tug,
She'll bait herself.

A fisherman's trick
Ghost gills for Hamlet
Gertrude can't see her dead fish's soul
"Alas, he's mad."
Hamlet hooks himself.

More and more line—Fisherman's generosity.
Hamlet hooks wherever he goes
It's a web of fish line
Pulling from Fisherman's pole.

Set up for the fish finale.
Snags into Laertes, Gertrude, Claudius, Hamlet.
The Fisherman's waiting for a hit
And, it happens.

Laertes' catch
Into Hamlet
Yanks the line
Through Gertrude
Claudius, himself . . .

Just reel them all out, Fisherman.
Out of the bed
You wished to sleep
If you can't have
A goodnight's rest,
No One Will.

Harriet wrote a reflection on her poem. I have included excerpts
to give a flavor of her understanding:

The guts first sparked with Maynard Mack's sentence: "The
young man (Hamlet) growing up is not to be allowed simply to
endure a rotten world, he must also act in it." Why? Because Hamlet has promised his father he will not forget his murder and will
revenge it. . . . Ghost Hamlet tells Hamlet he is "Doomed for a certain term to walk the night/And for the day confined to fast in
fires,/Till the foul crimes done in my days of nature/Are burnt and
purged away (Act I, Scene v, 9–13). The ghost will be tortured until his death is no longer a secret unavenged. . . .Ghost Hamlet con-

vinces Hamlet with his parting words in Act I, scene v "Adieu, adieu, adieu. Remember me." Hamlet is snagged with loyal obligations, whether literally or metaphorically, to carry out his father's orders. What Hamlet does not know is that it is impossible to kill Claudius without snagging anyone else in the court. . . In the final scene—the fencing match—it is only certain that now the dark will come to life. All the hooks are ready to be gouged into flesh as the truth becomes known. And everyone does die. . . . . Once the line is set and pulled, no one can continue living in the world he was so unjustly forced to leave.

I'd suggest that Harriet is educating her eye to see not only her own vision but to be sensitive to someone else's.

Stephen King (1984) writes in "Imagery and the Third Eye" that the image is "the bright picture that glows in the physical eye or in the mind's eye" (p. 74). He goes on to suggest that "our eyes convey images to our brains; if we are to convey images to our readers, then we must see with a kind of third eye—the eye of imagination and memory. Writers who describe poorly or not at all see poorly with this eye; others open it, but not all the way" (p. 76). King's article on learning to see was helpful to me as a teacher and a writer. He prods his reader to "follow the running man or get into that car and see what's in there; see who grabbed the child, and try to find out why. You can do it, if you care to open that inner eye just as wide as it will go" (1984, p. 79). We have it in our hands to help our students see further out into the world than they have before, to be more aware of other's visions, to attune their third eye to the spiritual and geographic landscapes in which they walk, think, and imagine.

Letting Loose the Stories Behind the Literature

Stories come in all shapes and sizes—fibs, folk tales, ad-libs, lies, and fragments from our experiences and imaginings—but I was particularly struck one day when I walked into my sophomore English class and overheard Kristie saying, "My Uncle Edward watched . . ." and Daniel's voice across the room, "When Julie left, then it all started . . . ." and Sam telling Charlie, "Yesterday when it rained my Mom saw . . . ." Each storyteller inspired attentive and eager listeners. Story inventions were being spun throughout the room. The classroom brimmed full of stories until I opened my mouth and the official class began.

I thought afterward how often we tell stories to justify our actions, to rehearse an upcoming event, to daydream, or to explain something we've experienced or read. Many people, given a responsive audience, will tell a story. These inventions fill our lives, but they are cut short sometimes in school environments. Certainly the power of narrative to sort through and make sense of images, thoughts, and imaginings is well documented, yet most writing or discussion about literature tends to be more expository and critical than narrative. This may demonstrate something about the bias in our discipline for criticism. Exposition and analysis represent the discipline of mind and the proper diet for classroom activity while story is entertainment and a bit suspect.

After hearing the stories that surrounded me before the bell rang, I decided to expand the ways in which students wrote and talked about literature. The narrative voices of Kristie, Daniel, and Sam led me to rethink the practices that were validated in our classroom and to find ways to bring narrative into the basic framework surrounding our study of literature. I am still finding ways to ferret out the stories in our literature study. Here's some of what I learned.

Stories of personal experiences with literature. I wondered what stories students would tell about their personal experiences as readers and writers. Students' story histories offer interesting glimpses into the strategies they use as readers and the experiences that may influence their attitudes toward reading literature. Sarah Graham, age 14, is a particular case in point. When we began writing transformations of fairy tales (much in the fashion of Anne Sexton's transformation poems), Sarah began to tell the story of Rapunzel:

> I remember my mother read Rapunzel to me every time we went to visit my uncle's house. I can't quite remember, but I guess there was a book of fairy tales and it was a change from most of the reading we did at home. So, I'd always ask my mother to read "Rapunzel," and I'd get a cold chill when she'd let her hair down. I'd get dizzy and weak in my stomach. I was certain Rapunzel's head would fall off. I kept thinking, somehow, that the story would change and I always entered it anticipating the worst. Now, as I think back on that, I almost wish it had changed. I kept hoping that the words on the page might shift and crawl into other pages while I slept at night. I wanted the words to change and create new stories that could surprise me. Rapunzel was my way of always wishing for that. I've found that it is true in some ways. When I keep myself open to new ideas as I read, or when I listen to what others have to say about how they understood a story, I do think the words are not as certain or black and white.

From high school students like Sarah, I learned it was important to build this awareness of story history and how such history explains an individual's reactions to literature as well as how that literature is interpreted.

I have extended the use of story histories to include the student teachers with whom I work. They will enter the teaching of literature with more sensitivity as a result of what they learned about themselves as readers. In Chapter Three, several of Beth, Jane, and Joe's experiences with literature demonstrated how their personal histories informed their teaching. Jennie, during her student teaching experience, wrote:

> By the time I was five my mother and I had traveled far and wide. We had visited cities, countrysides, jungles, castles, and many other exciting locales. Although this might seem rather unusual, it was made even more unusual by the fact that my mother had been paralyzed from the chest down since the day I was born. My mother and I traveled together through books, forsaking more traditional modes. I remember sights and places, real and make believe, as if I had actually witnessed them with my own eyes. My mother told me that I would read with other children when I went to school. What she failed to tell me was that there was a difference between "school reading" and the times we'd shared at home.

Linda, also a student teacher, wrote:

> Then came Wally. Wally Schlitz. He taught my first memorable literature class. Wally was informed in current events and his literature reflected it. I was on my way to becoming a "liberated woman" in 1972, and that year we read Gloria S. I'd been wanting to read pieces about and, better yet, by females since I was young. I felt that Wally picked these pieces just for me. An exhilarating class discussion would ensue after the readings between Wally, Tim Barr (a fellow student), and me. Unfortunately, the rest of the class suffered through our three way discussions in silence, bored to tears.

When it comes to seeing principles about teaching in these stories and considering how their own experiences inform their practices, prospective teachers have indicated that they have deepened their own understanding through not only the power of their personal histories but also the power of narrative to inform their teaching.

Stories about the processes of reading. Literature study involves more than explaining the meaning that a reader elicits from a text. Students and teachers alike have found it helpful to tell the stories of the types of inquiry in which they engage to make meaning as they develop and deepen their knowledge of a particular text. Such stories offer a vision of the processes and modes of inquiry that are available to readers. Inviting readers to pay attention to that other journey, the one that starts within, is inviting them to explain what they care about in a text and why.

Such stories may tell us what readers come to know and where and how they acquire that understanding. What classroom experiences facilitate their understandings? How does their work with other students help them build social understanding? This may appear a departure from literature studies where the meaning of the text is central. In this case, students study the story of their experiences with a piece of literature. Wittgenstein's (1974) ideas of the "criss-crossed landscape" is a metaphor that guides my work in facilitating literature studies or preparing methods students. To crisscross private and public meanings, words on the page with images in our minds, to cross again with first thoughts and developed reactions, and crossing again with quotes and visual images, and characters—all of these approaches inform the developing readings.

I ask students to reflect on their reading processes frequently. From high schoolers to student teachers, each finds individual ways to question, connect, and create texts for themselves. Tasche Streib, a twelfth grader, writes:

> Two days, five acts. *Hamlet*. We all know how that goes. On Monday, most of us came into class the same way we always do—sleepy. The majority of students had a good idea of what the play was about. There remained a few of us who had not even begun to read. We sat in the back that day.
>
> We started acting out scenes that we remembered, started trying to figure out just how to read some lines—what tone of voice would Fortinbras use in his triumph? Poor, poor Hamlet. Really? And Gertrude's description of Ophelia's death—sugar sweet, sarcastic? The main point is: we couldn't ignore all the possible ways to read those lines. Almost everyone said, "Oh, wow! I didn't think of it that way." We began to look more closely at the play in our own ways.
>
> I started thinking about Hamlet's soldierly qualities. Hamlet was like a chess player to me—he used lots of strategy, cunning, a split-second decision to kill the pawns. I noted the backdrop of war, the possibility of Denmark being overthrown, Hamlet's fencing abilities and his strategies.
>
> I noticed how intricate the play really is. Not only do you have a play within a play, but you also have Fortinbras threatening to invade, a lover's quarrel, three revenge plots by sons whose fathers had been killed, a murderous uncle and a score of other things. The play caught me; I was interested.
>
> I wasn't the only one to get into the play. Beth came in about ten minutes late one morning. Her face was flushed from the cold and

she was slightly out of breath from the climb up the stairs, but she started to roll off things like, "He talks alot about brains and stuff. He uses body parts as metaphors all through the play." This, all the while she was getting her notes out of her bag. By bringing up this aspect, we all learned something about *Hamlet* as a play. No one else thought about the use of anatomy. Since then, every time I read a passage with a body part mentioned in the conversation I think, "There's an example of Hamlet's use of anatomy in metaphor." Thanks, Beth.

Each person taught us about another line of thought. *Hamlet* according to Mia, *Hamlet* according to Jason, or *Hamlet* according to Matt would become a topic for group exploration and learning. . . .

This notion of students teaching students expanded when we worked on a visual representation of the play. The assignment required us to combine our thoughts into one, neat presentable package by creating a visual representation of our interpretations of *Hamlet*. This allowed everyone to show their particular way of seeing *Hamlet*. My project was to show the different "fingerprints" that Hamlet had. I drew a large hand on a piece of posterboard, and then drew symbols on the fingertips to represent the different traits that Hamlet possesses. These traits included his swordsmanship, his revenge plots, and his scholarly qualities. . . . Having everyone present their project to the class, explaining the reasoning behind the visual, benefits everyone. I kept finding new ways to see the play. Laura made plaster faces with gauze masks that would fold away to show that the characters all had a thin veil over themselves to conceal their real character. Bob's chessboard with the characters in appropriate positions, Jeff's use of gears to show the interworkings, and Jen's piano keyboard made me think of new ways to see the play. . . .

All of these different views of *Hamlet* were taken from words written on a page. We'd all read the same words but found our own meaning. We cooperated and shared many ideas throughout our discussions. . . .

As a class we learned to look at things with a more questioning eye, following someone else's line of thought. We didn't need much prompting to dig into *Othello* after our experience with *Hamlet*.

I asked students to reflect on their reading experiences more frequently throughout my teaching years. These young readers helped me understand the effect of the choice of classroom practices. Asking students to reflect on their reading experiences helps them articulate the strategies that work for them. They grow as readers with this meta-thinking that requires them to bring forward the activities of mind. By listening to their voices as they journey through the many landscapes of their imaginings, I found new ways to encourage them to reflect on their reading and learn from it. I learned many more practices that helped them experience literature. Their insights helped me refine my practices. I have it in my hands to ask them.

I've taken what I learned in the high school classroom into my work with pre- and in-service teachers by encouraging them to share their stories of the search toward understanding. Students and teachers alike can record such reflections in reading logs, as personal narratives they tell to others, or in visual presentations that map their journey. Reconstructing their own processes of reading specific literature selections allows them to consider how different genres, styles, subjects, or cultural and historic experiences affect their reading. Such experiences bring them to consider how their own experiences and processes will affect the way they teach.

Exchanging stories. I see a literary text as ideas, events, experiences, people, images, and places that are evoked into life through reading. What is created in the transaction has proven interesting. For this reason, I'm looking more carefully for practices that facilitate the making of stories from stories. These "readings" that become new stories take many forms that are common enough: retellings, genre changes, visual depictions, tableaus, film productions, or interpretive dance. From these, I'm becoming more aware of the power of story to provoke new story. I think of Harriet's "Guts of a Fish Tale" poem. *Hamlet* provoked a new story. New stories were written out of Faulkner. Several students began to tell their stories of childhood when reading *A Portrait of the Artist as a Young Man.* I saved several of these to remind myself of what the students found in the opening chapter of Joyce's novel. Brian, a high school senior, wrote:

> Once upon a time blocks fell from the sky, down and down they came, "Humpty, Dumpty sat on a wall." Brian knew about this and remembered "had a great fall, had a great fall from the wall . . . had a fall from the wall." Your name, your name, oh who knows? You were small, smaller than Brian and you leaked. Smack dab in the middle of the floor. You didn't care who watched, you just leaked. A puddle between your chunky little legs. "All the kings had men, all mean men. Poor Humpty . . . Humpty, Dumpty . . ." Brian doesn't want to go to bed. Kaye says he must. His soft yellow P. J.'s with Winnie the Pooh patch on the chest caught his poor "tinkler" in its zipper. He cried, yelped, and turned red. "Couldn't put Humpty together, together, together, oh, no more Humpty for a story, no more Humpty."

What Brian does is a direct play-off of Joyce. Often students told the stories they wanted to tell to classmates first and after the oral tellings, began to shape their written work. For example, Shaunie, aged sixteen, told a story about her mother's illness to her peer response group:

> Mom spends most of her time locked in the bathroom. I try to see her through the keyhole. It is one of those old keyhole locks, the skeleton key type. I put my eye against it and see in. Everything is fuzzy—the red of my mother's robe, the mirror behind, the lines of bottle after bottle in the medicine cabinet. I try to imagine where she hurts and how it feels. Sometimes my legs go numb when I crouch long enough, and I feel good about hurting."

The next day Shaunie tells her group that the word "hurting" triggered another story that she wanted to tell them. "I remember riding my bike around the block. It was a new Schwinn. I crashed on a piece of broken cement. I could see the corner of my house about a block away. I screamed for my mom but she didn't come. I knew she could hear me. She was inside the house. I was trapped under the bike and couldn't escape and she couldn't help. It's like now. My mother isn't really hearing me." Shaunie went on to describe how this had given her an idea for a story to write about her mother's present illness. She tells the group:

> I think that Michael Water's poem we read in class a few weeks ago is still in my head, because I can see now how I might connect the two stories. Remember? In his poem two stories are told. The incidents blur. The boy is reading a story of drowning but his mother is packing to leave after something has gone terribly wrong in the house. I assumed it was like a divorce or a fight with the father. I've decided to try to write the poem of my mother, so it isn't sappy, by bringing together the incident from much earlier when I fell from the bike and now when my mother is so focused on her illness.

The results of Shaunie's oral telling and talking with her group about what her plans were led to the following poem. She brought it to her group several days later:

> I don't remember
> dying in front of
> Darren Wilson's house.
> I heard the crashing
> of metal on asphalt.
> Twisted handlebars.
> Rocks in my palms.
>
> Crying without moving
> my pants caught
> in the chain and

my mother hurting again.
She'd locked herself
in the bathroom.

Moans drifted from
our keyhole eyes
while rocks dug
deep blood soaking
through my pantleg. The blur
of pills and needles.
Mother sick and lying
in hospital beds.

Father hugging
her motionless hand
no longer clenching,
Repeating and calling her name.

As I lie
under the frame
screaming "Mother!"
and no one coming
down the black road
to fix my scratches
and free me from
the pinching chain.

I watched Shaunie closely through this process as her poem unfolded. I often recorded peer response conversations as a way to learn more about how to help groups. At times I captured gems like this one of Shaunie's.

Robert Scholes' (1985) notion of textualization seems related to the ideas I have been describing in this whole section on "Stalking Visions from the Masters." He suggests that we must "learn to help our students unlock textual power and turn it to their own uses. We must help our students come into their power of textualization. We must help them see that every poem, play, and story is a text related to others . . . to encourage them to cast their own strands of thought and text into this network so that they feel its power" (pp. 20–21). Additionally, literature becomes an enabling device that facilitates an understanding of the ways language in literature creates impressions, meanings, and effects for the readers. Literature enables students to experiment with a wide variety of forms and language options in their own writing. Thus literature becomes the enabler of expressions and brings continuity to the reading and writing acts. Barthes (1974) states that "the goal of literary work is to make the reader no longer a consumer but a producer of text" (p. 34). I know that my classroom of years ago is not the same as my classroom today. To borrow again from Barthes (1974), I work with students to "set the texts going" (p. 67). We have it in our hands to do that.

Challenging Ourselves to See Differently

The possibility of reading the particular incidents of our teaching lives is endless. To write this chapter I rummaged through multiple file cabinets of student work and listened again to audio tapes from at least ten years ago as well as prowled through the recesses of my mind to capture these few readings. How many and complex they are! It's nearly impossible to articulate what we learn as teachers, how we learn it, and what we do subsequently to reflect that learning. It seems nearly overwhelming to do what I have suggested: "read the text of our teaching life as we would any text." Of course, it isn't just any text, and it can't be read fully. But, I hope this chapter will affirm how much you really know, how much we all know.

We should be presumptuous enough to suggest that we create possible worlds through our transformation of what *is* into what *can be*. The world of the classroom is not rarefied. It's a place where the rhetoric on education gets close and personal. It is in the classroom where we participate in incidents that inform us about teaching and learning, where we take risks, struggle to understand why some explanation didn't make sense to students, and where we get our hands covered with chalkdust. From teaching we learn that teaching is messy business and the practices within it are not easily labeled. Looking again and again at what we do and what we can do, we challenge ourselves to unlimited possibility. We need to be challengers of others as well. Maxine Greene (1986) said it eloquently: "It is when people become challengers, when they take initiatives, that they begin to create the kinds of spaces where dialogue can take place and freedom can appear. And it is then, and probably only then, that people begin thinking about working together to bring into being a better, fairer, more human state of things" (p. 73). We have in our hands the potential to open the dialogue.

Reading the Metaphors of Teachers

Metaphors have been said to help us create definition, as Bruner (1990) suggested, out of the wide array and complexity of what we do and who we are. Metaphors can be useful in self-exploration. "A large part of self-understanding is the search for appropriate personal metaphors that make sense of our lives" (Lakoff and Johnson, 1980, p. 233). This chapter has offered a variety of influences that have engaged me in reflection, encouraged change in practice, and brought forth a deeper understanding about teaching. I remember what Joe Conrad, the experienced teacher whose reflections you examined in Chapter Three, said at one time during the study, "I take a mental stroll through a class period sometimes to see how it will play out. I rehearse lines. I'm a kind of dresser. Yes, that's it. You know, from the movie. The dresser for Prospero. I've become more like the dresser than the star attraction. I started thinking I was the star. Yes, now I'm the dresser. Maybe, I'll become the stage hand next. Behind the scenes, you know? I'm waiting. The possibilities are endless."

This excerpt captures Joe's metaphor of self as teacher as he conjures up his evolution as a teacher. In a fashion that parallels Pinar and Grumet's (1976) *currere,* an autobiographical telling of past, present, and future, Joe captures his triple telling through past (star attraction), present (dresser), and future (stage hand). As Pinar suggests, *currere,* or the triple telling, offers up multiplicitous ways of seeing the self. Teachers have been conceptualized in the educational literature as applied scientists, moral craftsmen, problem-solvers, hypotheses makers, clinical inquirers, radical pedagogues, political craftsmen, scholar-teachers, performing artists, and reflective practitioners. The list is long and rarely exclusionary except to hear the metaphors that teachers use to define themselves. Metaphors of teachers are part of the heritage that influences conceptions of teachers as enablers, liberators, nurturers, or tyrants.

I'd like to postulate that the metaphor of the known can anticipate the unknown. Metaphors have the ability to mobilize not just represent. Metaphors that visualize proposed action can be important to transformational or transgressive thought. Viewing metaphor-making in this way leads to an emphasis on the function of metaphor rather than on its specific structure. Metaphors can help us not only represent who we are but also rename us. Metaphor, as it works in literary text or in defining ourselves as teachers, can: (1) create tension of consciousness between what is and the possibility of what can be; (2) illustrate multiple representations of the self; and (3) add a "shock" or what Kierkegaard called the "leap" that compels us to break through the limits that we may have been experiencing. Bruner (1990) suggested that we can learn much about people from the metaphorical crutches they use to construct understanding of abstractions (p. 29).

I'd suggest that metaphors such as those Joe uses to describe himself as a teacher—star attraction, dresser, and stage hand—are generative because they shape and alter our actions as well as our perceptions. Our choice of metaphors may reveal how we think about ourselves and may define the mental maps or schemes through which we interpret who we are and what we do as teachers. I would like to end this chapter by posing a few of those metaphors that I am learning to live by.

Teacher as archaeologist. In the graveyard scene when Hamlet cradles the skull of Yorick, looking in and through the remains of what once was a man who "hath borne me on his back a thousand times," I hear and see saliency in the artifacts of past human imaginings and actions. Literary texts are such artifacts in a shared culture of what it means to be human. Through these, we nudge students to unearth the shades of human folly and invention and to think through their personal experiences and those of others as part of the larger culture and history of humankind. If the purpose of literature education is to provide representations of personal, social, or cultural conceptions of the artifacts of human imagining, then we might conceive of ourselves as archaeologists—taking care to preserve and build knowledge of where we have been and how we have represented ourselves.

I do believe in this metaphor as one facet of who I want to be as a teacher. However, as purveyor of culture, I sometimes feel with my students like the old woman, Koi-ehm-toya, in N. Scott Momaday's *The Ancient Child* (1989). Seeing the children at play and outside her grasp or influence, she suffers some anxiety:

> From the opening of her tipi, from the highest point in the camp, the old woman Koi-ehm-toya saw the children moving across the wrinkles of a meadow toward the trees. Zeid-lebei! she thought; a bad business, dangerous. . . . The children bobbed and skipped and tumbled away in the distance. Oh, they were only at play, she decided, running around and wasting their time, as children will do, giving not a thought to their safety. She clicked her tongue and set a mask upon her face, a perfect scowl. And in the way of an old woman she wondered aloud what was to become of the people, they had grown so careless (pp. 23–24).

I confess that I've felt this way as students weasel their ways and minds out of my control, particularly when I am teacher as archaeologist. Nonetheless, I want to assist them in finding the craft of culture, in cradling the skull of Yorick, in seeing what life must be like for Pecola, of learning the importance of the Phoenix as a symbol for a people's spirit. Who is to decide what artifacts, what literature students will read and study? Who can tell someone else what should be important to them in a reading experience?

The purposes and content of literature education have been vigorously debated. From the traditional canon, with its narrowly defined fundamentals of great books in Western civilization (Bennett, 1984; Bloom, 1987; Hirsch, 1987), to the assertion that the world is rapidly becoming a global village filled with pluralistic perspective and experiences (Freire, 1971; Shrewbury, 1987; McIntosh, 1981; Winkler, 1986), the legitimacy of whose literature should be taught has been called into question.

As the arguments become higher pitched, teachers often yield to the textbook writers. Curriculum is supposed to be a socially constructed artifact, the intellectual baggage built up over hundreds of years. We must take the responsibility to cradle curriculum in our hands, question what it should be and for whom. As Florence Howe (1984) writes, "teaching is a political act: some person is choosing, for whatever reasons, to teach a set of values, ideas, assumptions, and pieces of information, and in so doing, to omit other values, ideas, assumptions, and pieces of information" (1984, p. 282). John Locke wrestled with similar issues in the questions he asked: Should classics or sciences be the foundation of curriculum? Should formal logic be stressed or the study of mathematics? Should teachers emphasize obedience or freedom? Is general education more important than the development of specific skills?

The concern over what should be included in the canon, the particular interpretive strategies valued, the ideology embedded in literature curriculum—we can study these as artifacts of the history of literature education and teachers within the tradition. This is another dimension of teacher as archaeologist—we need to be informed on the history of our debates. The debate over canonicity has taken on new meaning in the political arena, reminding literature teachers that we must question whether or not our students can or should study Homer, Shakespeare, Aristotle, Balzac, and Sartre or Momaday, Morrison, Alvarez, and Allende. Unfortunately what is posed in this list is typical of the dichotomy present in the argument. Is it either/or? A Great Books or a multicultural approach? Who is included and who excluded? Concerns about representation of race, ethnicity, gender, sexual orientation, age, and class are at issue. But, I worry that if we polarize the argument we will not ask the essential questions about the texts we or our students choose. In the process, I hope we do not allow for the acquisition of knowledge of one tradition at the expense of others—across the lines of ethnicity, race, gender, sexual orientation, class, and age.

As Peter Taubman (1993) suggests in "Canonical Sins,"

> But in a classroom, we can talk about those relationships. We can discuss why Albert Tylis falls asleep over certain chapters in *The*

Scarlet Letter, why I like the novel this year but didn't last year, why *The Awakening* evokes such rage among many boys, and why *The Women of Brewster Place* upset Asaki Johnson or why Nowar only reads fantasy. We can discuss how Karen Factor's tenth-grade reading of *Native Son* bumped up against her eighth-grade reading of *To Kill a Mockingbird* and sent her into her own past as well as into the reality of her Bensonhurst neighborhood. And we can read as a class not only the historical and social contingencies which affect our reading but also the psychodynamics of that reading (p. 50).

I am cautious about the trend to provide students with literature anthologies labeled multicultural. Many are no more than a shopping mall approach—Native American literature in one section, Puerto Rican in another, and enough African American writers for Black History Month. There is a danger that we might be in the process of creating another monolith. Both within and outside of the canon, we have important considerations about what is assigned, what is self-selected, how we discuss and question what we read, and how we teach others to do that. Are we only replacing one standard with another? We cannot confuse the canon with the curriculum in literature education. We can investigate what it means to teach literature and examine the complexities of making choices in content and practice, often within competing and contradictory intentions and means.

The teacher as archaeologist needs to know the history of education to understand curriculum as an artifact. The competing and emerging voices of curriculum continuously shape the social construction of knowledge about teaching and learning. But, we must decide for ourselves, be able to fully articulate and to take a stand on what curriculum is and can be. This requires a long-term commitment to the hard business of inquiry and a willingness not to hold our tongues or our energies from the enterprise of critique or creation.

Teacher as anthropologist. The anthropologist brings to mind an image of one watching, recording, living in a tent with mosquito-net draped over a cot, surrounded by dark jungles and exotic birds. I've always had a fascination with the work of Margaret Mead and Gregory Bateson. I used to imagine them sitting by a fire in some faraway jungle, daughter Catherine cradled between them, as they created theory out of everyday human action and artifact. But an anthropologist may research in corporate boardrooms, hospital operating rooms, or factory assembly lines. Anthropologists live among their subjects, observing and collecting and rigorously analyzing the data gathered. Educational anthropologists conduct fieldwork in classrooms, faculty rooms, and other educational sites.

Teachers can look through an anthropological lens as one way of investigating the culture of schools. Much of our job is to collect information before we act on it. From attendance-taking to copy-machine bottlenecks, we can study particulars as a way of interpreting meaning from the fragments of culture that surround us. As anthropologist Loren Eiseley (1975) suggested, we are inculcated with certain attitudes: "Then some fine day, the kaleidoscope through which we peer at life shifts suddenly and everything is re-ordered. A blink at the right moment may do it, an eye applied to a crevice, or the world seen through a tear" (p. 25). I am suggesting that as teachers we need to put on our anthropological glasses and force ourselves to move beyond the familiar boundary of what is clear and known. We need to stand outside and look within as if for the first time so that we might see more or see differently than we have before.

By interpreting data from the field, we can better understand the culture in which we work. By wandering the maze of our meta-phoric streets and squares, searching out the coffee shops and sub-urbs that are the cultural life of our schools, we can anchor our personal experiences to the larger culture of school. The teacher as anthropologist can explain, celebrate, excuse, and define teachers' work through a broader understanding than the Monday-to-Friday reality of the classroom.

Some of the places we visit will not make us proud of ourselves. The faculty room may engage us in a cultural critique. Examining a policy on tracking may force us to re-examine our taken-for-granted assumptions. The artifacts of our own teaching life may suggest how much attention we've given to various facets of our discipline. Student product may reveal what we value and celebrate as learn-ing. Even the way our classrooms are organized suggests the types of exchanges and interactions that are valued in the setting. We learn from the artifacts in any classroom what is valued, honored, and celebrated. The excavation of our file cabinets or an examina-tion of what is displayed on the walls will yield information about what we do and what is important. We learn from the wastebasket what students do and do not value. Look around your own class-room into the crevices and study the territory where you and your students live. What does it reveal?

If necessary, it may be time to renovate the place. The teacher who is an anthropologist should engage in deliberate and serious talk about how we've mitered, jointed, and polished the culture of schools we've constructed. As anthropologist Clifford Geertz (1983) has suggested:

It is not a new cryptography that we need, especially when it consists of replacing one cipher by another less intelligible, but a new diagnostics, a science that can determine the meaning of things for the life that surrounds them. It will have, of course, to be trained on signification, not pathology, and treated with ideas, not with symptoms. But by connecting incised statues, pigmented sago palms, frescoed walls, and chanted verse to jungle clearing, totem rites, commercial inference, or street argument, it can perhaps begin at last to locate in the tenor of their setting the sources of their spell (p. 120).

Teacher as artist. My grandmother, Helen, was a potter, mostly for self-satisfaction. She supplied her ten children with dinner plates, bowls, and goblets long before it became fashionable to have anything other than Haviland in the china cupboard. For me, her potting fired my imagination. I would sit by her side, the moist clay in hand, and fashion, at my will, colonies of imaginary beings—extraordinary people, demonic animals, or peaceful creatures who roamed the caves, hills, and valleys of the civilization that I constructed in the corner of her garden. I'm aware now that it was the feel of clay in my hands that exhilarated me. I named, and maybe I, like Pan-ku or Prometheus, breathed imagination, intellect, and much dissatisfaction into the minds and hearts of these creations.

Not long ago, after my grandmother's death, her dresser was carried to our family home. I opened the bottom drawer. Carefully wrapped in tissue, and arranged in upwards of thirty cigar boxes were the actors and actresses of the civilizations I'd fashioned, along with the artifacts of their culture. Seeing these again, I felt the power of such shaping, the exhilaration of my imaginings, that brought life and stories into the long hours of one seven-year-old's days.

I was the shaper not only of form but also of culture—albeit a snug and insular one. Now, from my vantage point in the broader currents of culture that I've been keeping—Wittgenstein, Vygotsky, Gadamer, Frye, Barthes, and Kuhn—my shaping seems small and insignificant. But the metaphor of that seven-year-old experience brought me to think again what teaching is and is not.

To be a teacher is to be part of a constructive and shaping enterprise. The story of teaching is a personal story of creating, of composing, as personal as the worlds of imaginings I created in clay. Are we the awakeners of student desire? Should we nurture students into making their own art? The art of teaching rests on the fulcrum's balancing point—awakening the imaginings on one hand, allowing students the freedom to shift and move in their own direction on the other. The current educational literature is full of plans and recommendations for reshaping. But we must always ask whether those most affected, students and teachers, are part of a shaping enterprise. The art of teaching cannot be reduced to, as the first year teachers introduced in Chapter Two found it to be, a staged performance acted in front of spectators.

I've come to realize that I left behind my seven-year-old impulses to create a civilization for another type of composition. This came to me, when I opened the drawer again, through this story of my grandmother's dresser. I have been asked numerous times why I teach. Perhaps the beginning of my answer starts in the story I've told—that of my grandmother, the clay, the garden, and the shaping. Perhaps this chapter should end with why I became interested in teaching in the first place.

There is a long accounting of students with whom I have shared a brief moment—Sarah Benedict, Tim Oakes, Marshall High, Susan Stradler, Scott Smith, Ted Faulkner, and Susan Fowler. Perhaps they remember the day in class when we discussed the fate of Tess of the d'Urbervilles. Some may remember that Othello killed Desdemona. All will know that revenge and greed as well as charity and forgiveness have consequences. Nowhere in the history of education could another teacher construct this same list of names that sums up what was partially in my hands. They're with me still. It isn't just memory. It's the feeling of having been an aerial for ideas, awakenings, and imaginings. Drawing those students into themselves and through themselves somehow drew them right through the marrow of me. We must keep the learning and imagining. That's what we have in our hands—the responsibility to do just that.

PART TWO

LESSONS FROM THE CLASSROOM

I'll never really know what method Mr. Duerksen thought he was using as he stood up there at the front of the class, eyes blazing, one lethally tipped finger in the air, sonorously declaiming Matthew Arnold's bleak lovely poem, "Dover Beach." I do know that when I'm honest with myself, I can trace my love of words and writing to his class. That which endures, endures because of the strength of his lessons, a combination of learning, erudition, the hard-won knowledge of experience and passion—honest, vulnerable passion.

Paul Sullivan, "Mr. Duerksen's Magic Word"

Chapter Five

Teaching Mindfully

Throughout my experience as a student, I had no idea that teachers planned what went on in classrooms. The idea was simple: they came to class and so did I. I assumed teachers drove their '56 Chevys from white picket-fenced houses to the school parking lot, and walked the long corridor to the teachers' lounge where they sipped coffee and caught up on the latest gossip or talked about how teachers' pet Sarah Provost won a blue ribbon at the City Music Festival. Then they arrived in the classroom as the last bell rang. Whatever was in the book on teaching or ingrained in the walls of classrooms was what teaching had been and would always be. Day-to-day life in English classrooms fashioned my belief that the selections studied in literature, the writing that we were asked to do, and the grammar drills were the same in every English classroom. It was taken for granted that teachers didn't have much to do with the process except to lecture or lead a discussion, assign the pages that should be read, give a test, and put a grade on a report card.

This view of teaching goes well beyond my own. In his study of junior high boys, Robert Everhart (1983) points out that they see the "teacher's world . . . straightforward and linear, hardly complex at all" (p. 74). This image was trapped in my mind, even during my teacher preparation program. I didn't understand until I began teaching that what happened each day was a construction that resulted from an interaction between many competing and often contradictory forces. Very different outcomes resulted between what I intended to put into practice day after day, hour after hour, and year after year and what actually occurred in the classroom situation.

The Importance of Situated Knowledge

The events that take place in the classroom are a complex series of situations and negotiations making difficult any simplistic or singular interpretations. Classrooms represent the intentions of many interested parties—students, teachers, parents, and administrators. For teachers, there is, behind each class session, an implicit conversation between content knowledge and pedagogical understanding. If we see a teacher lecturing to students about the symbols in *Moby Dick* or the dramatic irony in *Oedipus Rex,* we can assume that behind those actions are beliefs about what is important in literature study and how students learn literature. Teachers rely on their personal beliefs and understandings to interpret the various situations and dilemmas that routinely confront them in planning or teaching classes.

Yet, any act of teaching also has a historically determined situation, comprised by the stock of experiences that informs it. These experiences refer, at least indirectly, to all the past and present acts that contributed to the making of knowledge about teaching. This includes what the teacher learned from other teachers, what those other teachers learned from their teachers, what was constituted as meaningful from prior teaching experiences, and what has been appropriated from others. The bulk of teacher knowledge is socially derived and hybrid. Homi Bhabha (1990) explains the concept of hybridity succinctly: "For me the importance of hybridity is not to be able to trace two original moments from which the third emerges, rather hybridity to me is the 'third space' which enables other positions to emerge" (p. 211). The act of teaching engenders a continual contestation beyond teachers' present and future knowledge—challenging, mixing, testing, and ultimately transgressing what the teacher knows "how to do" or has ever done before.

Contesting Present Knowledge

Consider, for example, how contemporary reading theories that focus on the role of the reader have led many teachers to work out a strategic framework that privileges certain intellectual, affective, and social readings that may not have been overtly considered even fifteen years ago. Although the belief that individual readers particularize readings has influenced the ways in which many literature teachers conceptualize what reading literature means, these teachers may not be relying on the knowledge of any one particular theory such as Bleich's (1978) subjective criticism, poststructural, or feminist approaches. What has happened instead is a crossing over, a hybridity bred from many facets of several theories that come together and are interpreted through a teacher's understanding of readers as gleaned from day-to-day interactions with students. What often results is a unique blending of influences that distorts any one construction of theory or practice nearly beyond recognition. I do not mean to suggest that distortion is negative, simply that it changes as it is filtered through a particular teacher's situated knowledge.

Contemporary theories provoke literature teachers to tease out strategies that might help readers create *reflexive* rather than *representative* meaning and *generative* rather than *definitive* meaning from a text. From this perspective, rereading might be seen as a strategy used to understand *differently* rather than *better.* As Rosenblatt (1978) observes, "The reader's attention constantly vibrates between the pole of the text and the pole of his own response to it "(p. 129). This dynamic process is "the game of the imagination" as Wolfgang Iser (1978) calls reader participation in the production of textual meaning (p. 108). Iser's (1978) "repertoire" theory and Barthes' (1974) "referential code" emphasize the role of social, historical, cultural, and personal knowledge that leads readers to engage in the dynamic process of constructing meaning. For example, there is no overt connection between shadows and lurking evil, yet the network of symbolic codes suggests associations in the reader's mind only if certain knowledge of literary conventions exist. Reading, then, is conceived as associational. Such connections produce a text that weaves and interweaves cultural, historical, and psychological bases and biases into a cloth that becomes the fabric of meaning for the reader. The most apparent result of the reconceived roles of reader, text, and context is that literature teachers have responded with a variety of practices that take into account the central role of the reader in making meaning. A curriculum and practice built upon these concepts result in a series of experiments and enactments of working hypotheses that are tried out in the classroom.

Teachers shift their attention from particular texts to experiences that help readers effect meanings that are multiple and dynamic. What readers bring to their readings, the feeling or associations evoked, the contested interpretations leading to critical readings, all and each promise a fruitful means for producing more self-aware and socially aware meanings from literary texts. These directions aren't part of the repertoire of principles or practices for many literature teachers, but for those who are influenced by the theories, there is an entirely different set of notions about texts, readers, and teachers as well as about structures and experiences enacted in practice. For some, reader-response signals a liberatory pedagogy;

for others, a cognitive consequence; for still others, a critique of culture, power, and ideology; yet for others, an experiential foray into self-understanding. How these theories become understood or enacted in practice is quite a different matter.

Literature anthologies, for instance, suggest activities that are deemed appropriate to elicit student responses. The selections that are used and the methods that are set forth tell a great deal about the principles behind the literature education as put forward in the anthology. Consider these examples:

1. In Harcourt Brace Jovanovich's *Adventures in World Literature,* copyright 1970, the introduction to excerpts from Homer's *The Iliad* provides readers with information considered important to foreground the reading selection. A brief historical overview introduces the legends and historical events that led to the Trojan War. General rules for pronunciation follow, along with names of gods and goddesses. Then, a brief summary is given of the scene before students read any of the text. *The Iliad* is excerpted for forty pages, interrupted by periodic summaries of text and a nine-page insert that describes and gives examples of some masterpieces in Sumerian, Greek, and Roman Art. At the end of each excerpt are a series of questions. Exemplars include: "In Book 1, find several reasons for Achilles' anger. Identify those which are based on specific grievances and those which are mainly about honor." "Do you think Achilles was justified in his wrath and in his subsequent withdrawal from battle? Explain." The questions are mostly text centered. A few deal with how *The Iliad* is representative of the larger culture of the Greeks. A brief overview of classical conventions and the characteristics of epics ends the study of *The Iliad*.

   I wonder if the excerpts and the activities that accompany the anthologies will engage students in a chain of speculating, connecting, reflecting, and inquiring. Will students experience a vicarious world that intensifies their perceptions and their ruminations about the events and mysteries of life? Will they, as can often happen with a literary text, feel like they are entering another world? I think not. Two hundred years ago Wordsworth gave an account of what reading was, using words such as "devouring," "appetites," "passions," and "possessions." The spell that *The Iliad* is intended to precipitate is broken into fragments through the excerpted text and commentary that interrupts the flow of narrative.

2. By 1990, many literature anthologies shifted the emphasis in their series to reflect the current focus on reader-response approaches. For example, the textbook by Tchudi, Tchudi, Yesner, and Yesner (1990) *Literature by Doing: Responding to Poetry, Essays, Drama, and Short Stories* is exemplary of this shifting of attention to the student reader. Beginning with a one-page introduction to students on "Keeping a Reading Journal," the textbook sets into motion the idea that the student reader's "feelings, thoughts, associations, and insights into the worlds and the ideas of the writers whose works are included in this book" are inexorably linked. Each selection is introduced with a brief synopsis of the story or poem. After each selection, three types of activities organize response: "Discuss," "Explore," and "For Your Journal." A careful examination of what student readers are asked to do in each of these sections evidences how deeply ingrained are the habits of the past. Although the language of the textbook smacks of reader emphasis, the actual activities do not contest or challenge past practices. After reading Alice Walker's "A Sudden Trip Home in the Spring," students are asked in the "Discuss" section to answer the following question:

    1. Sarah refers to the U.S. author Richard Wright a number of times. Which statement best describes what she feels she has in common with him?
        a. Both Sarah and Richard Wright attended all-white schools and felt like outsiders.
        b. Both Sarah and Richard Wright felt alienated from their fathers.
        c. Both Sarah and Richard Wright felt anger that the white world did not appreciate their art (p. 27).

I'm not sure what to make of an activity like this one that is placed under a rubric titled "Discuss." Identifying a statement which "best" describes "something" seems a pale rendition of "doing," as the title of the textbook has promised. The conception of what and how a discussion might support student construction of knowledge is very narrowly defined in this example. The other two questions included in the "Discuss" section are every bit as limiting.

In "Explore," five questions are presented that ask students to examine particular topics that the textbook writers feel are important: irony, motivations of the main character and her relationship with the family, and the significance of Richard Wright in her life. Is "doing" literature a matter of doing what is interesting to someone else? In the third and last section, "For Your Journal," the students are asked three questions to respond to in their journals. I looked back at the inside cover page where the textbook writers had promised students that the journal was a place in which to "capture ideas, a place to record your feelings, thoughts, associations," and "Your journal is also a place to experiment." I wonder whether in writing this textbook the authors questioned whether or not the experiences they created for students actually did offer what was claimed: "an innovative, hands-on approach to literature, *involving* students in poetry, essays, drama, and short stories (italics mine)." A close scrutiny of the textbook led me to ask: What is the hands-on approach and what does the term *hands-on* actually mean? How are students "involved"?

Corcoran and Evans (1987) outline several "classroom reading events" that support students' engagements with literature. They detail four stages wherein teachers can help students negotiate the terrain of text:

> "(1) foregrounding and introducing the text; (2) encountering and reading the text (especially a novel) to allow the aesthetic interplay of picturing and imagining, anticipating and retrospecting, engagement and construction, and valuing and evaluating; (3) providing sufficient time and space for the individual to express, in a variety of ways, the essence of an immediate and unique transaction; and (4) creating subsequent opportunities after the expression of an initial response, for teacher and students 'to extend each other's seeing' through a series of collaborative explorations, allowing as well for revisiting and reflections of a primarily personal nature" (p. 54).

Much of what Corcoran and Evans suggest is an interpretation of reading as a process of encountering, transacting, negotiating, and exploring experiences through the medium of language. Teachers can nurture such literature-in-the-making. I don't know how this can be done with literature anthologies, and I worry about the manipulative and commercial aspects of those disseminated by publishing houses. Anthologies are used widely and teachers can challenge the forms, processes, content, and values represented in the textbooks, but I don't know with what regularity or how formally that occurs. I believe that teaching mindfully requires that we contest our present knowledge by examining the provision of activities, materials, and practices that need to be set in the context of a deeper, developing rationale for eliciting response from our students.

Enacting Purpose and Principle Through Curriculum

A developing rationale is probably implicated in thoughtful articulations of curriculum. Although curriculum has traditionally been defined as a sequential product, more recent theorists consider it a construction reflecting ideological and theoretical stances, a process of learning to make meaning from ideas and experiences that "rests on teacher judgment, rather than teacher direction" (Stenhouse, 1975, p. 96). Conceptions of curriculum have important consequences on what happens in classrooms. As Ken Kantor (1990) suggests, "curriculum needs to be defined in terms of personal, lived experiences, rather than through some set of objectives, strategies, notions of scope and sequence, and artificial scenarios" (p. 71). Reconceptualizing curriculum has led to diverse ways of interrogating its representations. Alternative theories focus on different purposes for and practices in curriculum, including development of the self as learner, processes rather than product-oriented education, ideo-political education, and liberatory education. Each version of curriculum demonstrates the ideological base of theories and models and the constructed *isms* that lurk behind each representation.

By stepping outside the classroom texts they have created and inquiring into their guiding principles and beliefs about curriculum, teachers might use such inquiry as a means of rooting out the challenges in and possibilities for curriculum composing. "Teaching itself is a constantly evolving form of curriculum, a particular way of interacting, interpreting, questioning, and re-visioning" (Miller, 1990, p. 86). We do not often talk about curriculum as composing or curriculum as belief. Doing so is beset with subjectivity, and it is easier to consider curriculum as a compilation of objective statements about what should be taught. When one walks into a school as a new teacher, it is likely that the first things placed on the desk are an attendance/grade and lesson plan book and a curriculum guide. The guide is mostly filled with what students should *know about.* Of course there is seldom time to teach all the *know abouts* that the guides include. These usually represent a motley array of traditions, innovations, desires, and beliefs. They are the product of near Sisyphean labor, but not always mindfully constructed to represent beliefs about the purposes and principles that are important to the enactment of any curriculum in the classroom.

Literature curriculum as ideology. If literature curricula are viewed as representations and systems of reconceptualized beliefs, these beliefs may reflect traditional assumptions about literature as program and knowledge in which text, the canon, literary criticism, identification of elements, and understanding of conventions are central. Other representations may reflect more personal, social, or cultural conceptions of curriculum in which reader and societal control of text, politics, power, and emerging voices are central. These dichotomies in literature curriculum are simply more specific curricular cases exemplifying the polemic oppositions housed in our conceptions of curricular content and purposes. This covariation in vision leaves literature education hovering among static, progressive, and reactionary phases. We cannot seem to get our *isms* in sync, to agree on which ones serve our purposes, or even to establish what those purposes are. As Bill Green (1990) suggests, the result of these differences is "an endemic feature of English teaching right from the outset: its internal history of conflict and struggle, and secondly, its role in the (re)production of larger, more systematic forms of social difference, discrimination and domination" (p. 136).

The particular evolutions of ideology in literature curriculum go beyond the dichotomy between Dixon's (1967) model of "personal growth" and the "cultural heritage" model, beyond literature viewed as "what the authorities call literature" (Hirsch, 1975, p. 206), and beyond reader response, transaction, and subjective criticism. What is beyond these dichotomies is blurred by unclarified issues and stakeholders, but the inquiry cannot be sidestepped. However, one way of beginning to see what literature curriculum means and the complexities in composing it is to ask the teachers of literature who struggle with its composition and perpetuation each day.

Personalizing curriculum inquiry. What, then, is the unique contribution of the teacher to curriculum construction? How is this best characterized? As an art? A competence? A task associated with the job? How does a teacher shape his or her interpretation of events, choices of action, and intentions into a curriculum. I asked the experienced teachers—Beth, Jane, and Joe—to describe their own personal inquiry into curriculum construction. They detailed their beliefs about literature curriculum, considered their processes for composing literature curriculum and described, whenever possible, the constraints and freedoms that guide their decision making. This inquiry led them into a maze of tensions and dilemmas. They considered how their reading, theorizing, and teaching informed their beliefs about curriculum. They examined how workshops, curriculum guides, and administrative and peer support or antagonism informed curriculum implementation. Beth, Jane, and Joe questioned whether and in what ways their curriculum planning was productive rather than reproductive. Beth described how Michael Apple (1985) informed her view of the latent power of curriculum to suppress, change, or to mindlessly reproduce what is. "I came across Apple's books after reading an *English Education* article that dealt with curriculum. I started reading and thought about how I'd taken curriculum for granted." Beth goes on to describe that while she had not taught someone else's curriculum she "hadn't realized the power."

Jane described her dissatisfaction with the goals and objectives outlined in curriculum guides. "I couldn't understand purposes behind those lofty statements. I need a big picture . . . a way of seeing what, how, and why together." For Jane, curriculum guides do not help her to resee herself or her work. "I do that better through my reading. For example, Glenna Sloan's book, *The Child as Critic,* challenged me to look at myself as a teacher." Joe pointed out that his reading about teaching continues to force him to rethink his understandings of curriculum. "Some books help me find language through which I explore ideas. I'm thinking about my reading of the Corcoran and Evans (1987) book, *Reader, Texts, Teachers.* I found a language there for what I'd been struggling to articulate about teaching or experiencing literature."

This inquiry led Beth, Jane and Joe to further sort through some of the complex negotiations and competing views and values that play a crucial role in their and their students' participation in composing, negotiating, and implementing curriculum. As they inquired, their views became more clearly represented as a dynamic production of personal, classroom, and societal readings of teaching and learning literature.

Jane connected curriculum to the selection of literary texts:

> Oh, I don't select literature. The students select. I've really tried to avoid forcing literature on them. They seek it out themselves. That doesn't mean I don't recommend. We do share pieces. I read aloud each day and they're invited to do that for the class as well . . . But, they have the ultimate responsibility. . . . Sometimes it's comics . . . Calvin and Hobbes is quite popular. Sometimes it's books on nonfiction topics they've taken an interest in. The rain forests and wolves were big ones this year. Of course, there are children's novels that are perennial favorites (Roald Dahl, Katherine Patterson, Lois Lowry). Some go on poetry binges. It's part of learning to read—deciding is.

Believing this, Jane must confront the issue of knowing how to step back effectively. As she describes it, "I know what I want to do, but it isn't always easy." Jane's dilemma illustrates something similar to Broudy's (1977) "knowing that" and "knowing how" distinction. Jane illuminates that distinction as she considers: "When you deliberately set out *not* to take a center role it doesn't mean you don't plan ways . . . I mean . . . it takes more planning and that planning to erase yourself from the center and finding another place to fit into the classroom becomes part of your curriculum." Knowing that she wants students to become lifelong readers, Jane must explore ways to facilitate and encourage that development.

Jane helped me further understand that what might appear to be an easy way to teach requires more thought and skill than planning controlled or predetermined activities. The idea of erasing the self has seductive power. Behind it is the image of a seesaw balanced on its fulcrum. On one end is the teacher in full charge of events, on the other end, the teacher has given up charge of the classroom. The challenge in Jane's conception of curriculum is not how to sequence content but how to find her place within the context of student and teacher roles. The mutual commitment of students and teacher to learning and sense-making is part of her literature curriculum.

Beth considers "themes as the organizers . . . themes that connect pieces together with their experience . . . To see relationships . . . There are a certain number of pieces that are part of the curriculum including *The Diary of Anne Frank, Rebecca* and *A Tree Grows in Brooklyn.*" The teachers in Beth's school have agreed to teach a certain number of literary selections that students will share as common reading experiences. "We've agreed to teach those, and they've become favorites of mine. The better I get to know them the more I've found ways to get students involved." Beth's selection of text is a part of curriculum planning. Additionally, Beth organizes her teaching around themes because she believes her middle school students have an easier time connecting literature to their personal lives through themes. This approach emphasizes Beth's belief that the purpose of literature study is to help students examine important lessons in how to live.

Beth knows what she hopes to achieve; the question becomes how to nurture her students' awareness and understanding. Creating relationships among students and between herself and students is central to her planning. "That requires carrying on conversations together . . . getting to know one another's opinions. Listening to others." Beth finds that students can relate easily to themes because they find connections with their personal lives in the literature. If students are interested in the themes, it motivates them to share their opinions and to listen to one another. Beth believes that students spend too much time in school memorizing facts and that a thematic study of literature helps students become more involved in the subject rather than in trying to remember the literal information given in a literary selection.

Beth wants it otherwise. "Looking back, I think over the years I've come to realize that students have separated themselves from each other. They didn't have outlets for meaningful talk together. Literature is a good way to open that space." Beth led me to further realize how knowing the context for a teacher's decision making gives new insights and richer ones. Context may inform our understanding of curriculum composing and certainly has an important role in generating curriculum. Making the contexts accessible and articulable, through examination, mediates the reconceptualizing of what curriculum might include. Both Jane and Beth enhance the definition of curriculum by focusing on different contexts in their deliberations. Jane concentrates on teacher and student roles as part of the composition of curriculum. Beth attends to relationships among students as relevant to shaping the content of curriculum. As Beth sees it, the relationships between peers is particularly tenuous during the junior high years. Knowing this, Beth facilitates ways to nurture those relationships.

Joe's approach is based on exposure to genre, which includes media other than literature:

> I keep thinking that if I can get them comfortable reading or viewing almost anything . . . starting to appreciate different genre as a way in. I select pieces that will tie to their interests, but also ones that show the genres and how they work and the possibilities within each so they see the processes of not only reading but writing.

For Joe, the curriculum is not directed essentially toward the production of knowledge about genre although on the surface it may look or sound that way. It is aimed at ends beyond itself, developing and exercising the right to read, the right to express opinions, and the confidence to do so. It is not a curriculum driven by the need to know genre or understand craft. Once reading means something to students, they find themselves involved in processes of questioning ideas, disclosing opinions, and listening to others' opinions. There is room for interpretation.

Finding truths, searching for what the author means, or examining authorities' opinions are left behind as the exclusive ways of interpreting text. A new and consoling security comes to students who feel they have a voice in the construction of meaning from a literary selection. For Joe's curriculum plan, genre is a way for students to begin studying literature in much the same way that theme is used in

Beth's class or individual selection in Jane's. Joe facilitates students' performances of literature in various genre to stress the differences in how public readings offer another way to understand a text. Performing the literature is also a way for students to celebrate their personal readings. What may appear as text-, theme-, or genre-driven curriculum on the surface may not do justice to the complexities. The following discussion presents the participants' extended initial definitions of their constructions of curriculum.

Beth: It's how we read text. Beth stresses the importance of helping students learn different ways of reading text. This becomes one of the ultimate purposes in Beth's curricular planning. Beth does not equate reading with reading literature, reading skills, students' literal or metaphoric understandings, or their ability to predict or evaluate text. For Beth, "It's what we make of the reading that's important." Beth plans an overall curriculum component that gives students a variety of opportunities to perform or celebrate multiple readings of texts. Her curriculum includes a forum in which students share the meaning they have discovered from various readings. Through a variety of forms, including sketches, tableaus, video or audio scenes, reader's theater, original writing or imitations, the students' learning and meaning-making are valued. Beth takes deliberate care to design this sharing into her daily, unit, and yearly plans. She believes:

> When all is said and done, it's what you take away from the reading, not what you read. Even if they read Stephen King or a how-to manual (although I cringe saying that), they take away certain attitudes or feelings or ideas from the reading. I mean really reading. We learn how to read for someone else in school, but we need to read for what we take away. It isn't instruction that teaches that. It's the spirit of instruction. The curriculum must engage readers in an apprenticeship with the soul or the spirit of literature.

For Beth, literature is not a subject but a medium for expression of human spirit and experience. The important outcome of the curriculum is not knowing certain texts. It is nurturing the reader's sensitivity to life. "I'm concerned with bringing experiences to young readers, enriching their lives, helping an adolescent understand and feel what it means to be an outcast, fear for her life, have a handicap, or live in poverty. That's the basis of reading literature—just open their eyes and hearts to see and feel more."

According to Beth, the curriculum surrounds and promotes the learning; it is not the content of learning. Curriculum holds separate experiences together by illuminating different layers of meaning.

Through curriculum, Beth provides opportunities for students to hear other readers' readings and from that understand that more than one meaning resides in a literary text. Her implementation of a reader-response approach emphasizes how multiple responses to a text produce a knowledge base that is then studied by the class.

Joe: Undoing the fear. Joe's central concern in curriculum planning is to get students beyond the barriers that their school experiences have created. He finds that by senior high many of the students are "downright afraid of literature or hostile toward it." Joe points out the irony in this and senses that many of his students have had enough of assigned reading, finding deep and hidden messages in text, and fighting to make sense out of a language that seems spoken in tongues.

> It's ironic, really. Here they were as children loving language (maybe not always but I'd like to keep that myth alive) and loving stories, and school requires them to perform incantations with reading until by the time they get to me, where for some of them, it's the end of their school career, and they're fearful, really feeling that literature is beyond them or just plain turned off.

To help alleviate or undo what has been overdone, Joe's overall curriculum plan is to create experiences with literature that give students the freedom to search out ways of engaging with text.

Joe brings in texts with ambiguity. For example, Henry James' (1898/1966) *Turn of the Screw* helps demonstrate multiple readings. "Students can see right away, once they get through the language, that there are many roads to Rome." Joe encourages students to trust uncertainty and respect opinion. He exposes students to literature from diverse time periods, and in various genre, but he relies heavily on contemporary authors and issues. He extends his texts to include magazines, films, and dramatic performances. "The curriculum can't be dogmatic and formulaic. We're good at making formulas out of text, but the issues that kids care about offer richer text for exploration." For Joe, a good part of the first nine weeks is spent getting students to trust their opinions and to trust that Joe will listen to those opinions and validate their searches for understanding. To accomplish this, Joe segments reading texts into units by genre. Students not only read but also write in the genre. Within the genre are smaller sub-units organized thematically or by literary conventions. Essentially, students concentrate on learning to trust their interpretations with minor emphasis placed on the study of literary conventions. "Whatever surfaces for students is the direction in which the discussion moves."

Joe described his curriculum composing as full of "tentative starts and stops. I'm a small bit kind of person. I keep trying little steps, subtle changes. I play around more." Joe gave one example in which he used "To His Coy Mistress" to introduce the idea of persuasion and logical argument. He explained that he often used film or photographs to introduce literary conventions. "I change plans quickly by watching faces. Faces in the classroom." Joe goes on to suggest that "I need to know if this idea will play in Boston." Planning as he does, Joe examines ways in which his curriculum can hold together. Joe identifies several outcomes that he hopes to achieve. These include ways to help students develop self-confidence, learn to read carefully and honestly, experience many types of literature, and connect their reading to personal experiences. Joe hopes students will see "the big picture. What literature is and how it's important to our lives. I hope they will come to enjoy it, but there's no grand design."

Joe indicates that he has stopped looking for a grand design but instead finds ways to lead students through a number of different experiences. "They need the chairs, and I think they ought to go through them. I think there ought to be a Shakespeare chair, but I think there ought to be some contemporary chairs as well. I think there are writing chairs. If they haven't written a short story, have them write a short story. If they haven't written a personal narrative, they need to try it." But Joe reminds himself that all of this must be done with respect for students' experiences, interests, strengths, and weaknesses. "There's potential in a curriculum that's open to chance and change." That attitude has enabled him to explore, review, and examine the possibilities of what, where, when, and how real learning of literature takes place.

Jane: Reading lessons. Jane's literature curriculum is based on exposure and experience with literature that is heavily dependent on students' individual reading and selection of reading materials. Students come together to read and to share what they read. Individual instruction in elements or conventions of literature and reading strategies complement the individualized program. The traditional elementary school reading program complicates Jane's curriculum plan. It is expected that she will teach reading. She adamantly refuses to teach a reading curriculum based on a scope and sequence of skills. Jane believes that can be accomplished through a reading workshop approach.

For Jane, reading instruction is not packaged into programs, sets of readers, worksheets, or comprehension tests. Jane will not rationalize that reading literature in basals is the same as reading literature. Jane's curriculum is based on what learning to read means. Margaret Meek (1988) suggests a similar philosophy in her work on reading. Meek maintains that reading lessons grow out of the act of reading. Jane's curriculum is based on a similar concept:

> I need to find ways to help students tie their own knowledge and experience with what they find on the page. When a reader needs a skill or strategy, I take a few minutes to teach that individually. A few things, they all need. It's having a full range of strategies that makes a skilled reader.

"Reading lessons," Jane states, "happen when students read."

Jane takes a deliberate position outside the role of lesson giver, designer, controller of text and meaning, director of discussions, or leader in selection of text. Jane watches, monitors, facilitates, and nudges. The students plan their own learning, uncover their own meanings, and share those meanings with others. Students evaluate their own progress through joint conferences with peers or teacher. It is in conferences that Jane teaches. She questions, advises, models, and probes.

Jane seeks ways to help students work toward more fully understanding what they are doing:

> I need to find ways to help them investigate and explore what it is they're doing when they control the reading . . . that they can reflect freely on what and how they learn and what that learning means. I'm working on it but still haven't figured it out. It's helping them and me develop a new consciousness.

Jane demonstrates that the nature of her work and her questions change each year. As she refines her curriculum to empower students, she is working toward what Grundy (1987) describes as an emancipatory curriculum that engages "both teacher and pupil, in action which attempts to change the structures within which learning occurs and which constrain freedom in often unrecognized ways" (p. 19).

Lasting lessons. What I describe as these teachers' principles for curriculum composing demonstrates that their concepts of curriculum are far more centrally connected to learning and understanding literature than what sequences of texts, activities, or tests will be given, or whether students will be asked to explain what theme, plot, or characters are central to understanding *Moby Dick*. For these teachers, the curriculum process extends beyond controlling the objectives, the knowledge, or the procedures for learning. Curriculum composing is more than what Giroux (1981) describes as the "culture of positivism" where "Knowledge, then, becomes not only countable and measurable, it also becomes impersonal" (p. 53).

Beth, Jane and Joe raised important questions about literature curriculum that led them to examine their principles for curriculum composing as they began to articulate the processes through which teachers might engender students' engagements with literature. Beth, Jane, and Joe described the typical processes of arriving at district curriculum in language arts: teachers "generally get together and talk about what ought to happen. That *ought* is skills, texts, selections, and sequences that a group of teachers agree upon." Sometimes this includes remote references to the methods of teaching certain topics. For example, "Our last curriculum revision included ways to teach poetry through the use of traditional forms. It's limiting to teachers, and it doesn't encourage thoughtful work. We get beaten down in those meetings until we give up." Joe suggests that, "we need to ask more questions and find ways to answer them."

Jane said that the types of questions she was asking about literature curriculum had changed. "I'm not concerned as much with what is going on as how it goes on. I'm more reflective . . . I mean, I ask about how I can validate diverse interpretations from students rather than whether or not the students see . . . say, . . . something like foreshadowing in a certain chapter." Beth, Jane, and Joe catalogued some of the questions that were important in their planning. They listed, sorted through, and categorized their questions:

Table 2. Critical Questions in Learning Literature

Phase I—Content
Are there certain literary selections all students should read?
Is there knowledge about literature that readers should understand?
How or do readers need to know conventions?
What is the student's role in selecting texts?
How much information do students need about authors?
Are literary terms important to know?

Phase II—Purpose of Literature Education
What does learning literature mean and to whom?
Does early literature experience have the deciding influence on students' attitudes toward reading or studying literature?
Why study or learn literature?
Is it essential to study literature rather than just enjoy reading?
Is entertainment, enjoyment, and nurturing lifelong readers the ultimate aim of literature education?

Phase III—Contexts for Learning Literature
What are the conditions that nurture learning literature?
What obligations do we have to develop cultural literacy and whose literacy do we validate?
Can curriculum guides that are static serve the needs of groups that are dynamic?
How can students develop a class community that is supportive and open to diverse ideas?
How can teachers organize their classrooms to promote open exchanges without the teacher as center?

Phase IV—Ways and Means of Learning
How can a teacher preserve yet extend individual interpretation?
How can we learn literature?
Do we learn processes for reading literature?
Do certain activities promote learning literature?
Does meaning reside in the text, in the readers' experiences, or in both?
How can literature learning be evaluated?
Are there sequences that promote learning literature?
Are there literary concepts that promote understanding?
How does writing nurture reading?

As Beth suggested, "It's possible to look at these questions as more than categories of the types of questions I ask about literature curriculum." Beth maintained that these questions work in phases hierarchically. "I spend much more time thinking about Phases III and IV because I'm trying to understand learning. I probably spent more time on Phases I and II in earlier years when I was more focused on what and why." As Mayher and Brause (1991) have pointed out, "Evolving toward individualization and student-centered modes of teaching is not an easy process, but the constant challenges it presents make teaching continually fascinating" (p. 25). Beth, Jane, and Joe raised questions that make explicit the uncertainty of what literature education is, its purposes, and the struggles and complexities associated with composing curriculum for classrooms.

Joe summed it up this way: "Curriculum is not a course of study or your favorite English literature anthology. That doesn't suggest anything about how people learn. It's a course of action that a teacher takes to help students learn." Beth added that "Curriculum is not a sequence of skills or content. It certainly isn't a textbook or how we teach. It's the experiences that students generate into new meaning. And that new meaning brings about change—a new way of feeling or hearing or seeing." For Jane, "Curriculum isn't replicating or giving back someone else's knowledge. Curriculum is the children and what they make of their learning." Jane went on to suggest that curriculum has outcomes. Students will know something or be able to do something because of the learning experience that they could not do before. "It's what is in the learner's head or heart." Joe felt that "curriculum gets distorted into what we gotta teach and into formulas of what constitutes knowledge. It's the Hirsch like lists." Jane indicated that the focus in curriculum design is misplaced: "It isn't what we teach that needs to be planned. It's stepping to the other side and thinking about what children learn."

These ideas have powerful implications for planning. Such principles postulate a configuration of qualities for composing; not planned outcomes of actions, skills, or content knowledge, but dispositions and ways of thinking or deliberating that will inform the teachers' learning. Beth, Jane, and Joe's inquiry demonstrated that the product of reflection, which is curriculum-as-a-course-of-action, results from these teachers' dialogic relationship between beliefs about content, teacher, students, and their methods of acting those meanings into practice.

As Boomer (1988) notes, "Teachers teach most profoundly what they are at the core. The lasting lesson is the demonstration of self as it handles its authority and those under its authority" (p. 31). Jane is more than willing to relinquish teacher control, encouraging children's intentions to guide them into literature lessons. She retains a role that prods and facilitates. Jane's conception of curriculum is inextricably linked with her image of the ideal concept of teacher that she retains from the image of her father as "a model for me of someone with such great passion and reverence for literature. How could I resist?" What is essential for Jane is that she not give into complacency. "I keep reading. I use *Language Arts* as a touchstone. I read Moss' (1984) *Focus Units in Literature,* participated in one in-service class on literature this semester, and I read Bruner's (1986) *Actual Minds.*" Jane is, profoundly, a seeker and a searcher.

Beth retains a central role in planning particular literature experiences, and she works together with students to create a context where everyone shares in the construction of meaning. As Beth attempts to collaborate more with her students, she continuously reexamines her beliefs to formulate a more accurate understanding of herself and her students. Each new formulation leads her to new questions and concerns. As she said: "I keep pushing at the edges of the familiar. It's risky sometimes, but I keep learning."

In a quest to save readers who have overdosed on school reading, Joe starts with a fundamental question: How can I get students to trust their own opinions and shed the witch hunt through text mentality? Joe retains a control similar to that demonstrated in Beth's curriculum planning. He gets students started. He gets them to trust themselves as readers. Then Joe steps back to become observer and questioner. Joe's expressed commitment is to nurture student learning. He sees the curriculum as something that happens between the teacher and students. There is an image of the lighthearted atmosphere, the play and enjoyment in sharing language and literature. Listening to Joe talk about his practices, I could not help but notice that his involvement touches significant facets of his personal identity. He is relaxed and casual in his inquiry. "I had to wonder the other day after I talked with you about Rosenblatt's work, knowing it has made a difference in my views of response from students. Well, I wonder if early in my career it would have had impact? I had a long road of learning from students before it could ultimately make any sense to me." As Garth Boomer (1988) suggested, "When all the surface features are stripped away we teach profoundly what we are, what we know, what we value and what we believe" (p. 104). This inquiry revealed that Beth, Jane, and Joe's principles of curriculum composing are dialectic with their beliefs on learning.

These beliefs may not appear radical unless viewed through a lens similar to the one posed by Mayher (1990) as common sense teaching. As he describes it, common sense teaching generally turns students off to reading literature; it does not value student knowledge; it justifies the *what* rather than the *how* and *why* of text. It must be remembered that Beth, Jane, and Joe's beliefs are in sharp contrast to much of what curriculum has come to represent. Lists of facts, rules, activities, and seat work dominate history, science, and math. Joe's experience with students reaching high school turned off in mind and spirit is what led to his search for better ways. In this sense, the participants' beliefs about literature curriculum are more in keeping with what Mayher (1991) defines as the uncommon sense approach to teaching literature in which "every time we teach a text, it becomes a kind of hypothesis generating research project in which each reader generates hypotheses about an interpretation based on his or her individual transaction with the text" (p. 15). The interrelationship among acting and reflecting informs the learning.

Examples of these principles are summarized in the table that follows. These principles are the foundation on which Beth, Jane, and Joe plan and implement classroom activities and serve to define strategies for learning literature that they hope students will take into their lifelong habits of reading literature:

Table 3. Principles of Learning Literature

Beth stresses that students learn literature by
- investigating issues and problems.
- negotiating and renegotiating meaning personally and socially.
- involving themselves actively rather than passively.
- rehearsing ideas, making connections, exploring relationships.
- reflecting deliberately and carefully on what has been learned and what can or needs to be learned.
- taking present knowledge and applying it to new situations.
- consolidating learning through application in performances, celebrations, or writing.
- trying out ideas and testing opinions.
- reflecting on what has been learned.

Jane emphasizes that students learn best when
- working with intention, motivation, and judgment.
- designing, planning, and setting goals for what is to be learned.
- discovering and using strategies to further understanding.
- receiving instruction as it is needed.
- reflecting on what has been learned and what can or needs to be learned.
- defining and constructing their curriculum.
- setting goals for solving problems, answering questions, and finding new information.

Joe believes students learn literature when they are actively involved in
- puzzling through, sorting out, and investigating.
- feeling empowered to have opinions, attitudes, and beliefs.
- interacting and collaborating with others' thinking, writing, and reading.
- inquiring, questioning, testing hypotheses, and reflecting.
- interpreting and applying knowledge.
- constructing their own meanings.
- performing their meanings for themselves and others.

These teachers' conceptualizations of curriculum illuminate the principled ways in which curriculum is shaped out of their own personalities, commitments, styles of action, and decision making. The way these ideas play out in their classrooms shows that finding and framing a class lesson is a creative act, an act of professional imagination. In what follows, I will illustrate these teachers' implementations of curriculum in particular class sessions. I highlight how Beth, Jane, and Joe enact lessons in their classroom as the flow of meaning and discussion is situated in the teaching moment.

Reading the Classroom as a Text

Due to the extensive amount of time I spent in the classrooms of these teachers, I learned a great deal about how they implement their intentions into practice, structure not only the events that transpire but also the learning environment, and observe how their intentions are enacted into a lesson. I have written narrative reconstructions of the fourteen class sessions I observed, using my fieldnotes and audio tapes to present the dialogue, sequences of events, and interchanges as accurately as possible. However, these narratives are not a simple chronicle but a configuration of people, intentions, and actions (Polkinghorne, 1988) and as such are highly personalized accounts of reality. I include one of the narratives from each classroom as a case to highlight the subject matter, classroom structures, and the educational strategies conveyed through each class session.

Lesson 1: Joe's Alternative to the Class Discussion

1:00 P.M., February 13

As the bell rings, students lean across aisles, chatting with friends. A few open their binders. Fewer still are reading the story assigned for today, John Cheever's "Torch Song." As Joe walks to his podium, the chatter subsides and these twelfth grade students reach for notebooks. Joe begins: "Let's start with a quiz. I'll ask four questions, so one sheet of paper will do." Noticeable groans, shoulders shrug, and Ray sighs before he buries his head in his arms on the desktop. Joe asks the following questions: What was Jack's attitude toward Joan at the end of the story? What was Joan's most common way of helping the men in her life? Why did Jack lose his job? Where did Joan and Jack meet?

After students hand in the quiz, Joe asks: "What did you think about Joan?"

"She's weird," Jeff answers.

"Well, the guy has an overactive imagination," Rita retorts.

"This lady is seriously weird," Jeff persists.

Joe asks again. "What about the rest of you? Is Joan weird? What makes you think so?" Stephanie answers, "I wouldn't say weird. I thought she was mysterious."

"Okay," Joe says. "Let's take some time to figure her out. I'd like you to get together in groups of four or five and sort this out, talk about it and see if you can come to some agreement. Then, get some quotes to support this and narrow what you're thinking into a simple statement about Joan. Make that statement into a cinquain. Do you remember the form? I want you to give a concentrated portrait and the cinquain is a way to give impact to your impression of Joan. Anyway, get together and start. There's butcher paper on the wall for the quotes and cinquains. If you have questions let me know."

Joe walks over to Ray. "Hey, Ray, are you feeling okay?" Ray lifts his head momentarily. Then slumps back to the desk top. Joe persists, "I know you worked late but you need to get the work done. Come on, at least listen to the group. Do a quick read while they get started." Ray grudgingly gets to his feet, surveys the groups, and gets in with four other boys.

By now, one group is writing quotes on the graffiti wall. Denise writes in large green letters, "It troubled Jack to see in these straits a girl who reminded him of the trees and the lawns of his home town" (Cheever, 1980, p. 58).

Jason finishes in bold red calligraphy, "Her voice was sweet, and reminded him of elms, of lawns, of those glass arrangements that used to be hung from porch ceilings to tinkle in the summer wind" (p. 59).

Audrey and Bob leaf through the pages for another quote. "Oh, here it is. Let's put this up."

Bob begins to write in purple, "she stood by the hat rack, bathed in an intense pink light and the string music of heartbreak, swinging her mane of dark hair" (p. 57).

Scrawled in black above, "He began to think of her as The Widow . . . She always wore black" (pp. 56–57).

Again, in black: "He had the impression that there had been a death there recently" (p. 60). Kate and Elizabeth finish writing this cinquain above all their quotes:

> Black Joan
> dealing slow death
> caught in her serene web
> lured by her despairing "Torch Song"
> Jack's trapped

To the side of their work, Andrea and Sue are searching for a final word for their cinquain:

> Sweet Joan
> a trail of men
> nursing them through sickness
> drugs, meanness, selfishness, greed, spite

"I've got it!" Sue yells as she scrawls:
> Victim

"Perfect," Andrea steps back to admire the work.

Joe brings the class back together. [Approximately 30 minutes were devoted to the discussion, quotes, group cinquain] "Now then," he surveys the graffiti wall. "So, what have you learned about this character?"

Sue starts. "Andrea and I discussed how Jack is confused about how he feels from the first. He sees her as black and associated with the undertaker from the beginning. She's also serene and oblivious to the faults of the losers she's with . . . I think there is an attraction."

Tony interrupts, "But death is everywhere and Jack finally catches on. It reminded me of the knitting women in *Heart of Darkness*. She's just fate that he doesn't want to meet. Joan is death and that's dark and serene too."

Joe sits on a stool, the graffiti on Joan as a backdrop.

"It's a beautiful set-up job. Cheever lures us into the trap. I admit it. I thought Jack and Joan would get together . . . You know, the happily ever after story. Weird. I didn't expect it to turn out the way it did." Randy looks around for a reaction to what he has said.

Trina chimes in, "What do you mean how it ends? I don't know what is going to happen to Jack. Will he die? The story ends while he's trying to escape."

"Yeah," Randy is thinking about it. "Well I just assumed because he packed up and was getting out that he might escape her."

Kate adds, "At the end he's flushing nail clippings . . . wasn't it Pythagoras who believed if you left hair or nail clippings exposed the evil spirits could enter? I mean, he gets rid of all the signs."

Lillian adds, "It's just too, I mean like we don't know about those powers."

Morgan asks, "What was that deal with Pythagoras?"

Kate clarifies, "Well it's just about superstitions, like we just don't know."

Cyndi says, "Well that's just the point. We don't know and that's the way Cheever wanted it."

Joe ends, "Think about how Cheever can make us feel so many ways at the same time. You've shown that here."

The bell rings.

Exploration. It seems most appropriate to begin the discussion of Joe's class session by encouraging the reader to spend time reacting to and reexamining the events, the assumptions behind the events, and the congruence of these events with what has been learned about Joe's purposes and practices in teaching and curriculum construction earlier in this chapter and in Chapter Three. Describe and analyze what took place, the motivations and assumptions that led Joe to design the session in the way that he did, and how the students' reactions indicate what they took away from the lesson. Avoid the inclination to reach hasty judgments about the lesson. The following questions may serve as a guide to your exploration. You may want to write out some of your reactions to the following prompts:

- What are your questions about what took place during this class session?
- List and describe the representations of Joe's key principles in teaching literature (from Chapter Three and the previous section of this chapter) that you see in this lesson.
- List and describe incongruities between the class representation and Joe's key principles of teaching literature and between his planning (In Chapter Three, "Planning of Class Sessions") and what occurred.
- Describe the level of student participation and teacher directives.
- Is there evidence of competing agendas? Resolution of competing agendas?
- What did students learn from this lesson? Are there practices, strategies, and/or structures used in this class session that would be helpful to you in your own teaching?
- Describe what types of assessment or reflection you think Joe was engaged in during the class session.

Commentary. Rarely do teachers have the opportunity to spend much time in their colleagues classrooms. Although the narrative reconstruction of a class session cannot show the complexity of the actual events as they transpired, I hope an examination of Joe's lesson helps the reader consider how Joe's conceptions of teaching are connected to what actually took place in the classroom. My goal in what follows is to extend the discussion by analyzing four forms of reflection-in-action that Joe described while he was teaching. It might be interesting for the reader to compare what Joe remembered with what you imagined as you answered the last question in "Exploration."

First, Joe stated that his reflections focused on how students were understanding the character of Joan as they created the graffiti wall. "Actually, I can see how they formulated and reformulated their views." He illustrated with this example: "I learned some very particular things while they were working. I knew that Sam hadn't read the story. He became the recorder for the group because he couldn't help them find meaningful quotes. He didn't contribute one idea about Joan as a character. Most groups were interested in Cheever's use of black and of the multiple personality they ascribe to Joan." One of the particular ways that Joe monitored this lesson was by studying the quotes students selected. The structures and activities that Joe put in place gave him a means for such monitoring. He watched students for other reasons as well. For example, Joe knows Ray's habits: "After he's worked all night he tends to be confrontational. He does one of two things typically—goes to sleep or gets in somebody's face. I won't let him sleep, so I need to be ready to step in if he gets down on somebody else. Today he was quiet; mostly he was reading to catch up. He wasn't in the group actively, he was just in the geographic proximity." Joe believes that structures such as the graffiti wall have moved the responsibility for discussion to the students. Class became a "puzzling through and sorting out."

Second, Joe analyzed the congruence between his plan and what actually happened. He explained that he likes to "test hunches. I find that one of the most valuable aspects of planning is to see how much I can predict how things will go. I study where things were different and I believe that I am fine tuning my skills at having two or three alternatives in place." Joe pointed out that after the students came back together to talk he simply got them started and stepped out of the discussion. The students created their own momentum. As he began to describe his plan, he thought of the cinquain. "I don't know exactly why that struck me. We'd just done those a few days before and the form is perfect—it stretches syllables out to eight in the fourth line and then snaps back to two. It carries a punch and it seemed perfect. Actually I liked the way it worked out." Joe had not predicted the intertextual references to *Heart of Darkness* and Pythagoras. Hearing what students said gave him an idea for future discussions. "They still want to deal very much with what happened, and I must remember not to take the plot of the story away too quickly. They lose some of the pleasure of the reading when I do. I think I'd slow that down next time." In reminding himself of this, Joe challenged certain assumptions about what he was doing and how that fit with his students' desires and motivations.

Third, Joe predicted possibilities from what had taken place. Joe predicted what students might focus on:

> From the looks of the wall, they're going to bring up the Fates— *Heart of Darkness, Macbeth* and they'll take that back to their own lives and talk about fate. This would be my prediction of how it will go. I've started them. Most of it will unfold now. We'll end by writing original character pieces where they'll show multiple sides of a person. They'll write or create performances of multiple faces.

In keeping with his planned objective, "to have students create characters," Joe began to forecast possible means that would lead to that end.

Fourth, Joe evaluated his role as teacher. In the interview after class, Joe suggested that he may have guided too much. "We lost steam before class was over today. I realized it was happening and thought how I'd completely set the agenda and they followed." Joe stated that he wants to be a teacher who "facilitates entrances through which students can make the bridge between what they know and do not know. I need to find ways to get them into conversations with what they're reading. I'm still searching for how to do that better." Joe recognized that his agenda, even with the appearance of active student involvement, created constraints on what students could do. "As free and open as I've thought I am, it's my agenda, my ways of learning literature, what I think that's important that gets put into place as rituals. I'm rethinking how to help them find their own ways in. I can't quite imagine how to do that. That's the tricky part." Joe suggested that he thinks about this while he's teaching, but that he is still learning to challenge his intentions and balance those with better ways to understand students' intentions.

After observing the lesson on "Torch Song," I asked Joe about his use of reading quizzes. "Easy," he said. "If they haven't read it, there's not much point. There's always a reading quiz before we get on to the real stuff."

Ruth: Do you ever question whether there are other ways to accomplish the same thing?
Joe: Not really. I've concentrated on other areas. I don't know how to do a song and dance for them to get this done. So, I do what's worked.
Ruth: Is this quiz representative of most reading quizzes you'd give?
Joe: Sure. I mostly ask literal questions. I'm not trying to get them into . . . like the Bloom thing. They're not ready. This is a fragile reading and I don't want to make much out of it.
Ruth: I mean you've said, and I've seen that you want students to read in thoughtful ways. Is it possible that knowing they'll have a literal quiz encourages them to do a literal first reading?
Joe: (after a long pause) I hadn't thought about that before, so the question spins around in my head. I alternately say: 1) Literal is ok for a first reading 2) Is it? Or do we need an engaged read? 3) It works so leave it alone. 4) How else would I do it? 5) How much time would it make if I changed? 6) Do I even know how to change it? It gets complicated.

Through our collaborative exploration, Joe was challenged to take a closer look at a particular class routine that he had created to motivate his students. He began to consider, through the six questions he asked, an expanded repertoire for dealing with first readings. Joe took the issue to his students for their reactions. Interestingly, one of the students said, "Oh, you mean you have a choice. I thought that was something you were required to do." The students' perception of the teacher as technician is definitely alive in schools! Joe's openness in discussing this issue allowed the students to reconsider Joe's role in planning, and they were invited to participate in reflection as well. The students could not suggest with any definiteness how reading quizzes affected their first readings. Jason suggested that the class could experiment with various types of quizzes in order to "distinguish different ways of reading. I need to think about how I read now that I'm aware." Elizabeth stated that she's "learned to read for the quiz and I can pretty much take any story and skim it in ten minutes and get the grade." Joe cringed. Randy said that the quiz gives him "a focus, a starting look, and it doesn't usually hurt my grade." The answer of whether or not to give reading quizzes wasn't solved, but through reflection Joe was led to consider the impact of his quizzes on students' reading of text. As Joe stated months later, "What happens in these conversations is that they create an uncertainty, a disequilibrium and that's the kind of situation that I reflect on over and over again."

Lesson 2: Beth's Strategy for Understanding Layers of Meaning

7:50 A.M., May 8

Sometime before the beginning of first period, I walk the halls of Eastman Junior High. Accompanying the drone of ceiling fans, I hear typical school sounds. Mr. Butler stands in the hall talking with a cluster of students about last night's homework; someone in the next hall slams a locker door shut, a notebook thumps to the floor, the rustle of papers and finally, the single horn blast from the bell. Then, the rumble of students as they spill from the halls into classrooms, looking like streamers of color. I stand back, as close to the wall as possible, to let them pass.

I turn around and find that Beth's classroom door is closed. There is a note on the door: "Ruth, we're on the practice field." I find thirty students and one teacher in various postures. Nate and Craig on hands and knees, Jen and Susan stretch out looking skyward; Dan, Brian, and Andrew sit cross-legged in a cluster. Everyone has marbles. Beth sits with a huge basket of them by her side.

Rosie takes one from the basket, looks it over carefully, puts it back, not quite satisfied. It sounds like someone's walking through gravel as she digs through the mound for the perfect one.

"Once you've found one, examine it and then write a description of it in your journal. Dig for details. Do you see anything inside? Does the marble remind you of anything?" Beth takes her journal and begins jotting notes. Everyone has settled into the writing except Sarah who is back at the basket, hoping to find the perfect one.

"Take a few minutes to share what you've written. Then talk about other ways to see the marble. Talking may help you find more things to say. Jot those down so you don't forget." Beth moves toward Harriet and Rosie. The three read what they have written, look over each other's prize marbles, and work on further descriptions.

After fifteen minutes or so, Beth suggests they dig deeper still. "Set up some metaphorical statements to push yourself into new ways of seeing." She gives an example: "The marble is a planet, dying from lack of oxygen."

Students begin to shout other possibilities: "The marble is a crystal gazer's key to the future." "An egg with a fetus." "This marble is an eyeball."

Beth asks the students to jot some possibilities in their journals. They share in small groups, then Beth asks them to get in a circle.

Beth hands out Edward Lense's (1988) poem "Marbles." They read it in pairs. It begins, "The marbles I have just won brim in my cupped hands." They finish reading the last two lines: "inside . . . is a boy's face" (p. 23).

"Hey, I've got the one with the bands of cloud," shouts Jeremy.

"Mine's like strands of blood in milk," Jen says, turning her marble over and over.

Susan holds hers toward the sun: "I've got the transparent egg."

Beth picks up the basket and passes it to Jim who is sitting beside her. "Take a handful of those in your cupped hand." Jim takes more than he can hold. Some fall away. The lost ones look like Easter eggs hidden in the grass.

"Let's see if we can find all the different ones the poet describes," Stephanie says taking the basket from him. Several others join her. Beth sits back, waiting for a few moments. "Look through the basket, look at your own marble again, read the poem again, and see if you've found new ways of seeing your marble. Jot down what you think of." Students test their marbles against the light, look through the basket, jot notes, and talk.

It is nearly time for the bell when Beth says, "Andrea said yesterday that some poems have layers of meaning and that reading poems is like stripping off layers. How do we find those layers for our own writing or for our reading?"

Sue: First I noticed just the color, the design, how the marble felt. Why are they always cold? The things I can see right now.
Harriet: I agree with Sue. Then when we talked I got to describing it with different words and Stephanie said something about the rings around Saturn and that got me going.
Stephanie: I used that in one of my metaphors. That's when I

started to see another layer like Andrea said—something beyond a marble.

Colin: Like this poet dude really knows how to describe but some of the ways he describes like mysterious fog and smoke-veils and then blood and the chick's embryo. I thought about birth. It's really beautiful.

Rosie: Then that line about broken pieces of a face is another level . . . another story in the poem. I agree, Colin, there's something beautiful.

Jamie: It's sort of like all the layers of meaning tell different stories. Each story is there waiting like Andrea said to be stripped back.

Brian: Yeah, cool.

Susan: That reminds me of Anne's idea, you know when we were reading [reference to *Diary of Anne Frank*]. She had this idea about "thinking oneself out" and that's really what happens when you start peeling back the stories. I think Andrea's idea helps me see that there are a lot of ideas in something and we sort of strip one away and tell it and then maybe find another.

Andrea: Well, I'll take applause.

Exploration. Again, it seems appropriate to begin a commentary on Beth's class session by encouraging the reader to spend time reacting to and reexamining the events, the assumptions behind the events, and the congruence of these events with what has been learned about Beth's purposes and practices in teaching and curriculum construction earlier in this chapter and in Chapter Three. Remember to examine what took place by both describing and analyzing the lesson. What were the motivations and assumptions that you think led Beth to design the session in the way she did? How did the students' reactions indicate what they took away from the lesson? The following questions serve as a guide to that exploration. Again, you may want to write out some of your reactions. Refer back to prompts included after Joe's lesson. Additionally you might consider comparing this lesson with the class session on *A Tale of Two Cities* that is included in Chapter Three.

Commentary. As with Joe's lesson, I'd like to follow the readers' description and analysis with some of the issues that Beth raised about the lesson by presenting what she describes as her reflection-in-action and her reactions to this lesson. Again, it will be interesting to compare what Beth has to say with what you imagined she might feel about what took place.

"What is remarkable about what happened out there," Beth stopped and took a sip of her coffee, "is not that the lesson itself is anything special . . . although it did turn out well." Beth paused, searching for the words. "I really listened to what Andrea said yesterday and rather than saying something like great idea or good thought, I came back on it in a serious way." Beth explained that she had planned the lesson after the previous day's class session. "I just stopped where we were and extended. I validated Andrea's comment which in no small way validates all the students' ideas. I really have to work on that because I have my agenda." Beth's decision to follow up on Andrea's point with a subsequent lesson suggests that she is experimenting with how to link students' understanding and intentions more integrally with her own. This is one move Beth makes toward a more student-centered classroom. Although, as she admits, "It is a small start, but I think it is an important step."

Beth explained that part of the discussion that took place the day prior to this lesson focused on different ways that individual students read poems. "Some like to dig out meaning and others said they like to hear poems. Others talked about the language and images. Andrea commented that all of those ways of reading are like finding different layers of meaning. Different people will find different things." Beth indicated that she was listening more carefully and thoughtfully to students and acting on what she heard. "I just wouldn't have done this a couple of years ago . . . I'd rationalize about time and plans. But the bottom line was fear. I was afraid it might not work." Beth's planning has taken a new turn.

Beth facilitated students' explorations into ways of reading a poem through a concrete application of "layering." Their descriptions of marbles, from the literal to the metaphoric, was a direct application of Andrea's concept of layered meaning. Lense's poem "Marbles" supported both the descriptions and the concept with a literary example. The students engaged in ever-changing hypotheses about layering as they engaged in writing, reading, and talking through their developing understandings.

Consider the students' moves: Students have a concrete object from which to begin their explorations of the abstract concept of layering. They write, discuss, and share. They respond to a series of additional prompts; they read the poem and write additional descriptions as ways to carry forward the construction of meaning about layering. Consider the teacher moves: Beth prompts them to dig deeper; she models ways of seeing, gives directions, pushes them deeper still. She writes with them and facilitates a meta-conversation on the layered meaning of poetry, then summarizes. If what has taken place is a reading lesson, what has been learned?

Beth extends Andrea's idea that multiple levels of meaning exist by demonstrating the abstract idea in a concrete fashion through the use of the close observation activity. By pushing students to add layers of description and metaphor to their original descriptions, Beth encouraged them to dig deeper into layers of description and metaphor. The students created their own concrete examples of multiple layers of meaning. The primary purpose of this lesson was to make explicit a number of reader moves: readers examine descriptions carefully, question descriptions to see what is buried beneath, look for answers over time, pose alternative ways of describing, and think metaphorically. Beth's reading lesson helps make concrete what Andrea suggested about finding different layers of meaning. Through this particular lesson, students demonstrated that meaning taken from a text is not fixed; it is created. When Beth's participation in the exchange is examined, she guided the students' explorations but they had the responsibility for carrying the discussion forward. They talked to one another and did not funnel all information through Beth. Beth hoped to open up rather than close down opportunities for students to wrestle with their ways of making sense of what they read.

Beth suggests that "Kids come up with things that never occur to me. If I listen it actually gives me a better understanding of how they work, how what I try to facilitate helps or hinders them, and what they need to do when they get stuck." In discussing her own understanding of how these lessons unfold, Beth referred to her habit of "explaining things to herself, of questioning herself when she reads." Taking into account her own ways of engaging with text, Beth discovers ways to encourage her students to do the same. As Beth suggested, "The trouble is, I don't always know where to look." Saying this is not enough for her, and she remains concerned with finding ways to promote learning that go beyond what is in a particular text. For students to understand reading strategies presupposes their having developed an awareness of how to read in multiple ways. Beth tries to objectify her knowledge of this through the reading lessons that are acted into meaning in her classroom. The classroom becomes a philosophic laboratory where "forming, thinking, knowing, abstracting, meaning-making, acting, creating, learning, interpreting: Imagination names them all" (Berthoff, 1984, p. x).

Obviously this lesson can be read in multiple ways. For example, it was difficult to know without hearing all the small group talk whether or not students were connecting this particular activity to a strategy for reading. Observing this one lesson without knowing the preparatory work and explanations given in previous days, Beth's intent in teaching this strategy, or how she follows through with the strategy in subsequent days and discussions might render very different readings. It became clear to me that the interpretation given to events, attitudes, or settings were interpretations of choice and required careful crafting and consciousness. There is no sure-fire and right reading of any of these lessons. My depictions of what I saw and heard are as much my interpretation of the experience as they are the reporting of what seemed to take place for the teacher and students in the class.

By developing a classroom experience that engaged students in investigations of meaning, active involvement in understanding abstract concepts, and reflections on what they were doing, Beth acts into meaning many of her principles. Beth's practices are best understood against the backdrop of her stated purposes for literature education, "where they can learn to actively question and get at meaning for themselves." Her image of the role of teacher "as a model really of the questioning attitude," and her emphasis in curriculum that "leads students to generate new meaning" are evidenced in the lesson. Even though Beth states that she encounters many difficulties in determining what and how to teach, she takes seriously her responsibility to reflect on her practice, to remain alert to ways in which she can further her beliefs in practice to monitor the practices to discern their effectiveness.

Beth shares some of the difficulties. She wants students to talk about multiple interpretations of what they read. The problem is: Students resist this idea. Beth said her eighth graders assume that there is *a* secret in every text. If they find the right key, they will unlock it. Beth expressed her frustration with breaking those attitudes. "I've realized that *saying* they bring part of the meaning to what they read just has not convinced them. I hope a concrete activity like the one with the marbles helps them see the concept. I find they resist the idea and still want to know if they're right." We continued the conversation:

Beth: I try to get at the idea there are lots of secrets in a text. They'll each find different ones, and we'll share those.
Ruth: Do you use the word 'secrets' with them?
Beth: Yes, I do. I've said that for years I think because I want them to get excited about what they'll find in whatever they're reading. I used to believe there was one secret myself, and I'd guide students by the nose to get them there. Now, I really try to say let's look for lots of secrets.
Ruth: I guess I'm wondering what the word *secret* means to them. If I tell you, I've found out a secret for making good spaghetti sauce, isn't it still spaghetti sauce in the end? I'm wondering what connotation they carry for that word *secret*.
Beth: That you've unlocked—oh, I wonder—I mean, *maybe I'm passing on that fraud*. I know I've opened up and want to honor as many different

meanings . . . Maybe I'm carrying my old language with me as baggage that sends different messages than what I think I'm saying.

Together, Beth and I focused on her students' resistance to accepting that a literary text may have multiple meanings. Beth struggled to discover *why* students have those perceptions and was led to consider how her language may have informed them. Our discussion led Beth to an inquiry of possible causes for students' reactions. Beth can now consider alternatives, and she suggested that "through being constantly aware of my language and the messages it carries I can begin to think about how to move students beyond their resistances."

Lesson 3: Jane's Blueprint for Reading Lessons

10:30 A.M., February 11

Jane has a cup of coffee waiting on the back table when I arrive. "I'm feeling overwhelmed with the schedule. We have children pulled out all day. She hands me a list—band, choir, special needs, and a meeting for the committee on recycling. I hate to lose them during reading." Jane walks back to her files and collects these fourth graders' reading folders. I look around the classroom.

Carey, John, and Sarah are reading, bellies flat, legs extended, lying together on pillows. Todd and Shawn are sitting at their quad. Todd is reading *The Witches* while Shawn is writing something in his journal. A copy of *Hatchet* lies open, next to him. Most everyone is absorbed in reading. Ryan and Russ are reading together from Roald Dahl's *BFG*. They read in unison at times, taking turns at other times. They do this in a corner behind shelves of books where they will not disturb other readers. Jane moves into the conference corner with Jen. Jen tells Jane that she thinks, "Jess Ahrens really changes. At first he's just interested in winning the race but after Leslie wins, funny it was a girl, he is nicer then and cares more about other people." Jane has her note pad handy and jots a note or two. Scott rummages through books in the class library. He is itching to walk around and check in with everybody. He can't get into reading today. Michael, Jeremy, and Jamie curl into a single tangle under a table.

Jen leaves the conference corner, walks over and taps Mary on the shoulder, "Ms. W. wants you." She nods toward Jane. Mary finishes the paragraph she is reading, gets up and heads for her conference. She tells Jane, "I just finished the part where Annemarie pulls the Star of David off Rachel's neck just before the soldiers walk in. That was so tense. I really like the way the author describes the dark room and that little gleam of light, then

Annemarie sees the necklace and knows it will give them away."
Jane studies Mary's face. "Would you rather go back and keep
reading than conference today?" Mary beams, "Oh, yes, Ms. W."
She races back to her desk and picks up *Number the Stars* by Lois
Lowry and resumes her reading.

When Jane finishes conferencing with Bob, Tony, Russ and Ryan
motion her to their corner. "We'd like to read some of this to the
class. It's so funny." Their faces are flushed, and they begin laughing all over again. They read her a few lines. She laughs with them.
Jane makes the announcement. "Russ and Ryan would like to
share what they're reading. Write in your reading logs for a few
minutes before they share. Think of some things you want to say
about what you read today." A few students write, a few linger
over what they're reading; others rustle papers. After a few minutes, Russ and Ryan walk to the front of the room. Everybody's
laughing. Tears roll down Becka's cheeks. Scott cradles his stom-
ach in his arms. Andy asks Ryan if he can have the book next. Jane
looks at the clock on the wall: "Time for recess. We'll have more
reading time after the break, and I will have more conferences."

After recess, Jane conferences with Hannah.

Hannah begins by reading two or three pages, picking up from where
she was reading in Beverly Naidoo's (1986) *Journey to Jo'burg.*

Jane: Did you figure out answers to your question from the other
day now that you've read more. You asked: "Why do the black
people tolerate the white people being so mean?"
Hannah: Well, yes and no. I just read the part where Tiro and
Naledi see all those people being hit or screamed at. Some were
arrested and taken away in vans because they didn't have passes.
The whites have money and guns. The blacks don't. That helps me
see why Tiro and Naledi's mother must obey her boss. I couldn't
believe the white lady wouldn't let the mother have her own children sleep where she is living . . . after the long journey . . . I mean,
none of it is fair, but I see now . . .
Jane: What do you see now?
Hannah: That they don't have choices. That they might as well be
in prison. Their life isn't very good. I mean they walk miles and
miles because they don't have money, very little food, and the doctor is far away.
Jane: How does the author help you see all this?
Hannah: Well, it's like we talked about with *Black Stallion* . . . It's
the way she describes things and telling little things that make you
think about how hard life is . . . like the children are cold and hungry and don't have enough milk. Their stomachs hurt because
they're hungry.
Jane: I'm curious to know, because I haven't read this book, and I'd
love to hear some of it, maybe one place where you noticed that.

Hannah: (searches through pages before reading) "The children weaved in and out among people as they ran along the stony road, between rows of gray block houses all looking exactly alike. No great leafy trees here, only gray smoke settling everywhere" (Naidoo, p. 30). It's just sad they live like that.

Jane: I love the image of the stony road and the gray houses and smoke. I can see how gray life is.

Hannah: I didn't know that people live like this.

Jane: Do you think this is an important book to read?

Hannah: Oh, yes, because it's hard to imagine that kids, I mean my age, live this way, and it's not their fault or their mother's fault. They can't do much.

Jane: Why don't you read a chapter of this to the class. Would you like to do it? It's so opportune, here we have Mandela and South Africa in the news constantly, and yet we don't know what it's like. Literature can help us feel those feelings.

Hannah: Today?

Jane: If you'd like. Choose a section and practice a few minutes. If you'd rather wait until you finish that would be nice too.

Hannah: Yes, I will . . . I'll read today about when they find their mother. It's sad and so weird that they can't live with her. Maybe I'll read later about what happens . . . after I've finished. Do you think life can get better for them?

Exploration. Again, it seems appropriate to preface commentary on Jane's class session by encouraging you to spend time reacting to and reexamining the events, the assumptions behind the events, and the congruence of these events with what has been learned about Jane's purposes and practices in teaching and curriculum construction earlier in this chapter and in Chapter Three. The prompts after Joe's class session may again serve as a guide to your exploration.

Commentary. In our follow-up discussion, Jane described three concerns that struck her during the class. First, she monitored how students used the time while she conferenced. She explained how she watched Scott, hoping he would settle into the reading. She indicated that she was prepared to stop her conference and speak with him and help him find a book if necessary but that he "didn't disturb others, so I decided to let him keep looking. I think the time was wasted for him today, but he needs to monitor himself sometimes." As Scott's case illustrates, Jane has learned to focus her attention selectively on students who may have particular needs. Jane remarked that she monitors whether or not students are working productively if they work together. She explained that Russ and Ryan were working although "they were having a great deal of fun at the same time.

Many students have the routines down, so I don't watch them but I watch others closely." As she monitored individual cases, Jane described how she had prepared students to work within the structures of the reading workshop that have been established. "I reflect on how that's going every day and make adjustments or work with the students to make the workshop work for them."

As Mary's case illustrated, Jane was forced to decide how she could balance their competing agendas. Mary wanted to continue reading and Jane wanted to conference with her. Jane determined that Mary's immediate needs were most important. Jane described that many situations occur like Mary's and much of her own reflection time during conferences centers on how her intentions and the children's intentions can both be met. Although Jane sees her job as one through which she instructs and guides young readers into increasingly sophisticated ways of reading, she believes the students can and do direct their own learning.

Jane described reading conference sessions as times to "consider what is being learned and to generate further learning or the motivation for it." Jane outlined her mental blueprint for conferences:

> First, I ask them to read a few pages to keep a feel for how fluent, expressive, and sense-making their oral reading is. I have notes from previous conferences and try to identify a critical concept that the child introduces there. Take Steve. He notices that the main character acts differently in different situations. This may seem easy but not for fourth graders. Steve can't elaborate on when or how or why. I encourage him to follow-up by saying, "Think about that as you read the next few chapters and see if you can figure it out." Or I'll say, "Think about what would happen if the character didn't act differently in different situations." Sometimes it's a strategy. Some children don't visualize when they read. If I figure that out I ask questions such as: "What do you think the character looks like? What did you see on that hillside? What color do you think the buses are?" Anything to get them seeing.

Implicit in Jane's use of conferences is the introduction of a range of strategies and understandings about literature that she monitors in her discussions with her students. "I've learned that I need to listen to them and pick up from where they are. It isn't simple, and it's indefinite. I'm not always certain we're making progress. My heart tells me we are. It's central to develop private reading habits, and it's hard to know how to help with that."

Jane described another concern that was exhibited in her conference with Hannah. Her reflection was more centrally located on what Hannah was actually saying. As Jane indicated: "Hannah, well, she was right on track and had interesting questions. I wanted to push her to think about the writing and once I saw that the reading was enjoyable and she was really into the book I felt comfortable moving ahead as I had planned. I wanted to have her start focusing on details and it seemed right to move ahead with that." In the following excerpt from the interview she explained the dilemma: "I'm constantly imposing on students when I ask them to stretch farther—to focus on a passage or character and study it in ways they haven't or to encourage them to read something harder. Is intervention a good thing? But, I'm learning as I teach to make decisions—like Mary. It wasn't the time, so she's an example that there isn't one way or the other. I'm trying to make decisions as they occur and using my intuition as guide." Jane worked through this dilemma by suggesting that it isn't "one way or the other." Jane continued to struggle with her role of teacher. She "imposes" and wonders if "intervention" is a good thing. In part, she reconciled this role by suggesting that judgments in particular contexts are important and that her experience leads her to feel more comfortable in making those judgments.

Jane has her students keep logs in which they react to what they are reading. She uses these to determine issues for the conference, but as she reflected on the class session, she indicated that the students don't seem motivated to write in their reading journals:

Jane: I've said this to you before in different circumstances but I'm starting to realize that students aren't very interested in writing in the reading journals and I'm getting closer to understanding why. I do think their real journals are the writing ones and that is where they expend their efforts—I mean, like I said before, on their own writing.

Ruth: I'm interested in how much you value their writing. What do you do with their writing journals that you don't do with the reading journals? Is there a difference?

Jane: Well, I always carry on a dialogue with them about their writing. I mean, I write back to them about their pieces. They use their reading journal when they peer conference but I haven't shared with them that I read those to prepare for a conference with me. I mean, I spend all my time reading and writing in their writing journals. Maybe I need to write in the reading journal—carry on a dialogue or at least let them know I read those.

Through this discussion, Jane questioned how her lack of input on the children's reading journals may affect their motivation. "I could begin to carry on a dialogue on paper. Would I want or need the one to one conferences as often then? Maybe I just need to let them know I read what they have written before we conference. I could create a mini-lesson to show them how I use their journal to prepare for a conference. Maybe then they would take that more seriously." Jane reflected on alternative strategies for dealing with the students' motivation to write in their reading journals. She continued this inquiry during the remaining months of the study and began to write responses to their journal entries. She demonstrated through a mini-lesson how she uses their journals to prepare for conferences. Whether or not this motivated the students is hard to say, but Jane believed that a few students did write more and referred more often to their journals during conferences. By the end of our time together, Jane didn't have an answer to her dilemma, but she was willingly engaged in the recursive process of reflection as a way of assessing various approaches.

Thoughtful Action

Beth, Jane, and Joe's class sessions and their reflections indicate how thoughtful and vigilant they are about their work. They do teach mindfully and whether or not we might agree with the particulars of pedagogy, interaction, content, or classroom rituals or structures, it is clear that they take the composing of their teaching lives seriously. Beth, Jane, and Joe shared several common features in the way they think about their teaching: (a) they monitor students' reactions, and are aware of problematic students, students' progress, or situational contexts; (b) they consider whether what they teach is integrally related to students' intentions, hence, questioning the role and authority of themselves as teacher; (c) they study present events as a way to predict how to move forward in future class sessions; and (d) they examine if their rehearsals and actual classroom events were congruent, leading them to elaborate on their developing knowledge of teaching. Analyzing a single class episode for each participant, even in the depth gone into here, can only suggest what assumptions, knowledge, and beliefs about the purposes of literature education are embodied within.

I have sought to describe some of the defining principles and practices in Beth, Jane, and Joe's teaching. One of the challenges was how to do justice to the complexities without attempting to codify what was idiosyncratic and often circuitous. On one level, these teachers' reflections were *informative*—taking the form of internal talk meant to examine ideas or to create or clarify meaning. Whether such reflection took place in the classroom amidst the confusion and activity of real classroom life or in the teacher's den, the faculty room, at her desk, or in his car, I'd suggest that such reflection proceeds with a critical interest in thinking through problems or plans that will bear on the work of teaching. Like the reflection described in Schön's (1983) work, the deliberative process takes place in "the action present" and presumes to have both educational means and ends. But, reflection has *transformative* potential as well. Reflection relates to the struggle that teachers undertake to construct a life in teaching and to constantly consider or revise their conceptions of what will take place in the classroom, or their need to shape a teaching identity. That power, as Kincheloe (1991) described it, offers the potential to transform teachers from "classroom technician to active political agent" by considering "the indispensable qualities that are mandated by knowledge production: critical reflection, a desire to act, discomfort, uncertainty, restless inquiry" (p. 21).

The informative and transformative power of reflectivity was never more poignant than when Beth made the following observation after a particularly problematic class session:

> Two voices in me were working simultaneously. One voice kept the class going forward on the path that had reached a dead end. The other voice kept asking: What's gone wrong here? Where was the wrong turn? How can we get out of this? Searching for options . . . trying to think of a . . . well . . . a spark of an idea to get us back on track or to think of a way to stop this and reorganize. I was caught between the thinking and not being ready to act on it. That was the time to stop the class and say: What is going on here and how can we get this working better?

Beth's statement encapsulates the dynamic between thinking and acting. The product of Beth's lesson, from the teacher and observer's standpoint, was a sluggish and dull discussion. But the reflective inquiry that Beth described was a dynamic going on beneath the action. Perhaps teachers might be encouraged to see their work as transformative as well as informative—as comprising more, for example, than how one thinks about particular classroom events, what to do tomorrow, or how to deal with Billy. Such a habit of mind requires that teachers take charge of their own looking. I might add that realizing the possibilities to inform and transform depends on whether or not one has the habit and will "to see again."

Beth, Jane, and Joe's strong sense of an individual teaching identity correlates with their habits of "seeing again" and taking charge of their own looking. Understanding oneself can be enabling. This principle was illustrated by Jane:

> The narratives help me see myself in significant ways. When you can step back to observe yourself, it can be intimidating but exciting. Reading about oneself through a writer's eyes provides an

interesting start at introspection. How many times do we have a chance to stand back at a distance? I found myself wanting to do each day what you managed to capture in the scenes. What amazes me is how simple it looks or sounds here and how hard it is. Essentially there are so many things happening at once. I wouldn't want to give the impression that this is easy. In a way I see how I construct my own visualizations of what has taken place in class and from these I stretch myself to try new things. I try to see how I must look to the students and imagine how I might create a different place in the future.

Jane continued to describe this sense of identity by suggesting that experimentation builds her confidence and provides the motivation to push her inquiry even further. "And when I do, I'm more critical of accepting someone else's formula for doing things. I'm learning to define myself." It is absolutely crucial to say that these teachers struggle to personalize teaching and avoid anonymity, as exemplified in what Jane said. To do this requires a degree of thoughtfulness that leads teachers to acknowledge their individuality and uncertainties, and to value their experiential knowledge. Hearing Beth, Jane, and Joe discuss their practice-centered reflection shatters the image that teachers mindlessly, rather than mindfully, attend to their teaching lives.

Yet the notion of informative and transformative reflection raises many questions for further inquiry. Among the most pressing, in light of the argument here, is whether teachers can learn to examine their teaching practices and interrogate the unintended consequences of what they do. And, if they can, how? Even with the extensive information that I collected and the numerous occasions in which I observed Beth, Jane, and Joe, I cannot describe with any certainty why or how they developed the self-conscious intent that each brings to the teaching act. What certainly happened was that they brought their reflective capabilities and strategies to conscious awareness, and they and I came to see that their teaching repertoire developed in a haphazard way through spontaneous as well as deliberative experimentation. It would be interesting to compare the phases, forms, or emphases of their reflectivity with that of teachers in other disciplines or teachers who face situational contexts very different from those that Beth, Jane, and Joe confront in the community and schools in which they live and work. Different methods of eliciting the teachers' reflection could be brought to bear, and we could hardly predict the endless variations. It is difficult to catch such intangibles and hold them up to the light for close inspection. What I do know is that Beth, Jane, and Joe exhibit tolerance for multiple perspectives and advance conceptions of meaning that are temporal, not terminus.

What, of course, has escaped scrutiny in this chapter is something so fundamental as to be preconscious: it is something to do with not only the habits of mind but the habits of heart that Beth, Jane, and Joe possess—the pleasure they get from being with students, of enjoying students' energy, frustrations, laughter, and the sound of their voices. The contrary exhilaration involves reaching beyond the known and into risky territory. When I think of such fearful pleasure I can't help but remember Sam on a first day of a school year. Sam walked into the room and breathed a huge sigh, expecting the worst to happen—course requirements, class rules, too much writing, and the dreaded peer response groups.

Sam's class participated in self-chosen studies, individually or in small groups. I planned book talks to get them started thinking about authors, time periods, genres, and topics they were interested in. They shared these in pairs, small groups, and with the entire class. They spent time in the school library browsing (much to the horror of the librarian who wanted them to have a clear-cut agenda or a book title before entering her lair), talking to friends and parents, and reading the *New York Times Book Review.* We all read together too. Some short stories, nonfiction, poetry—contemporary and not-so-contemporary. We waited for ideas to germinate. Most of the time the students were engaged in this laissez-faire work, my heart was in my throat.

Someone in Sam's class studied the role of women in Shakespeare's tragedies—for a whole semester. Another student examined Soviet youth as portrayed in fiction and magazines from the U.S.S. R. His Russian grandmother helped him with translations. Sam, whose father was killed in Vietnam, began a study of literature written about Vietnam vets. He began to search out and record oral histories from local and regional vets. He found literature written in or about Vietnam during the war—both sides. The journey into this landscape was emotional, arduous, filled with frustrations and dead ends, but Sam got hooked. I got a rush from his successes. Last I heard he was in an Eastern Studies program. He received a Woodrow Wilson grant to compile oral histories of South Vietnamese survivors. He lived in Saigon. Sam was a reminder that in spite of my fear of doing so, I needed to keep the agenda open. The risk is great—sometimes there is chaos; some students get lost and lose motivation and do shoddy work; some find a lifetime passion. For all my plans and need for the known, for structure, and for my agenda, I couldn't fail Sam. He was one of many adolescents who came in with expectations of requirements and rules but left with a new idea of what it means to learn in school. Over the years, I learned to challenge myself as my students provoked me to keep learning how to teach and as I became more adept at discovering how they learned.

I met Sam during my seventeenth year of teaching high school when I had developed habits of mind and heart that allowed me to continually experiment with different ways of working in the classroom. His experience in this class in 1982 was a far cry from the experiences of those students in the classes I taught in 1966. As I remember Sam, I hope to remind other teachers, as Beth, Jane, and Joe reminded me, that we all have the possibility of stretching into zones of uncertainty. Through such experiences, we develop theories of practice based partly on what takes place in the classroom and partly on how we scrutinize the results. The sheer pleasure is in the possibilities.

Chapter Six

Developing Habits of Mind

Much of the first year of teaching for Avis, Stephen, Sarah, and Ben was experienced in the agony of possibility, as I suggested in Chapter Two. As Ben said, "I recognize that most of my students think school is irrelevant, but I keep hoping to arouse their interests and get them involved in their reading and writing lives. I hope they'll find pleasure and get hooked." It was in these first-year teachers' classrooms, no matter what the feelings of uncertainty or possibility, no matter how much agonizing or reflecting, that they found themselves in a position where they must take action in the present moment. These four teachers learned that it was in the classroom where they had to take action simultaneously negotiating the multiple motivations, intentions, and demands. As Sarah suggested, it is "the place where I realize how much teaching involves thinking on our feet."

Avis, Stephen, Sarah, and Ben increasingly understood the classroom as a complex cultural setting in which they must take some responsibility for shaping as well as being shaped. In short, they began teaching with the implicit understanding that there are practices, traditions, and expectations that constitute the culture in which education takes place. Yet, the knowledge of this culture that they learned as students must now be reconceptualized and possibly transformed as they learned to make reasoned pedagogical and management choices within the classroom community. Learning to be a teacher involves knowing explicitly that the learning environment as a social construction can be recreated or changed. This knowledge enables teachers to reflect on what is going on and to imagine how it might be otherwise. I would suggest that these first-year teachers understood early on that they must develop the ability to reflect during the teaching act itself. As Avis reasoned, "It is easier to think about what will or did go on when the classroom is empty or when I'm sitting with a late-night cup of coffee. It's much harder to assess what is going on when I'm actually teaching."

What's Going on Here?

Avis, Stephen, Sarah, and Ben gained knowledge about the life and learning that went on in their classrooms by identifying and examining the multiple intentions and agendas that contributed to what took place at a particular moment during a class session. They learned that their beliefs and priorities as well as those of others were inextricably interwoven and that whatever planning or predicting they did was ultimately subject to improvisation as the events of the day unfolded. Recognizing the importance of articulating the mental activities behind their actions, Avis, Stephen, Sarah, and Ben recognized how important it was to their future practice to constantly ask: "What's going on here?" In so doing, they began a critical study of both their practices and the school culture in which those practices were conceptualized. This principle became a habit of their *praxis* as they continually struggled to clarify and to pattern events out of their insights.

In October, Avis, Stephen, Sarah, and Ben suggested that it was time for me to observe their classrooms for the first time. In the section that follows, I have reconstructed these class sessions. The commentary provided after each scenario highlights some issues that demonstrate how each of these teachers reflected on the events that took place during the class session. As I suggested in Chapter Five, part of the process of examining these scenarios is to read the class session as a text, subject to multiple readings and interpretations. Or, as Gayatri Spivak (1990) argues, to be open to "a weave of knowing and not knowing which is what knowing is" (p. 78). Reading their classroom as a text enabled these four teachers to position themselves so that they could examine, as inquirers, what went on there. It was in their classrooms that they learned to enact what they had been so carefully prepared to do as English teachers—read a text while remaining attentive to setting, various events, themes, characters, metaphors, irony, and style.

Sarah Martin: "Learning to Talk Beyond Myself"

9:25 A.M., October 16

The first girl I commandeer has on a sleeveless T-shirt with *Save The Earth* stenciled across the front. She probably paid extra to have the Levi cut-offs shagged at the bottom. "Can you tell me how I get to the third floor, Ms. Martin's room?" I ask her.

"Uh-huh," she motions for me to follow. "I'm headed that way." I scramble to catch up with her. "Thanks, this is a new school for me." She glances over and eyes me up and down, then up again. "What ya here for?"

"Ms. Martin asked me to visit." She looks away. "You a teacher?"

"You got it. High school for a long time; now it's university."

She smirks as we begin to climb the stairs. "So, you taught her I'll bet." "Ms. Martin's cool and she likes us. She's okay. She's doing great." It sounds like a threat.

"Yeah, that doesn't surprise me. What's your name?" I glance her way.

"Tiffany. Tiffany Greenwood." She pauses. "She's good, you know. I'll be in here next period." Her outstretched arm points me into the room on the right. "Stick around. I'll see you then." With that she disappears around the corner.

Students file in. They notice me and pass looks among themselves. The bell rings as several make a leap for their desks.

"All right," says Sarah, followed by an introduction of me. One student is taking attendance; another reads excerpts from *The Crucible;* a third reads the minutes of what took place the day before.

Sarah begins. "Now that we've finished this play, think back to the part that you remember vividly. The one you drew." She gestures toward the wall where the art work hangs. "Could you think about how you see that scene now that you've finished reading the play? Take fifteen minutes to write about this in your *Crucible* log." Students begin to shuffle through their notebooks. Students laugh and talk and shuffle more. A few are writing. [Ten-minute interval]

"Whadda ya want us to do Ms. Martin? I don't get what we are supposed to write," Tim whines in exasperated tones. Sarah explains again. She walks toward the art work. "Now let's take Tim's as an example since he's asked the question. Tim, what scene is this?"

"It's the courtroom. I just thought about the time there."

"Why all the black and gray?" Sarah asks.

"I just thought the court was solemn and scary and colorless," Tim answers.

"Now write about your interpretation through the art for a few minutes," Sarah says again.

[Ten-minute interval]

"Ms. Martin?"

"Yes, Eliot."

"I think until a director can see how a playwright sees a scene, the play is still just words."

"That's a good point, Eliot. Let's take that idea for a minute. Is it how a director sees what a playwright sees? Is that what you said?"

"Yes." Eliot nods his head.

"Can the director decide what he or she sees rather than trying to imagine what Miller was seeing?" A few hands shoot upward.

"Lydia, what about that?" Sarah steps toward her.

"Well, like you've been saying, a reader sort of creates an interpretation. Directors do that too."

"Take a few minutes to discuss that idea with your study group," Sarah says walking back to her desk. [Eight-minute interval]

"We're not sure if we're discussing what you want us to Ms. Martin? Anything? Or is there a specific question?" It's Joseph asking. Sarah begins a more careful explanation. "This idea that a performed play is an interpretation of a script, like a movie is an interpretation of a book."

Marguerita interrupts, "Like *Hook*. Some director, huh? His interpretation. Not the story I read when I was a kid." Sarah nods, "Well, I guess, Marguerita, there are readings and there are *extreme* readings." She sounds weary now. "Anyway, talk about that."

Joslyn asks, "Weren't we supposed to write about how our interpretation changed? I'm confused. Are we talking about that or about directors or are we writing?"

"Well, it's related," Sarah suggests. "I mean talk now about how your interpretation changed from earlier. A director would have an interpretation too."

"But after he's studied a play," Ray suggests.

Sarah picks up on Ray's comments: "Well, then, how would any of you change the scene you drew earlier if you were going to film or put this play on stage. That helps, Raymond. Does that help?" Sarah asks the class. A few nod. Sarah glances at the clock. "You've got ten minutes before the bell." Students shift. They move into discussion groups but everyone is waiting for the bell.

Exploration. As in the previous chapter, it seems appropriate to begin the discussion of Sarah's class session by encouraging the reader to examine this classroom session through description and analysis. The following questions serve as a guide to that exploration. You may want to write out some of your responses to the following questions:

- What is happening, specifically in terms of identifying multiple intentions, agendas, or understandings?

- In what ways do you think Sarah is extending the limits of her present knowledge during this particular class session? For example, do you see her struggling with particular issues, moments of action, or student reactions?
- What are some possible moments during this lesson where you expect Sarah is working hard to determine "what is going on"?
- How might what is happening during this class session be informative to Sarah's future teaching?

Commentary. Sarah suggested during an interview later in the day, "Sometimes I feel like I'm treading water. I don't quite know where I'm taking them. I want activities that are enjoyable, but, more importantly, are meaningful. I'm not entirely sure I'm doing both. They had a great time drawing the scene, but then I wasn't certain what to do with it. I decided to get them to think about whether their way of seeing the scene changed after they had all the events of the play. They got confused about what they were supposed to do." Sarah expressed a common aim of most teachers—being conscious of the purposes behind their actions. Through her reflective inquiry, Sarah discovered that the cause of some of her frustration during this particular lesson was directly related to her lack of clarity of purpose.

Clarification of purpose. Sarah commented that she did "not have a clear idea, until I tried to field questions, that I hadn't really articulated what I wanted to do with this lesson." Sarah began by asking the students to use their drawing to test their developing interpretations. She gave instructions for them to write about the differences in early and later interpretations but lost track of this focus as students began to question what they were supposed to do. "Then, things got confusing," Sarah remembered. "I didn't know and the students didn't have any idea what we were trying to do." She explained that Eliot's statement, "I think until a director can see how a playwright sees a scene," confused her. As she said in the interview, "I led them [students] to a different issue, which was basically about interpretation and not changing interpretations. They got more confused then." After the exchange with Eliot, Sarah wasn't certain how to move the lesson forward: "I just decided to see if they could work it out together. I told them to just discuss this on their own. I just quit and hoped the bell would ring."

Sarah recognized that she needed to refine her purposes with enough clarity so as to articulate her intentions with more precision. During the interview, Sarah pinpointed particular moments from the class session where her responses or examples did or did not support her intentions. She then illustrated where and why students were confused and how she might have contributed to their confusion. Once Sarah determined the problem areas she speculated on how she might plan differently in the future in order to avoid confusion. "I'm thinking that it's important to write out the pivotal questions that will move a discussion forward. For example, I needed to have a particular question in mind that would make the connection with developing interpretations. That would be more useful planning than what I'm doing now, which is to list the sequence of what will happen in class." Through this inquiry, Sarah demonstrated her openness to critique her teaching and set future goals.

Modeling possible approaches. Sarah used Tim's question as a way to model how "students might evaluate their drawings as one of many interpretations that will lead to their final interpretation." What Sarah accomplished, however, was not what she had intended. Sarah asked Tim to elaborate on what he had drawn and why he used the black and gray. Once Tim gave the answer that "the court was solemn and scary" Sarah suggested that he write about that interpretation for a few minutes. What she didn't do was tie this idea to how his interpretation of the courtroom had or had not changed after he finished reading the play. As Sarah suggested in the interview, "I knew when I said that to Tim that something was wrong, but I couldn't quite figure out what. Now that I've thought about it, I didn't take him out of the old interpretation to think if he had a different view of the courtroom now. I could have asked: How do you see the courtroom now? Has that changed?"

Sarah suggested that she uses modeling as a way "to show I'm open and responsive to students' questions and confusions. I want them to know I take them seriously." The ability to "read" what would be an appropriate and effective way to elucidate the principle behind students' questions or confusions, however, is what separates an effective from an ineffective model. As a teacher learns how to read the particular configuration of needs, then a successful model can be implemented in order to aid students' understanding. Proceeding on the assumption that such modeling allows students "to be presenters of knowledge of their own learning," Sarah believed it was her responsibility to facilitate that effectively. Although Sarah takes a central role in the involvement and shaping of such modeling, she recognized during her reflections on this lesson that such modeling must clarify the purposes of the lesson. "I am finding that using their questions or their work to clarify a situation is a good practice, but I need to be clear on where the modeling will take students."

Future possibilities. What was particularly interesting in Sarah's pedagogical inquiry was how she used her experiences from the day to develop a plan for future action. For example, Sarah noted that she had not monitored whether any of the students actually wrote in their *Crucible* logs. "I just went with where they took me because I wanted to keep them thinking. I could have called for examples of what they wrote down and then used those to show examples that would demonstrate the assignment. That would be a more effective way to monitor than to use Tim's question to elaborate before I know if it's just Tim who doesn't understand or the whole class." Sarah's inquiry was a powerful way for her to bring to consciousness what took place during the class and what she believed might work more effectively. She decided that it would be helpful to find ways to evaluate how her assignments were interpreted by students. Sarah described this concern by stating, "I'm not sure that relying on their questions alone will help me know how the whole class is doing. I need to find ways to monitor what they are writing down as they're working."

Alternative conceptions of how to assess students' understanding will require experimentation with methods, but Sarah is engaged in the struggle to create and examine her practices. Her reflections illustrate that each teaching episode becomes a site for interrogation of her evolving actions as a teacher. She considered possibilities that might go unexamined if she were not an active agent in her own critique and subsequent action. At the same time, Sarah grew increasingly convinced that she wanted her students to take responsibility for moving beyond the structures she created. "I want students to set some of their own tasks. I would have loved it if they'd just ignored my questions and taken some direction of their own. Maybe it's early in the year. I'm trying to think of ways to turn over some of the classroom to them."

Procedural strategies. Sarah had structures in place that were intended to give students a part in managing the classroom. As Sarah explained it, various students are assigned different roles weekly. One student takes attendance. Another records what takes place in class and reads the minutes the next day "to remind the students what went on. This helps everybody refocus, and it's valuable for those who were absent." A third reads excerpts from the piece of literature that is being studied or a related text. "I know what I have in place is minimal, but it is a start. Even though I've decided what their involvement will be, they take the responsibility for getting class started."

Sarah struggled throughout the year with how to get students more integrally involved in their own learning. She analyzed the class session I'd observed to make her point. "They were just following and basically asking: What do you want us to do? They weren't involved really. Well, a couple of times when they thought about films and when Marguerita thought about the interpretation in *Hook*. How could I set up the class so they would keep moving forward without me always the central person? I can't figure that." Sarah drew on her own past experiences to recall that she did not have any models for getting students involved. Although Sarah's goals were to expand student control, she realized that she also was "a control freak. I want my expectations to be clear and consistent, but for students to adapt these to their own needs. I'm not certain how both are possible." As Sarah described it, "I plan for theme and structure. For the theme I come up with an idea that I think is important to cover. I pose questions, get students to write, and talk about what they write with partners or in small groups. Then, I deal with issues in the class. There's a sameness."

Sarah found that it was difficult to engage students when she exerted such control. "Ten seconds often seems like forever, and I can't stand that I'm always throwing out questions, and students seldom just take over. Their responses are short; they don't engage with a text. I want them to build a discussion from their questions and response journals, but it seldom happens." Thoughts such as these marked the beginning of Sarah's quest for a wider range of instructional approaches that would give students the space to invent their own learning. Confronted with this goal, however, Sarah was not certain how to move the class toward that end. Sarah noted, "The students resist freedom mightily. They remind me of my friend's terrier, Taffy, who won't urinate unless my friend is standing next to her. But my friend *trained* her. It's no wonder. I don't want to *train* students, but I haven't quite figured how to lead them and empower them. Learning to talk beyond myself. That's what I need to do."

Stephen Lyon: Patience and Resolve

10:35 A.M., October 16

Sarah walks me across campus to Stephen's building. She's analyzing the past forty minutes and intermittently greeting students. "You probably think I didn't learn anything," is the last thing she says as she holds open the door to Stephen's classroom. There are paneled walls and desks arranged amphitheater style. Stephen's desk is covered with stacks of student papers, folders, and notebooks.

Stephen walks in with some students, his face fixed in a frown. He is holding a squirt gun in the palm of his hand. "Water is one thing; clorox quite another, and neither are appropriate in school. I have to write this up. You ruined Lisa's dress." The three young men roll their eyes in unison. Stephen sees me and gives me an exasperated look. He shuffles through papers in his desk drawer for discipline forms as the rest of the students come in, including Lisa, tears streaming down her cheeks and bleached spots making geometric designs on her hunter green dress. The bell rings. Sarah tells Stephen "Good luck" as she heads back to the other building. A cluster of girls surround Lisa. The boys look smug. "Mr. Lyon, it's no big deal. Lisa was asking for it. Come on, let it go." Stephen jots notes on the form. "OK, let's get started." He looks right through the three culprits, then turns and says to them: "You'll be hearing from Mr. Anderson's office. Take your seats. We're wasting time."

The kid nearest Stephen steps in his path and pushes his over-sized fist into Stephen's face. I suspect his shirt size must by 17½ plus. "Wasting time? That's all we do in here every day. I hate getting in those groups. I hate this class. I don't know what the hell's going on in here."

"Enough out of you, Tom," Stephen says and walks around him. "Get with us or go to Anderson's office now and sit this one out. Either way we're going on."

"Let's settle down. Stephen wipes his forehead with the handkerchief he takes from his pocket. Tom leans over and says something to the girl behind him. They chuckle. Lisa flashes Tom an "if looks could kill glance." Most of the students just stare at Stephen. A few who want to be helpful open their notebooks and turn to the appropriate place in *Walden*.

Stephen continues. "How easy would it be to just drop out of society? I don't know about you, but I feel a bit like it myself." A few students laugh. Lisa is concentrating on the clorox patterns that are turning whiter. Tom's friend wisecracks something about how they'd love to have Mr. Lyon drop out too. Laughter.

Stephen repeats. "How easy would it be to drop out for two and a half years?" One hand. "What's your answer, Patrick?" Stephen looks hopeful as he asks. Patrick says, "People do it all the time. We call them homeless." Snickers from the inner circle of boys who are still fuming. The disrupters have asides for each other.

"Mr. Lyon?"

"Yes, Brady."

"Why are we reading this? This weirdo goes to live in the woods. So what's the big deal?"

"I guess that's what I hope you'll explore." Stephen takes a deep breath. "Maybe someone can tell us what they've found personally important."

Rebecca says, "I think Thoreau thought it was important to leave behind all of the distractions and get to know himself and nature better."

"I'm thinking he was self-centered. It's selfish to leave your responsibilities," Ron says.

"I think he's saying something to us about how we buy into and accept the conventional. We can be too conventional." Jamie leans over and stares at Ron.

"Yes. Does what you're saying give you any reasons why *Walden* has been important reading for many people?" Stephen says in a near whisper, as if his voice were an intruder. Take a few minutes and talk about that with your reading partner." [Fifteen-minute interval]

Stephen brings the class back together. "What did you decide Thoreau has to say that is important?"

"Thoreau dreams. We all do. But he chooses to live the dream. It's austerity for him. It's his way of giving up the material for the essential—planting, fertilizing and harvesting the crops. Enjoying the rhythms and worshiping the sun and poverty. I don't know if he's right but he makes me think it's possible." Rebecca finishes by saying she could make a list as long as her arm "of Thoreau's dreams."

Stephen asks the class, but mostly Rebecca, whether dreams are important.

"It's the pond," Tom suddenly enters the conversation. "The pond helps him figure things out. It's like the place he gets to know himself and the Universe. It's eternal. He says something about Walden Pond existed before Adam and Eve. Then, it starts to die in winter but by May it revives. It's rebirth, the cycle."

Everyone is quiet for a moment before Doug, a fawn featured young man next to the overgrown Tom, says, "Yeah, like Tom said. I was thinking how nature, I mean, anything in nature sort of helps us or at least me see myself."

Melissa interrupts. "I don't get why he tells about the bug at the end. What's that about?" Stephen writes her question on the board, then suggests that students meet with their dialogue partners. "Write a few questions and then select one to put on the board. From those, let's plan the last two days of our work on Thoreau's *Walden*."

Stephen eyes the wall clock. "You have about fifteen minutes before the bell. That should give you time to decide your most burning question." Stephen heads to the back of the room, down the aisle past Tom. He gives him a pat, ever so briefly, on his shoulder as he passes. Tom seems not to notice. He stops to ask Lisa if she's okay. She nods. Stephen shakes his head and says he's sorry it happened. Lisa gives him a tentative smile. "My mother may kill me."

Exploration. A close examination of the complex series of interactions that occurred during this class session is a reminder of how a teacher must observe students carefully and monitor their developing reactions. Take some time to reexamine and react to the events that transpired in Stephen's class. You might use the prompts after Sarah's class session to guide this exploration.

Commentary. "Whew. I wasn't certain I could get or keep control over the situation." This was Stephen's first comment as we began the interview. There was a fragile truce discernable in the room by the end of the period, but the beginning of the class period was nearly explosive. Some students were edgy and others mad. Stephen showed outward signs of frustration. He took on a role of disciplinarian, a role which he suggests "is frustrating, and I don't like to have that image with the kids."

Control over the situation. Stephen determined that it was best to move forward with the lesson. Part of his decision was based on his belief that "most of the thirty students in the room weren't really involved in the squirt gun incident. So I had some kids who were angry, others amused, and a few removed. It didn't make much sense to ruin a class period, so I just tried to get this under control and move on." What happened during this class session was an example of how a particular situation can influence a teacher's plans. Stephen indicated that his original intention was to have the students examine how Thoreau's closeness to nature led to his understanding about human nature. "I intended to give them some excerpts from Eiseley where he uses the lessons from nature to show something about human nature. Then, I hoped to get the students interested in writing an autobiographical piece on a time when they learned something about human nature from the natural world."

Stephen found himself in a difficult situation. He knew it was important to ease the tension, and he determined that the best way to do this was to move forward with the discussion on Thoreau. Stephen said, "I went with the thing I was feeling, ready to drop out and escape the situation." These feelings underlie much of what went on throughout the class session as Stephen attempted to "keep the work going so that tempers are kept under control." The ability to "read" student moods and attitudes is particularly crucial when an extremely volatile incident has occurred. Add to that the difficult task of "keeping the lesson going." Stephen suggested that behind all of this was a larger purpose. He wanted to "let the students know that I do care how they behave both inside and outside the classroom and that they have some obligations to each other to be decent." When Stephen said this I thought about what Vito Perrone (1991) suggested in *A Letter to Teachers:* "Teaching is first and foremost a moral and intellectual endeavor, always beginning with children and young people and their intentions and needs" (p. 52). In this difficult moment, Stephen attended to the students' needs on both an emotional and intellectual level.

Clarification of purpose. "Tom's comment really hit home. I know he was mad and wanted to strike out at me, but I think he's partially right. I'm not certain the kids do know most of the time what the hell's going on in here. I find that the hardest part." Stephen conceptualizes his plans day by day and week by week. He confronts the constant fear that "things won't hold together. I keep trying to think of how small group discussions are connected to dialogues or response logs are connected to content. I try to provide maximum experiences for students to connect and reflect. But, I haven't figured out how to create an environment in which that can happen." Stephen struggled not so much with specific assignments but with how to make all of the separate pieces connect into a conceptual whole.

For example, Stephen had the students keep journals with a dialogue partner as they read *Walden*. He believed the journal would help students monitor their own readings and provide a record for later reflection. The dialogue partner reacted and provided comments and questions. The partners examined their individual and shared modes of response and developing meaning. Stephen believed that asking students to connect with one another's readings gave legitimacy to personal responses and highlighted the active role of readers. But, as he suggested, "I still don't know how any of that procedure connects to what they learn or how individual assignments connect. It was easy to decide to use Eiseley and have students write autobiographical pieces, but how will that fit to a larger concept? That's where I'm puzzled. I can figure the day-to-day and some of that is good, but neither I nor the students know what the next day will bring." Stephen expressed his need for an overall plan that would make sense to him and the students. He wanted the work to be purposeful. "If I could figure out how to accomplish that I think it would exert a powerful influence on what curriculum means to my teaching." Stephen's concerns for a larger framework of understanding curriculum have led him to recognize the complexity of determining how specific classroom activities or events fit into the broader network of purpose.

Conscious involvement. Stephen's initial question sets the focus for discussion: "How easy would it be to just drop out of society?" Stephen described how those first moments were "rocky getting started. Mostly Tom and that crew wanted to torment me. Patrick with his homeless remark just wanted to show his loyalties to Tom. Then, Brady with the why are we reading this question." Stephen used Brady's question to move the conversation to students' personal reactions. This set off a series of responses before Stephen prodded students, through Jamie's comment, to consider why people might find this reading valuable. Stephen believed that his question on the importance of this reading to other people led the students to a "series of responses that were really important—Thoreau's dreams, Tom's reflections on the importance of the pond. I wish I'd picked up there with the Eiseley and student autobiographical writing. Doug gave me another chance to do it. His statement was just beautiful. It would have been perfect, but I was still rattled. I haven't had to deal with a discipline issue like that before."

Stephen recognized the importance of knowing where to lead students and of making effective transitions when the opportunity arose. Although Stephen did not funnel all responses through himself, he was still very much in control. He entered the discussion when he wanted to redirect points that were made, but he seldom repeated what had been said. One of Stephen's goals is "To stand outside of the conversation sometimes and let the students take over. I want the role of stepping in occasionally to redirect or focus their responses." He accomplished this at times during the discussion. For example, he used Melissa's question to redirect student attention to their lingering questions. These questions would guide discussion during the final two days of work on *Walden*. Stephen created conditions that promote involvement. As he suggested during the interview, "I can't quite figure out how to deploy everything at once—how to set agendas and have students refine or break them, how to model for them but not overcome them, how to get them started thinking but allow them to think for themselves. I just can't imagine how to do this all at once. I'm learning piecemeal as I go."

Making compromises. "Patience and resolve. Patience and resolve. I kept saying this over and over to myself as this class period began. I handled the situation well and kept the discussion going even if it wasn't exactly the one I intended to have. I'm proud of that actually." Stephen wasn't having much luck provoking more than oblique interest in *Walden* at the beginning of the discussion. Later in the class

session, students made assertions and moved toward some involvement with the discussion. As they focused their attention on the text,
the tension that had been triggered by the events at the beginning of
class began to diffuse. Tom's involvement near the end of the class
session could be interpreted in many ways. I found it an interesting
way for him to signal to Stephen that he was sorry; it was a peace offering of sorts. It might have been that he simply got involved in the
text and the discussion, but whatever the motivation, Tom found a
way to defer his anger, and he let Stephen know that.

Looking back at the transcript and my field notes, I realize how
inadequately I've represented Stephen. Teaching wasn't only the lesson, the classroom management, the content, or what happened in
the forty-seven minutes this group spent together; it was partly all of
these things and more. Tom's entrance into the conversation through
his underlying hostility, Stephen's pat on Tom's shoulder, and his
question to Lisa about how she was doing all reflect an underlying
environment of care and deference. I was reminded during this particular class session how affective, as well as intellectual, teaching is.
Structures, practices, and the best laid plans do not take place in the
abstract; they are situational. Stephen confronted his fear about "being in control. I worry that some situation will explode and I won't
know how to handle it. Much of teaching is about making compromises. I'm learning that and remembering that it takes patience and
resolve." Although Stephen wanted to make it clear that there were
limits to what disruptive behavior would be tolerated, his main goal
was to help his students work through their own problems and find
acceptable avenues for dealing with controversy. In this particular
case, Thoreau was an important source of helping the students
"read" beyond the present moment.

Avis Johnston: Foregrounding Student Responses

7:30 A.M., October 18

In fifteen minutes, I've driven from streets alive with honking
horns, the screech of tires on concrete, and the haze of industrial
pollution to a countryside tamed by earth plowed into straight fur-
rows, dried corn stalks cut down in a crew cut stubble, and hills, yellow with winter wheat. Last week, I read that a work of literature
comes to life only when readers bring their unique experiences to it.
What sensations and concepts and qualities of life will these students
bring to the literature? Even in this car, traveling at 55 mph, as the
landscape before me unfolds and reveals itself, I know more surely
than ever before that this landscape shapes the reading as well as the

writing of literature for those who have lived here. By the time I walk into the building where Avis teaches, I've imagined that I could find peace in this community, that the whirlwinds of dust or shallow backwash ponds swollen with mosquitos and cattail patches help build character. People here would be suspicious of a life too easy.

I suspect these thoughts were going through my mind when I bumped into D. J. Johnson. He raises his brows and breaks into a grin. "You a sub?" "Not me," I smile back and keep eye contact. He's a chunky kid with a blunt haircut. "Too bad, I don't mind sub days. No work, all play, and a little torment."

I nod at what is a major truth. "You know where Ms. Johnston's room is?"

"Yeah. I got her this period." He adds, "It could be worse—she's serious but nice. You a guest speaker?" He joins the stream of students in the hall. I follow close enough to answer. "No, just a guest." I'm almost running to keep up so we don't talk until we nearly crash through a door and enter a small cubicle of a room, empty rows of desks, one high window cut out of cinderblock walls painted pale pink. The fluorescent lights hum overhead. "You just came to school for fun?" He's put his books on a desk near the back. "Curiosity," I tell him just as Avis joins us.

She bites her bottom lip and smiles as color blooms in her cheeks. "I see you found D. J. Thanks D. J.," she says as the bell rings. Students spill into the room. Avis pulls on the door as she walks by and it sighs to a close. I sensed she was ready to begin. Students talk in hushed whispers until Avis introduces me. They stare or nod. Then Avis takes attendance.

"How many of you have known a person who is handicapped in some way?" Avis asks. "I guess we call it physically or mentally challenged." Several hands. "Do you want to tell us about the person you know, Kara?"

"Well," she says, "I have an uncle who had polio, and he still has a leg brace and one crutch. He works in a feed store because he can't work on the farm. It's sort of kept him separate from the rest of the family."

Walter interrupts her. "Talk about separate. I have a cousin who is Downs and it's weird trying to talk to him. We try to be nice to him but he gets mean and throws fits. He's fourteen now and getting too big to handle."

"You're the tough guy, Walter. Just beat him up," D. J. adds. The class laughs.

Avis intercedes. "Okay, let's keep this going and not get silly. I heard both Kara and Walter describe how the person is handicapped and the results of that. Maybe some of you could add other examples?"

Several more students tell about friends, relatives, schoolmates, or other acquaintances. Laura talks about the television series, *Life*

Goes On. She elaborates by suggesting that "the show has changed my image of what a Down syndrome person is like. Corky is warm and intelligent in his way. The family is so accepting, which helped me realize how much difference it makes to have people who care about these problems."

Michelle adds, "What Laurie said reminded me that part of what I learned from *Life Goes On* is not to be afraid of people who are different. Sometimes I get scared. I know that sounds stupid."

Jamie, who has been drawing in her notebook, adds, "I was thinking about all the technology that has helped these people lead normal lives. I have a cousin who lost both arms in Vietnam and he has, whatever you call them, fake arms and hands. He can do almost anything. It's really interesting to watch him eat or use his computer."

"That's for physical disabilities. Do we have advances that affect intelligence?" Avis maneuvers the conversation toward a different end.

"Like artificial intelligence," Jason says. "I don't understand all that but it's really interesting."

"Even computers and calculators are a form of boosting intelligence," Kathleen adds.

Avis asks, "How far should science go to alter intelligence? Do you think some of the advances are beneficial and others aren't ?"

The students list pros and cons with Avis recording on the board. [Ten-minute interval]

Avis asks them to write in their journals. "I'd like you to record some responses that you can look back at a few days from now. Would you list what you think the consequences of increased intelligence could be? Then, explain which consequences are positive and which are negative." [Fifteen-minute interval]

When a few students have finished writing, Avis asks them to share their entries in small groups and to come up with three pros and three cons from each group and list these on the board. [Ten-minute interval]

Avis hands out copies of *Flowers for Algernon.* "The writer, Daniel Keyes," she tells them, "speculated on this same sort of issue. Let's read the opening together." Avis reads the first two pages aloud.

"Now, let's speculate. What do you think will happen?" Students shout out possibilities. Before the bell rings, Avis asks them to read the first fifteen pages for the next day. "Record your reactions as you finish the assigned part and bring those back to work with your group." The bell rings.

Exploration. Take some time to reexamine and react to the events that transpired in Avis' class. Again, the prompts after Sarah's lesson may serve as a guide.

Commentary. Avis indicated as we started the interview that she felt good about the way things had gone during the class session. "It's high interest for them—technology and the idea of altering the mind or body. I'm finding that I can predict their interests better than I could even in the first month." Avis set her instructional goals for this unit and the day from her developing knowledge of student interest. Additionally, she predicts the students' responses as she plans. In this lesson, for example, Avis forecast that the students would move from issues of being physically or mentally challenged to the idea that technology makes it possible to alter those conditions. "I thought they might be more reluctant to use examples of the intellectually challenged from their own families, but Walter did that. That surprised me. I was delighted how they moved to the *Life Goes On* example. What's funny is that last night I thought that might happen. I nearly laughed out loud when Laura brought it up. I wanted to pat myself on the back."

Forecasting student responses. Avis intended to spend more time on the artificial intelligence example. When students became involved in the stories of family and friends, however, she determined that it was important to let that develop. "I could see the next move in my head. I didn't panic. I knew there would be enough time to push the idea into *Flowers,* and then we can come back to the artificial intelligence issue over the next few days. It was amazing. I played some of that out in my mind as the discussion was moving forward. I'm starting to feel how that works." For Avis, the most important aspect of her ability to forecast student responses is that she can relax more and let the discussion develop. When Jamie described the technology that allowed her uncle to be reasonably self-sufficient, she gave Avis a point for segue, and Avis was skilled enough to recognize this and use the moment to introduce the ethics of technology. Learning to predict how the discussion will develop has given Avis a sense of security. "That helps me with the flow of activities. I run and rerun a film in my head of how the class might go. I'm learning how students respond."

Avis' ability to anticipate students' actions, interests, reactions, and interactions gives her an understanding from which she can feel more at ease in the ebb and flow of discussion. She is not tied to her plans as she learns to predict how to make spontaneous choices based on her prior knowledge of how events in the classroom unfold and how students might react. Avis is learning to read the classroom through her critical observations and predictions. Her developing perspectives on what and why things happen as they do can aid her in understanding how to direct her actions and achieve her purposes.

Questioning techniques. Avis believed that her students would be motivated to read *Flowers for Algernon* if they had important questions and speculations that they carried into the reading. Although the questions Avis asks are open-ended, they are purposeful. She let the students shape the discussion, but she had signposts, places where she maneuvered the discussion to a more definite focus and speculation. She had structures in place that helped her students process their ideas—journals, small groups, and whole class discussion. Avis helped them to frame their experiences and speculations in ways that foregrounded the upcoming reading. She hoped that this would open up the possibility for continued personal responses. Avis did not want students to fish for answers to questions that she had raised. Rather, she wanted to "get them involved in the debate about the uses and abuses of technology. Then this story will be particularly relevant."

Avis indicated that she's learned that students engage more with literature if they hook onto some questions, beliefs, or speculations about life that they can "play out as they read. Their curiosities keep them going, and I'm finding that I try to prod them into their questions. I don't know how to do that effectively yet, but I have some ideas." Avis created structures in which she encouraged individual and group interpretations to develop over time (i.e., "record so we can see this later"). She tried to diffuse authority of meaning as residing in the teacher or any one reader. "I wanted them hungry to read and respond. I wanted them to think of the pros and cons. I wanted them to prioritize those." "Just experimenting" is Avis' description of how she is learning to question, but it is clear that she is doing this in the context of what she is learning about teaching. Her purposeful reflection reminded me of what Maxine Greene (1978b) stressed in her discussion about the personal reality of teaching: "And what we do cannot be simply routine and mechanical; it must be conscious, interested and committed" inquiry into the realities of teaching (p. 26).

Clarification of purpose. The key objectives Avis had for this lesson were to highlight students' experiences with disability, explore the challenges for the disabled, and discuss the ethical issues of altering intelligence through technology. Her purpose in structuring the lesson in this way was to provide opportunities for students to connect their personal experiences with those they might find in *Flow-*

ers. Avis hoped that her use of written responses, lists of pros and cons, and connection with personal experience would help students examine their developing reactions, connect the text to personal experience, note developing and potential meanings, and generate additional questions. As Avis said, "When I think of the educational experience in this class, I want students to have meaningful engagements with literature. The more they write, talk, connect, and think, the more they become readers. It's their responses that count."

Avis was alert to the dangers of staying too long with any one form of processing information. For that reason, she had students relate their personal experiences in the large group discussion for approximately fifteen minutes. Then students brainstormed a list of pros and cons on the board before Avis asked them to respond in their journals. She indicated that "it is important to give them something to work from. Otherwise they just don't have models of what to do. Then I get question after question, so I try to avoid that with a very careful set-up and example. That's really what we spent all that time doing on the board." Students did not ask for clarification on the directions and appeared clear on what they were supposed to do. It was obvious that Avis was sensitive to the rhythms of the students' work.

Avis scanned the room regularly to evaluate student mood and their involvement in the work. By the time students became restless with the journal work, Avis moved them into another facet of the assignment. They shared entries with small groups and were instructed to reach a consensus of three pros and three cons to list on the board. With this list as a backdrop, Avis began reading from *Flowers for Algernon.* She moved forward with ease and definitiveness. There was fluidity in the movement from one facet of the assignment to the next. As Avis suggested, "As long as I work off the student responses, the lessons go well. I'm learning." Her perspective on her teaching illustrates the importance of developing a conscious articulation of one's own classroom practices.

Ben Silverman: Connecting to the Landscapes

9:30 A.M., October 19

Rosalinda glances at me briefly and points toward the door. Without a word, she turns and glides from the room. I follow, then catch up with her. Ben told me the night before that he would send Rosalinda to the office, and she would escort me to the classroom.

"Mr. Silverman told me your name is Rosalinda." She nods. I can't help thinking what Gloria Anzaldua (1987) kept hearing as a child: *En boca cerrada no entran moscas.* "Flies don't enter a closed mouth." She is a respectful girl and doesn't look me in the face. Humble, *humilde.* Deferential. Distant.

By the time we arrive in Ben's room, Rosalinda is telling me that her youngest brother, the eleventh sibling, was born just last week. Her parents and older brothers work in the orchards. Rosalinda takes a deep breath as we step into the classroom. I can only think she is relieved to turn me over to Ben and end this conversation. She walks away.

Ben is a natural athlete. His handsome face has the sharp curves and crevices of workouts, sun, and a diet of little fat. Only his delicate hands betray the gentleness of his character. The room is yellow with a low tile ceiling, obviously added to what was once the higher, airier ceilings of schools built around the turn to the century. Near the single window are rows of nearly empty book shelves. As Ben tells me, "I've been haunting garage sales for any literature and trying to find some Chicano, Hispanic, or Latino literature as well. That I buy new. Nobody around here is reading it." Student biography poems and self-portraits clutter one wall. Some are written in Spanish; the rest in English.

The far wall is shedding its plaster; buckets and garbage cans catch today's heavy cloudburst. "Really," Ben tells me, "between puberty and the reverberations of rain in this room we're not making much progress." I'm thinking how much I'd like the State legislators and the lawyers and stock brokers on the school board as well as the Federal Senator who owns the orchard where many of these adolescents' parents work to spend a few days in this classroom.

Ben starts class by entertaining a question brought up the day before: Does the landscape on which we live affect how we act, feel, or believe? He asks them to report the results of their homework which was a search for examples of how the landscape does or does not affect people. First, they share in small groups. Then, Ben asks the students for examples that can be listed on the board. [Sixteen minute interval]

"Sunrise," says one young man decked out in a flannel shirt and worn jeans. "So much depends on what the sky brings. In my house, we gauge the weather that way—it's an investment in crops and livestock."

A plump girl talks about the rough, scrub desert. "It's a starkness and the intense smoldering of heat that keeps so many of the people in this place edgy. Take my father. When it's scorching, his mood gets short, his neck turns red, and there's no relief. The heat burns into us."

So softly at first that it was hard to hear him, Juan tells how his

Papa always talks about the Barrio. "He's gone ten years except he still lives there in his mind. He doesn't forget how things are. He sings the songs and promises to take us there for tortillas cooked on the iron stove."

Jeremy says, "My father's obsession is to buy up more land. He seems to think the more he owns, the more he can control what happens. It's like he gets some kicks from looking out over the horizon to see everything he owns. I don't get it. He doesn't want to go back anywhere. He wants to keep taking in."

Ben's eyes scan the group after he's listed their responses on the board. Most students are looking at their notebooks or the floor. No one else seems eager to talk so he asks, "Do you think a particular place, a landscape, I mean, could change the person you are or bring out characteristics that haven't necessarily surfaced in you?"

"Sure," says the boy the other kids call Monster. "People do weird things when they get away from the places and people they know. People we live with expect us to behave in certain ways and if they're not around, well, we can lose it."

"Does the landscape affect that as well as the people?" Ben begins to pace through the rows of desks. Silence. "I mean, what if you were suddenly trasported somewhere else?"

"Are we talking about science fiction?" Derek asks.

"Well maybe but not necessarily," Ben replies.

"Do you mean like *The Hobbit* or *Chronicles of Narnia?*"

"Well, I didn't have a particular example in mind. Imagine this. Your plane crashed on an island. Now the catch is—there are no adults, only kids your age and no hope for immediate rescue. The place is deserted. What do you think will happen? No, it's more than that—this is a plush island, so there is plenty to eat and it is covered with vegetation."

"Party time."

"Cool," Monster shouts. "Ultimate freedom."

"There's got to be a catch," Kathy says. "Like animals or cannibals or Monster would be there." Most of the students laugh.

"Let's think about the possibilities for a few minutes," Ben continues. "In your journal, just imagine that you've survived the crash and the adults with you died. Write about your first reactions and concerns."

Some students reach for their notebooks. "So, I don't get it," Brenda says. "We wouldn't have paper and pen. How could we write?"

Ben shakes his head. "I want to know what you might think. What's going through your mind. We'll write it down so you have it as we continue discussion."

"Why did the plane crash?" Jose wants to know.

"Well it doesn't matter for this piece of writing, does it?" A frown begins to take over Ben's face. "Just write about your first reactions."

"Mr. Silverman?" Richard has soft curls that fall in curves over his ears.

"Yes, Richard."

"Can I borrow a pen?"

For a moment I can see muscles in Ben's shoulders tense. Then he walks toward his desk and picks up a pen. "Let's see that back on my desk when the bell rings."

Some students are writing; a few chat quietly. Ben paces the room watching. Rosalinda looks out the window where telephone wires stretch from pole to pole, leading over the ridge of rolling hills toward other places. [Fifteen-minute interval] Laughter blares behind me as the bell rings.

Exploration. React to and reexamine the events, the assumptions behind the events, and Ben's particular approach to teaching. Again, use the prompts included after Sarah's lesson to guide you.

Commentary. Ben chose to engage his students in an exploration of the relationship between the landscape and people's behavior as a way to foreground *The Lord of the Flies.* He explicated that purpose in the after-observation interview. "I hope to get students thinking about the wildness and tangle on the island, the darkness and wild boars, and all of the things that are without civilizing influence and how we see the boys becoming more wild. If we start with how they see people connected to the land I'll have more chance of doing that easily."

Clarification of purpose. Ben's clarity of purpose kept the students focused. Students understood and could exemplify Ben's starting question: Does the landscape on which we live affect how we act, feel, or believe? Students were clear about what they were to discuss during their small group meetings. Ben made the shift from how the landscape influences people to how it might change people with the help of Monster's response suggesting that people act strange "when they get away from the places and people they know." Monster elaborated: "People we live with expect us to behave in certain ways and if they're not around, well, we can lose it."

Ben continued this line of thought by asking whether or not a new landscape might change people. Ben's additional comment "if you were suddenly transported somewhere else" seemed to confuse the issue momentarily. Derek's question about science fiction led the discussion temporarily to issues of the surreal or fantastic, but Ben brought students back to reality by suggesting that they imagine themselves in a plane crash. During the interview Ben described that moment. "I could see that it might take us away from the purpose. I was headed as straight line to *The Lord of the Flies* as possible. I didn't want to get off into the science fiction or fantasy genres. Their typical adolescent examples of 'party time, cool, ultimate freedom, and Monster would be there,' focused on the idea of how things would change. Now it was a matter of bringing that back to how the landscape can affect them and how it might change them. I decided that near the end of the period they needed time on their own to start imagining this. Brena's question about not having paper was a good one, and I can think how I could set that up differently another time. Certain items remain from the crash. Conveniently each survivor would have a journal. You know what I mean. Anyway, I think we are off to a good start. I got them connecting to the landscapes." Ben was ready to introduce *The Lord of the Flies*.

Frustrations with fragmentation. Ben derived his idea for introducing *Lord of the Flies* from an exercise he did when he was a student in a high school English class. "The teacher had us speculate on items that we would want with us if we were the last inhabitants on earth—only three that we thought would make a new civilization. I remember we read "The Portable Phonograph" and *Alas Babylon* after that introduction. I just thought about that with *Lord of the Flies* in a different way. I wanted students to imagine what it would be like to have a place to themselves without any of the previous restrictions. We've started to do that, but I'm not sure where it leads. I feel my typical frustration with where I'm headed. I plan a series of little things but without a larger purpose. I don't think that's curriculum." Ben articulated his discomfort with the sense of fragmentation and of not having a larger conceptual framework for curriculum in mind. The deep-rootedness of this desire to have a conceptual road map of the year is nothing new in the themes of Ben's inquiry. Ben consistently thought about a wide range of instructional options to choose from and his decisions were often highly successful. However, he struggled with how all of these tie together into some meaningful whole. Ben indicated that he hoped "to learn this in time. I feel like there is some missing link in how I conceive of all this. I'm hoping this fits together better, but I also sense that there is nothing easy in figuring this out. I have these books we read, a series of things we do with the books, some writing and language study that I try to tie to that. I don't think that makes a curriculum."

The influence of Ben's frustration on his practices was myriad and complex. He did not fall into an easy routine of conducting the day-to-day events with his growing consternation about where all of this was leading. He made constant references to how a particular day's activities grew out of something that had gone before and would be related in some way to what came after. His assessment of his own successes was typically measured by this articulation. "What I learn through teaching each day is invaluable, but the large picture is missing. I figured out how to start *The Lord of the Flies,* but how is this introduction extending something that went before? How will students be different readers when they finish this book than they were before?" Ben engaged in such deliberations because he was struggling to develop a framework of curriculum built on his conception of learning. For him, "learning happens when all the pieces are connected. I don't think it happens in segments. The moments of recognition grow out of a series of things that take place and finally make sense rather than the single incident we remember as important." It was within the multiple and sometimes conflicting contexts of the classroom that Ben engaged in the process of testing out his beliefs about learning and from that articulating what curriculum is and might be. Ben's assumptions about learning and teaching were strikingly consistent when it came to his assumption that there is reason in curriculum to connect all aspects together rather than dealing with discrete parts.

Separate and Distinct. One of the most striking observations I made in Ben's class was the elaborate demarcation of the two very distinct groups of students—the indigenous students and the migrant ones. Although all are rural, farm families, the Chicano families tend to migrate with the seasons and end up in this valley for various crop harvests. The lives between these two groups of students seldom connect. In Ben's classroom the Chicano students sat together, near the back of the room, and with the exception of Juan, did not speak except in small groups and even then the conversations were muted. Juan's participation was interrupted by Jeremy's response. It's difficult to know what all this means, but Ben had a strong opinion on the topic. "I don't think the school really tries to make these students feel a part of what goes on. In part it is understandable because most of them are here a season or part of a season. There is a small group of students from Chicano families who have made this valley their home. They don't fit into the community at large. There seems to be no attempt in the school or community to deal with this. They are the silent minority."

Ben indicated that he didn't interfere with the Chicano students' desire to sit together because "they feel safer and more comfortable. I do wonder, however, if I'm perpetuating a bad thing. It's a difficult call because on the one hand I don't want to throw them into an uncomfortable situation and on the other I feel like I perpetuate what already isn't good." There seemed no easy or possible solution that Ben could discover from within his own resources of imagination, from the other teachers in the school, or from Avis, Stephen, or Sarah. When he spoke of the situation, many people nodded knowingly; others expressed sympathy for what was a difficult situation; some railed against a system that creates such disparity; everyone seemed to believe that finally it was the school's problem and Ben's problem and life would go one without pain or death or destruction. Ben struggled with the issues and the options. "I don't know and can't make many recommendations myself. The situation bleeds into all of the issues of the school, but nobody is willing to talk about it."

Ben indicated that none of the Chicano students were on the track team or in any of the other extracurricular activities. He mentioned that the grade differential between the two groups of students was dramatic. "Many times the Chicano students aren't around for an entire marking period. I'm not certain whether we get or send along school records on many of them. I have a feeling they are a lost population in both the structures we've created for schools and in the paper trail that accompanies students' progress through school. Working with these students has made me wonder what options are available to migratory populations. Schools are created for students who live in one place and that may not be realistic in our society." The issues Ben raised, even in the articulation of them, are complex for the entire educational community let alone a first-year teacher who struggles with so many new demands. But it is clear that Ben is aware and thoughtful about the situation. That is a beginning. Ben lamented, "I just can't imagine how I can learn to handle this better. I don't know where to begin except to be warm and supportive and encourage their smallest attempts to reach out. It's another landscape to contemplate."

The Formation of Habits of Mind

During the observations, I imagined that these same literature texts on these same mornings were being studied in other classrooms throughout the country. In the classrooms where Avis, Stephen, Sarah, and Ben teach, I suspect that the learning of literature did not look much different from what we might see elsewhere. Avis situated her students' personal experiences and curiosities within the context of larger questions about the ethics of technology as preparation for their reading of *Flowers for Algernon.* Stephen engaged students in a discussion about how *Walden* might inform their lives. Sarah helped her students wrestle with concepts of how interpretations are supported, subverted, or changed as the events, characters, and themes of *The Crucible* unfold scene by scene. Ben led his students straight into the implications of *The Lord of the Flies,* a novel that will give them a reflection of human nature with a possible image of what lurks deep within. The events that took place are important, but behind what transpired in the classroom, Avis', Stephen's, Sarah's, and Ben's reflections on these sessions revealed their developing *habits of mind.*

Avis, Stephen, Sarah, and Ben *articulated and clarified their purposes,* and they understood the importance of doing so. Clarity of purpose was regarded as an essential part of planning if a lesson was to unfold with fluidity and direction. Sarah recognized that a lack of clarity in her purpose resulted in student confusion. Stephen explained that his purpose changed as he discovered how context redirects what takes place. Avis learned that student responses are often predictable and that rehearsals of possibility can lead to further clarification. Ben described how his plan for this day worked with some success, but he continued to search for a framework of curriculum that might help him to better structure his broader goals. In each case, these first-year teachers understood that their initial purpose was only part of the possible meaning that could be constructed when competing assumptions were taken into account.

Beneath the more overt understanding of purpose, Avis, Stephen, Sarah, and Ben are learning that in order to *enact* purpose in a lesson, teachers' knowledge about the discipline, curriculum, and pedagogy must *interact* with the immediate responses that express students' needs and desires. It is one thing to impose purpose on students and quite another for an *a priori* purpose to be woven with a *felt* purpose that develops as teachers and students create the direction of the interaction. What habits guide interactive yet purpose-oriented lessons? To be fully purposeful, teachers can develop habits of mind that engage them epistemically and contextually. To be mindful, therefore, is to have both the ability and the disposition to conduct transactions between representations in the mind and representations in the classroom. Such transactions allow teachers to see the teaching episode as a human construction that is rooted in the context of a particular, rather than a generic, time and place.

The ability to recognize the *viability of alternatives* revealed itself as another essential habit of mind. Such recognition enabled

Avis, Stephen, Sarah, and Ben to identify what happened, analyze why it happened, and speculate on possible changes. Doing so increased their insights about contradictory or conflicting intentions, created dissonance that enabled them to reconceptualize practices, and aided them in negotiating the complex social forces underlying teaching practices. They learned the value of entertaining multiple interpretations and varied lines of thought. Avis, Stephen, Sarah, and Ben began to build a pedagogical repertoire of alternative approaches that could be used as classroom events unfolded.

For example, Sarah pinpointed places where she had difficulty clarifying her instructions or intentions for students, so she determined ways to evaluate student understanding that would help her to monitor more fully how to move her lessons forward. Stephen described how the environment of his classroom did not provide students with the structures they might use to direct some of their own learning; therefore, he began to consider ways that he might stand outside the conversation. Avis was excited about her ability to predict student responses, but she was searching for ways to diffuse her control over meaning. Ben struggled to articulate how his lesson fit into his larger purposes. As a result, he determined that he needed to sharpen his understanding of curriculum.

Avis, Stephen, Sarah, and Ben examined the relationship between what they hoped to accomplish and what actually took place as they taught. Without exception, they searched for ways to refine and improve their practices rather than viewing any particular facet of teaching in a fixed or essentialist way. After only six weeks as teachers, they demonstrated habits of mind that helped them to identify problematic practices, imagine promising future practices, and consider how changes in practice might clarify their intentions, involve students more fully, and help them to understand curriculum more richly.

There are many habits of mind, but the ones discussed here represent those that exerted the most immediate pressure on Avis, Stephen, Sarah, and Ben to act on their beliefs rather than simply reproduce information about teaching. Behind what transpires on any given day in the classroom, there are processes that these first-year teachers use to interpret the discursive structures and practices they've implemented. In trying to analyze these habits, I found it important to consider how these first-year teachers think or talk about their practices and their developing knowledge of teaching. It is the way all four have learned to read the classroom as a text that, I would argue, allows them to interpret and create praxis.

In writing this condensed version of their habits of mind, I thought again about the hundreds of faces that I can conjure up from my own years in the classroom and how those students helped me develop my own habits of mind and theories of teaching. One of the faces I see is Lennie's. He must have been nearly sixteen years old the first time he took a seat in the back row during the first period of the first eleventh grade English class I ever taught. Lennie couldn't read. I thought he was stubborn and wouldn't read. I checked with the counselors. Beyond the figures and charts, the knowing looks and shakes of the head, I learned that Lennie had been passed along for eleven years. His parents were illiterate by school standards, so Lennie was an ipso facto write-off. It was general knowledge that the Murphy kids would drop out of school after eighth grade to work on the family farm. Lennie, it was assumed, was no exception. Yet, here he was still holding on to school in the eleventh grade.

Everyone in class knew Lennie couldn't read. He wasn't taunted; he was ignored. It was the way he'd sit in that stolid, silent way, waiting. Unnerved by my lack of knowledge, I began to wish he'd drop out of school. In the next moment, I explained to myself that this situation wasn't my fault. I didn't know how to be a teacher for him. Once I overcame my fear of talking with him, I started being his teacher. I began by searching him out in the halls or cafeteria to ask him about the difficulty of the riding trails in the hills behind his farm or to ask if there were rattlers in the sage. Finally, I had the nerve to ask him to see me after school.

Lennie appeared one October afternoon as I was gathering up my books and papers to leave for the day. I had thought it would be more dramatic—there'd be Lennie saying he desperately wanted to read, a magic moment, a sudden breakthrough. What actually happened taught me about the need for patience in teaching. "Lennie, do you want help with your reading?" I blurted it out before the words stuck in my throat.

"I know water moccasins from rattlers, deer track from elk. That's what I read," he said.

What I learned is that Lennie could read the weather, knew how to build a trap, braided marsh reed into beautiful baskets. He was also highly talented at sketching. Lennie and I shared stories about our common experiences growing up on farms and about the horses we each loved. He led me to the best fossil beds in the area. He came in a couple of times a week after school to share his sketching. He brought fossils, too, hoping I'd help with the identification. That's where I finally hooked him. We went to the school and public libraries and found book after book on fossils and studied the photographs. I read relevant parts of the text to him. He began to yearn for the information that was outside his grasp.

The most immediate strategy I knew for helping him was to read to him and to record reel after reel of books on tape. I started with the books on fossils. We'd check out books; I'd read on tape; he'd take the book home and follow along as best he could, by playing the tape on a recorder we'd checked out from the school library for him to keep at home. Other students joined in when they realized what was going on. Students recorded assigned books on tape for Lennie and other books they thought might interest him.

From Lennie I learned the importance of books on tape for students who want or need that resource. During the years that I served as advisor to the National Honor Society, we made a collection of tapes that were available for check-out in the school library. It was a practice that I kept going throughout my high school teaching career. Since I met him during my first year of teaching, I had few strategies in my pedagogical repertoire to help me know how I might best help him. I learned to listen to Lennie and to develop alternative strategies to meet his needs. He challenged me into uncharted territory, and I couldn't fail him. As I remember Lennie, I hope to remind other teachers just as Avis, Stephen, Sarah, and Ben reminded me that we all have the possibility of stretching into zones of uncertainty. Through such experiences, we develop theories of practice based partly on what takes place and partly on how we scrutinize the results.

Lasting Lessons: Ongoing Inquiry

In early June when the first school year was crawling to a close, I met with Avis, Stephen, Sarah, and Ben. We shared a bottle of wine in a local park to celebrate the upcoming week of semester exams and summer break. The conversation turned to the past year—a year of hopefulness, watchfulness, disappointment, and aching tiredness. Ben said, "I didn't think it would be so hard. I sort of had these visions of my English teachers just coming to class each day to talk about literature. I loved literature so that's what I thought I'd do: get together with kids and talk *to* them about some great literature. The *to* them really got me in trouble."

Stephen thought for a moment before saying: "When I was a student, I didn't ever think about all the decisions teachers make. My image of English class was that we read assigned books, discuss them, take a test, write an essay (with Cliff Notes as a guide). Then, take some time for grammar. I didn't ever figure out what I'd do with that knowledge. What the heck. It was easy. Then another book would be handed out and the cycle would start over. I remember that we mostly wrote essays about literature except for a senior research paper. I wanted to teach English because I liked to read, and I was good at the English game." Avis reflected, "Thanks to my stubbornness, I survived. I learned that I had to distance myself from what I was doing in the classroom or what I had done as an English student in classrooms. That enlarged my vision—the distance I mean. I could take a more critical look at what I'd thought were great experiences in school. There were some, but the majority of my high school experience was the close reading of literature. We spent time writing essays. It was passive in a way. Often it meant figuring out how the teacher interpreted the piece." Ben added, "Yeah, like I said before—there's a lot of talking *to* students about literature and writing. After teaching this year, I know that was my experience. I understand that more than I did before." Sarah contemplated possibilities: "I was just thinking how I assumed that literature study meant answering questions and writing essays and listening to lectures on authors' lives or the meaning of the work. It's been hard to stretch beyond that and find ways that get the kids involved." I learned from Avis, Stephen, Sarah, and Ben how important ongoing discussion is and how their collaborative inquiry helped them identify and deal with their concerns.

Throughout the year, these teachers made observations about their individual experiences that led all of them to tacit understandings about themselves as teachers. Their shared inquiry helped them bring what they were learning about teaching to a conscious level. For example, Avis shared the following log entry with Stephen, Sarah, and Ben:

> By the end of the class period we completed a discussion of Chapter 1 in *The Lord of the Flies.* I'd been talking about the characters and identifying the characteristics, describing the setting and clarifying the power struggles that were already shaping up. I looked up from my book and saw that Jeff, Chris, and Scott were asleep; Pat was talking quietly to Amanda. I'd been so involved in setting up what I thought was important that I'd completely forgotten the students were there. I'd been alone in the classroom. I don't know how to balance all of the jobs of helping kids learn content, finding ways to make it exciting, and being a caring teacher all at the same time. I realized this must have been a boring day but I was so wrapped up in being a teacher.

The desires to "be a caring teacher," "find ways to make it exciting," and "help kids learn content"—these dreams and hopes became all too fleeting when Avis looked up to see her students sleeping.

The description Avis gave was a reminder to Stephen, Sarah, and Ben of the tendency of teachers to be wrapped up in being a teacher. Stephen explained, "You reminded me of something that I hadn't thought about consciously before. I get so wrapped up in myself and feel self-confident, like this lesson is going great. Maybe I watch myself more than I monitor the students. It's an important point you've noticed, Avis." Ben indicated that it's nearly impossible not to look at the self when we think about "how many choices a teacher must make. I get hooked into whether or not I'm carrying out what I planned or how well I think on my feet about things. I do forget about the students sometimes." Sarah described her own feelings about this by suggesting that there is "always a state of flux and uncertainty. There isn't knowledge but knowledge within new contexts. Trying to work within what is constantly changing certainly makes me watch myself closely and in doing that I maybe don't pay enough attention to students." Avis' discovery is worthwhile not only because she brings to a conscious level something that is apparently an issue for these teachers—the focus on self—but also because she introduces an issue that all four of these teachers can examine together. As they examined this issue, Avis, Stephen, Sarah, and Ben fine-tuned the work they will do with students.

These first-year teachers' inquiry allowed them and me to examine the transition from a teacher preparation program to first teaching jobs. Their assimilation into the complex reality of schools forced them to reconsider their beliefs, face the daily challenges of coping with classroom management issues, relate to superiors and colleagues, and design and implement curriculum and daily lessons. By the end of these teachers' first year, they had come a long way from their first feelings of being thrown into the cold water to "sink-or-swim" or as Lortie (1966) defined it, "the Robinson Crusoe approach."

Relying in part on what Avis, Stephen, Sarah, and Ben taught me, I have reconsidered my own teaching of prospective teachers. I want to help prospective teachers develop a repertoire of strategies through which they can define, examine, and refine their work in schools. Many of the prospective teachers assume that they will be told how to teach. The drive for answers, concrete activities, and methods expresses their need for essentialist or categorical knowledge about teaching. This works quite at odds with what I believe is of primary importance: to create situations that help prospective teachers develop dialogic habits of mind.

I use Bakhtin's (1981) explanation of the dialogic principle as a way of conceptualizing how multiple and contested meanings "may be juxtaposed to one another, mutually supplement one another, contradict one another and be interrelated dialogically" (p. 291–292). Bakhtin indicates, "The single adequate form for *verbally ex-*

pressing authentic human life is the *open-ended dialogue* . . . . To live means to participate in dialogue: to ask questions, to heed, to respond, to agree and so forth" (p. 293). Dialogic interaction competes with what Bakhtin describes as monologism. Monologism "denies the existence outside itself of another consciousness with equal rights and equal responsibilities . . . Monologue is finalized and deaf to the other's response, does not expect it and does not acknowledge in it any *decisive* force" (pp. 292–293). This tension between the need for dialogic ways of thinking and the impulse for the certainty of the monologic cannot be eliminated, but it can be confronted if English educators find meaningful ways to move prospective teachers beyond essentialist and into dialogic renderings of their developing knowledge. In doing so, the habit of essentialized readings might be decentered by the continual flux of meaning represented by multiple perspectives.

Such theorizing about the dialogic takes several forms in practice. As I mentioned at the end of Chapter One, I ask prospective teachers to describe and reflect on critical teaching incidents. Unlike decontextualized descriptions of teaching techniques, critical incidents serve as occasions for individuals to reflect on the multiple and contradictory ways that any incident might be interpreted in relationship to the context in which it occurred. The creation of knowledge about teaching, then, can be practiced as part of an ongoing conversation without the need for a final or "right" interpretation of the critical events or issues.

Each teacher brings three copies of the narrative reconstruction and a reflective memo on the incident to class. Every week, one class member volunteers to bring copies for everyone so that the entire class can analyze one incident as a way to build a shared repertoire of inquiry strategies. After the whole class inquiry, small groups analyze their own individual incidents and reflective memos from several points of view and pose a range of issues and questions. I designed the critical incident experience to elicit as wide a range of perspectives as possible to represent how reconceptualization and analysis of incidents can elicit dialogic approaches.

Observing a classroom is not constructive in and of itself. Confounding what is seen and heard or considering the many angles of vision through which an event might be interpreted allows teachers to examine their own subjectivities. It is the dialogic relation between the multiple subjectivities that decenters unitary meaning. For example, critical incidents can be interpreted from multiple perspectives: that of the person writing it, a student's viewpoint, a cooperating teacher's perspective, or another observer's point of view. Other teachers who read the incident can offer additional ways of thinking about it. The range of often contradictory or competing viewpoints creates a space in which these teachers can reflect upon what has happened and negotiate possibilities of what may be yet to come.

To demonstrate how essential the interpretive community is to learning to read the classroom from multiple perspectives, I gave the narrative reconstruction of Joe's class session on Cheever's "Torch Song" (from Chapter Five) to four colleagues, who have all taught high school English and who have engaged in various forms of qualitative and quantitative research themselves. I asked them to write a brief reaction to their reading of the class session. The responses are as follows:

> *Reader 1:* Joe gives contradictory messages to students. The reading quiz (and he doesn't seem to know anything about higher level thinking) usurps the students' power to construct text. He turns around and gives that back in the graffiti wall activity. I'd suggest Joe is a teacher caught between two worlds, and with one foot in each camp he can't decide which way to go.

> *Reader 2:* Joe is very conservative as evidenced by the reading quiz that doesn't encourage individual interpretation, connections with life or experience, or attention to literary conventions. He encourages a literal reading of text. The graffiti wall doesn't fit with that. I suspect he has read about it somewhere and finds it a way to get students talking but may not understand why he does it.

> *Reader 3:* Joe encourages student responses to literature with the graffiti wall. He follows that up nicely with clarifying what it is they are trying to make of the characters. From this scenario I'd say Joe is reader-response oriented and interested in students' interpretations. The quiz seems a way to get students to read.

> *Reader 4:* The structure of the graffiti wall is much too narrow. Students are not empowered to determine what in the story is meaningful to them. The quiz is further support of this. This is the classical case of a very traditional teacher hiding behind a bag of tricks.

Four readers. Four interpretations. Four different portraits of Joe. Obviously these readings truncate the process, but are intended to demonstrate how essential it is to read a class session in multiple ways. All of this introduces a fundamental issue: How can we as English educators encourage ourselves and the teachers and re-

searchers with whom we work to confound what can too often become simplified or reified readings of classrooms and teachers? An
inquiry of possibility should keep pushing at the boundaries and
reframe the work and methods that can help us to understand teachers' work. It is important to know the possibilities and liabilities of
whatever stance is taken. I don't mean to suggest that learning the
lessons and practices of the dialogic is a miracle cure, but I hope
that we can all engage in mutually constructed interpretations as a
way to further build understanding of our work as teachers.

As with many other English education programs, our faculty is
attempting to create a curriculum that will link together a series of
experiences rather than merely provide a discrete set of courses.
These experiences contain vehicles of the dialogic that develop prospective and practicing teachers' habits of mind. We still feel frag-
mented in some ways as we try to understand ways and means
toward that end. In addition to critical incidents and collaborative
teaching, we deliberately juxtapose articles and books that pose differing theories or viewpoints on issues in English education or education in general. Rather than teaching *a* philosophy, our
curriculum is designed to complicate the discourse on how and
what to teach. We have our students engage in case and artifact
studies, videotape critiques of their own and others' teaching, and
self-assessment through portfolios. Additionally, the prospective
and in-service teachers design a case study in which they follow
one teacher through a semester's work and write up the findings of
their research; the next semester they write a case study on one student. We want a curriculum that resonates with the tensions of what
it means to teach and to learn. We feel certain that the teachers' experiences in the program will be a point of departure in the struggle toward becoming.

Seldom are teachers encouraged to share how they plan, implement, and evaluate the classroom text through reflection. Consequently, our "depth of insight" (Erickson, 1986) about teachers' work
may allow misconceptions about the extent to which they think
through their teaching decisions. What if teachers' reflections on
their teaching and the issues about their teaching were studied more
thoughtfully than the answers they give or the behaviors that can be
observed? Through their ruminations on decision making we might
see a wider range of thought processes and strategies than are easily
recognizable in the overt signs given from answers and behaviors.

Composing a teaching life, like composing any text, requires rehearsals of meaning, ways of reading and rereading the text as it is
written, explorations with revising, ideas thrown out and taken on,

and the mosaic of individual, collaborative, and public presentations that must be balanced. There is nothing linear or tidy in the process. As Mayher and Brause (1991) suggest in their depiction of "The Never-Ending Cycle of Teacher Growth," teachers develop and change through articulations of their beliefs and practices. As the authors demonstrate through their discussion, this is not enough. Part of the key is testing understandings by seeking out "colleagues, articles, conferences, books, etc.; in short to become aware of what is happening in the field and to use it to explore alternatives to our current beliefs and practices" (p. 29). If teachers engage in "a never-ending cycle" (p. 29) and a continual conversation not only with themselves, but also with their colleagues through study groups, in-service workshops, professional and personal reading, and continued course work, they are likely to suffer some discontent. As Robert Fulghum (1990) says, "Discontent and ferment are signs the fires of education are burning well. In education, look for trouble. If you can't find any, make some" (p. 92). As has been catalogued in multitudinous ways throughout all of the previous chapters, teachers continue to search, to learn, and to look for trouble.

I think what is important in Fulghum's suggestion is that we might want to value the dialogic tensions over the formulaic answers. Might it be possible to accept that teachers' work is chaotic, not easily defined by statistics of performance, lesson plans, or objectives? If we begin to look behind the act, the formula, the answers to the causes, conditions, and contexts; if we begin to describe and identify the multiplicity of causes, conditions, and contexts; if we recognize and value what is unsaid as much as what is said; and if we begin to refashion frameworks for exploring and understanding teaching as a composing process, then we might learn to challenge, reinvent, and retheorize what it means to become and be a teacher.

If we find that the articulation of these meanings helps us to actualize who we are and what we are about as teachers, then I suggest, again, that we learn to read our teaching histories in much the same way we read any text—to open a field of inquiry. If meaning becomes the product of our engagement with this teaching text, we are cast in the role of questioner, critic, and creator of our teaching lives. The competing and emerging voices in this inquiry will continuously shape and recast the habits of mind we bring to our teaching and learning.

Chapter Seven

Initiation into the Discourse on Teaching

Each society has its regime of truth, its "general politics" of truth; that is, the types of discourse which it accepts and makes function as true; the mechanisms and instances which enable one to distinguish true and false statements, the means by which each is sanctioned; the techniques and procedures accorded value in the acquisition of truth; the status of those who are charged with saying what counts as true.

(Foucault, 1980, p. 131).

It's possible that learning to teach is not quite so sinister sounding or definitive as learning what Foucault describes as a "regime of truth," but the "types of discourse" are well worth interrogating as are the "mechanisms and instances," "the means," and "the techniques and procedures" through which student teachers are initiated into the discourse on teaching. I'd like to take a closer look at some of the classroom lessons learned by the student teachers—Beverly, Jennifer, John, and Regina—who were introduced in Chapter Two. In that chapter, I examined several of the themes that surfaced as these prospective teachers expressed their concerns: adjusting to the change from the role of student to the role of teacher in the school environment, facing the unanticipated incidents that occur daily, and forging a teacher identity. I'd like to extend that conversation here by tracing particular instances that demonstrate the contest for authority that often accompanies initiation into the discourse on teaching. Sometimes the language in the discourse is one highlighting efficiency and classroom management; other times, the language challenges the *status quo;* often the discourse illustrates inherent ideological or pedagogical issues. What has become evident to me in observing student teachers in classrooms where they are teaching is that the wisdom of the discourse is passed out in dollops from which a student teacher must take disparate bits and try to bring them together in some coherent and relevant way.

What happens in the classroom to influence what student teachers accept as "truths" about teaching? What types of interactions with students and cooperating teachers instill lessons about teaching? How do student teachers shape, refine, or change their discourse on teaching as a result of the interaction with others in the classroom? The following lessons from the classroom demonstrate the ways in which a warranty of experience is pitted against the vagary of naivete as a way of maintaining the "regime of truth" about teaching. I suspect that part of the impulse to sustain and deepen any discourse is the desire to maintain some sense of continuity and order. As Foucault (1980) describes it, there are those rare moments that shatter the familiar landscapes of our thought, "breaking up all the ordered surfaces and all the planes with which we are accustomed to tame the wild profusion of existing things, and continuing long afterwards to disturb and threaten with collapse our age-old distinction between the Same and the Other" (p. xv). Part of the current discourse on teaching is about taming the impulsiveness of new teachers that arises, as wisdom would suggest, from lack of experience. For all the rhetoric on change, there seems to be some fear of taking that leap over the edge into what Foucault describes as "the stark impossibility of thinking *that.*" (p. xv).

"You've Come a Long Way, Baby"

In Chapter Two, Beverly Crandall expressed disappointment when she realized that her students did not just naturally like her, and that, in fact, they considered her an outsider. She described herself as an interloper in the classroom because she interrupted a routine that was well established, and she felt guilty that she took time and energy from her cooperating teacher, Mr. Sterne, that could otherwise be devoted to his teaching. During my observations of class sessions and in the discussions afterward with Beverly and her cooperating teacher, I saw how her fear of not being a central player in the classroom and her general feelings of inexperience led her to accept certain viewpoints on discipline or teaching that seemed at odds with what she had said about her philosophy of teaching in written work and interviews *before* she began her first student teaching experience. The old Virginia Slims slogan, "You've come a long way, baby!" came to mind as I chronicled the discursive production of knowledge about teaching that Beverly was expected to accept as "the regime of truth." Of course, that put Beverly in the position of straddling ideologies, pedagogies, and agendas. This can be seen very early on in her student teaching experience.

10:25 A.M., September 28

Beverly walks to the front of her eighth graders to introduce the guest actors and actresses who are about to perform scenes from Arthur Miller's *The Last Yankee*. Lulu cracks her gum as Beverly walks by.

"Lulu, stop cracking your gum," Beverly says with a scowl.

"Why?" questions Lulu.

"Because it's rude," Beverly retorts as she walks toward the actresses and actors.

Lulu rolls her eyes in disbelief and murmurs something.

"What was that?" Beverly turns toward Lulu and hovers over her desk. The visiting cast freezes at the front of the room, waiting for the introductions.

"Never mind," Lulu says, again cracking her gum.

"Thanks a lot for your consideration with the gum. I mean cracking it after I asked you to stop. Thanks a lot," Beverly says as she turns toward the cast.

The actors begin to whisper to each other.

Lulu makes a face in disbelief. "Aren't you goin' to introduce them? They're just waitin' on you. That's Rude! What a witch."

Beverly turns around to face Lulu again. "What was that you said?"

"Nothin,'" says Lulu smiling at her friend Robert. "Just nothin'. You got company here to introduce so get on with it."

"No more from you. Out you go. You too, Robert. You're encouraging this. I want you both out of the room." Beverly has one fist on each hip.

"You're just wasting everybody's time," Lulu says picking up her books. "I can't believe it." She slams a pile of books on her desk as she picks up her coat to go.

"Who, me?" says Robert. "I didn't do nothin'. Lulu looks at me and suddenly I'm guilty. Bull. I'm not goin' nowhere. I didn't do nothin' to you."

By now Beverly has escorted Lulu to the door and is headed back for Robert. The cast of characters decides to start a scene. "Now," one of them says, "let the play begin."

Robert and Beverly look at each other. He shrugs his shoulders. She gives him a nod toward the door. Robert raises his hands, palms up, in disbelief, shrugs, picks up his books, and slinks toward the door.

In our conversation after the class session, Beverly indicated that she believed it was necessary to handle this situation in the way she did so that she could be an authority figure in the class. "I think I didn't feel confident enough to do that until today, and I'm thinking it is very important. Mr. Sterne keeps telling me that I need to exert a presence, that teaching is about a presence and being firm in that presence. Throwing those kids out (this was the first time I did it) was a statement about what I'll tolerate and what I won't. Although I didn't enjoy the confrontation, I felt extremely empowered and justified in asking them to leave. To my surprise the class was grateful for my stern establishment of order and responded by being even more attentive to the actors afterwards. I learned not just to listen to the voices that distracted me but to know the other students needed me to keep order. Mr. Sterne tells me not to be worried about whether or not the students will like me, because in the end, my students will respect me more if I discipline them properly. Mr. Sterne has helped me see that it's important to use this power but in truth it makes me nervous. It doesn't feel quite right or what I'd imagined I'd want to be as a teacher. It does work though."

Beverly's responses both in and after class are complex, difficult, and layered with meanings. Her own beliefs are contradictory with each other: to exert control, to establish a presence, to be respected through "proper discipline," and to be more than either of these things in what she imagined she wanted to be as a teacher. Interestingly she concludes with the statement: "It does work though." Her motivations are many and her actions demonstrate a version of how competing forces of power and pedagogy are at work in the classroom. Finally, "what works" counts. All of the participants in the scene are struggling to be heard: students, actors, and student teacher. Behind those voices actively vying for attention, the voice of experience in the form of Mr. Sterne is drumming into Beverly's consciousness what he has said about "the need to establish a presence, be firm, and establish authority and power." Embedded in Lulu's comments is evidence that she is aware of her own power, particularly with the actors present as onlookers and the support of classmates as illustrated by the exchange with Robert, and she recognizes the fragile power of the student teacher's position.

Although this incident could be viewed as a classroom squabble that doesn't seem on the surface to have much significance to what Beverly might learn about teaching, I would suggest that it represents an example of how teacher knowledge is constructed by the many contributors to a particular event. What this incident demonstrates is one version of the axis of struggle for control in this particular class session, evidenced by the exchange that took place between Beverly, Robert, and Lulu. Everyone was resistant to having their power co-opted. This incident is an example of how the discursive practices of teaching are perpetuated. In this incident we find an example of the language of confrontation between a student and a student teacher, how far each will go in perpetuating the conflict, and the types of actions that can be taken to diffuse the incident. The particular language of the exchange between Beverly and Lulu or Beverly and Robert is heard often in classrooms. It's easier to suggest why it happened than to consider the unproductive aspects of the interaction, but reflection on the incident may suggest that we need to be more vigilant about how the language of power in the classroom is articulated and rearticulated by and for the range of participants.

This was particularly obvious to me when Mr. Sterne responded to Beverly's reflections on what had taken place in the class by reaching over and patting her on the shoulder as he said, "You see, you've come a long way, baby." I'm uneasy about the implicit message of Mr. Sterne's remarks and how the statement might be interpreted by Beverly—although it could have been taken as condescending, it gave Beverly a vote of confidence that she had indeed "come a long way" because her way of "being" a teacher was accepted and honored by Mr. Sterne.

I'm sympathetic to Beverly's pride in having "handled" the situation. I asked her how she thought the cast felt as they waited for the confrontation to end. "I talked with them afterward," she said with a dismissive shake of her hand, "and they understood that I wanted an audience that would be respectful." Of course they, too, have been initiated into the discourse of classrooms. Mr. Sterne chimed in: "It's an important lesson for Robert and Lulu to know that they won't get away with anything just because we have guests." Even the language, "respectful," and "they won't get away with anything," has a locus of meaning about the power relations as they "do" and "should" exist in a classroom.

Mr. Sterne continued: "Every time I come down on a kid, I know it's for the best. Sure, they bring the baggage of their lives into school, but I can't feel terrible about that. This is English class and finally we as teachers make decisions about what the kids will learn. You decide that they will get into writing in certain ways and you give them freedom sometimes and direction in others. Kids need to learn that both are productive. Lulu and Robert will cool off." Mr. Sterne leaned over and patted Beverly on the shoulder, "You've come a long way. You got some way to go, but you're getting there."

The politics of "knowing" here suggests that teachers must keep control, that if they let up on one student the desire for power and voice will spread to others, and that there isn't much room for difference in the domestication of students and teachers through classroom events and interactions.

The following is another incident from Beverly's classroom.

10:35 A.M., November 16

Beverly hands out two poems: "Nikki-Rosa" by Nikki Giovanni and "Theme For English B" by Langston Hughes. "Take some time to read these two poems and then identify what you think is the quality of life expressed in each poem."

[Students read for a few minutes]

"Now," Ms. Crandall asks, "What about Nikki-Rosa? Talk about what life is depicted."

"The guy's sayin' blacks only get the simple pleasures." Lewis looks around for approval.

"It's not a guy, Lewis. Nikki Giovanni is a woman. One of them hot women writers." Leticia can't resist reaching across the aisle and slapping Lewis on the back.

"This identifies racism as an issue, but don't do no feelin' sorry for us," Lulu adds.

"Yeah, the line that counts is that it sort of don't make no difference cause black wealth is just a different kinda wealth." Robert looks at Lulu. She gives him thumbs up.

"Now this other dude is whining about bein' black and in school," Leticia comments.

"Yeah, like it isn't poetry. It's tellin' his story, like I'm twenty-two and colored, so who cares? Let us figure that out for ourselves?" Jamal adds.

"Wasn't this dude famous, like one of the first black poets to make a reputation?" Robert asks.

"Do any of you know about Baldwin?" Beverly opens a book and reads a few paragraphs of biography.

"Yeah, you could say he sorta lived in our neighborhood, was our brother," Tyrone does a few gyrations and his desk quivers under the rhythm.

"What are some of the specifics then in these poems that help you see what life is like?" Beverly turns to list answers on the board.

"Hey, we're livin' the life and so are you. It's just a few crackers in this room who ain't." Michael bobs his head around looking for approval.

"Yeah, you should know that Beverly. You different now cause you're a teacher?" Lulu has her chin jutted out as she often does when she's ready to do battle.

"References to prejudice?" Beverly continues.

"Why we doin' this?" Tyrone asks.

"We're going to start a unit on African American literature." Audible groans from some class members. Others are silent. Beverly hands out a copy of Connie Porter's short story "Hoodoo."

"This is short so why don't you read it aloud in pairs." Beverly walks to the front of the class. "Any questions? Can you do that? There should be time before the end of the period."

Right before the bell rings, Beverly asks the students to tell her what they've learned and what their reactions are to what they've read. "Just write an exit slip and leave it with me.

As students write their exit slips, Leticia says loudly, "I'm offended." The bell rings.

Beverly reads through a few of the responses before we begin our conversation on the class session. Leticia wrote:

> It seems to me like many of the students seemed either uninterested or carefree about the lesson. I really enjoyed this and it kind of hurt to see that many of them felt that it was unnecessary or boring. Many of them talked and complained over how weird the story was. I've been learning European history, U. S. history, and Caucasian literature. Even though I am very curious about my own history and literature I respected all of the non-black stuff.

Barry wrote:

> "Why are we only going to do black authors? It's boring. I don't feel this is fair. Why only black people? Is that because you're black? What about white authors?"

Beverly began the discussion by asking both Mr. Sterne and me if it seemed unfair to do a unit on African Americans. "Do you think I'm shoving my literature down their throats? I don't want them to feel that way, but there are mostly black kids in this class."

I asked her: "What do you hope to accomplish in this unit?" Beverly suggested that she wanted to break what she saw as a myth that "black folks don't have culture except rap and blues. But, I didn't think they would oppose my agenda?" I asked Beverly why she thought they were opposing her agenda. "Well, what Barry said." I asked her how many of the students had the same reaction. "Well, none, exactly. Some didn't have questions. Others were confused by the story. A couple thought it was boring, but no other white student commented on the racial issue."

"They *need* to have this education," Beverly added. A "needs" discourse is a rationalization for curricular decisions, as was highlighted the moment Beverly made this statement. Mr. Sterne interjected, "Maybe cultural groups ought to be responsible for taking care of their own education in a specific culture. What kids *need* is a shared education, one that gives a common heritage and background to all students who are educated in our system. There's nothing wrong with a unit that concentrates on a particular group and it's ok if you try it, but I don't think it's essential education. You'll learn that individual communities must take some of that responsibility. You'll learn you can't cover everything in everybody's agenda. It will drive you crazy to try and the more you try the more people will crawl out of the woodwork with their agendas." The discourse of *need* can certainly be used to create an authoritarian legitimation of any agenda. What became increasingly clear is how precariously statements of need hover over the lines separating ideological camps. Beverly's conception of need and that of Mr. Stern's are at odds, yet both arguments are part of the ongoing battle for place on the ideological battlefield as is recognizable in the following exchange.

"Maybe I'll start tomorrow with them confronting the issue that they seldom study anything African American. Even the African American students were mostly neutral. I want them to have an agenda to speak out and change the typical white curriculum," Beverly suggested. "They *need* to deal with the issue. What if I have them write about their own stereotypes about others and then give them some black poems that may break some of the most common stereotypes? Or, I could read the two students' reactions and get them to talk about that as a class."

"I know you mean well," Mr. Sterne gave Beverly that parental look. "But I don't think it will help them to get all embroiled in political issues. Just stick to the literature and keep teaching it. If you want to do African American literature just do it. Some students will get into it. Others will blow it off. One or two might just think you read it because you're African American, and they'll resent or accept the agenda. It doesn't matter except you need to stick to the literature. You're getting there. Don't blow it now." This exchange illustrates an axis of need struggle. Any *needs* talk that defines, recreates, and contests the purposes and practices necessary to educate the citizenry should be subject to careful scrutiny about the political issues embedded in it, as well as the potential for reproducing or reworking old habits through the initiation of new teachers into the discourse on teaching.

"Do We Have to Work in Small Groups?"

Jennifer Martin found that as she tried to implement approaches she had learned in her teacher preparation program, the students resisted openly. Student resistance plagued her. She wrote in her journal after two weeks at the school: "Every day is a critical incident, really. They have handed in *0* homework, done *0* 'Here and Nows,' done *0* reading at home. They are late five days a week. They talk while I'm talking, while anyone else is talking. They don't follow directions. They don't stay in their desks. They don't stay in the classroom." Jennifer tried to keep them involved by including high interest material in her lesson plans from current magazine and newspaper articles on various people, including Riddick Bowe, Malcolm X, and popular rappers. She tried to set clear parameters—policies on behavior and lessons on how to listen and how to respond. She conferred with them on projects. Jennifer felt that no matter what she tried, however, the students would resist and question any method that wasn't, as Jennifer told it, "the sit down and fill in this worksheet that is due in fifteen minutes or you fail" assignments.

9:32 A.M., October 13

Jennifer begins. "I was just thinking last night about an incident that occurred when I was in third grade. I had a crush on this boy named Derrick. Derrick had jet black hair and big dark brown eyes. I would stare at him across the room and during recess I'd try to get in line next to him. I made the mistake of telling my best friend Lindsay that I liked him, so this one day I'm rushing right behind Derrick so that I can keep up and get right behind him in the lunch line. He stops to pick up a dime or something off the floor and I bump right into his butt and knock him over. He falls straight on his head and somehow cuts his eye right above his eyebrow. Blood gushes everywhere. Of course, I fall too, right on top of him and I scramble to get up I'm so embarrassed and there is Lindsay standing over us taunting me: 'Jenny's falling for Derrick. Derrick fell for Jenny.' I wanted to run into the girls' bathroom and cry."

"You must have some stories like that yourself," she asks the class.

"Mine is almost like the one you told," Tracy squeals. "Except the boy was Lance and I bumped him off the bars and he had to get about a dozen stitches."

"I remember wetting my pants in first grade. I didn't dare ask the teacher if I could go and finally it was too much. The warm pee just trickled right between my legs and down to the floor. I don't know why I thought nobody would notice but Aaron who sat behind me shouted at the teacher, 'Daphne peed her pants. Daphne peed her pants.' Everybody was looking at me!"

Arian described how a love letter she'd written was read to the whole class in fourth grade. "I didn't go to school for two days and my parents were mad at the teacher for doing it, so they had some big conference."

"What about you, Ambar?" Jennifer looks toward a frail boy in the first row who responds, "I don't remember. I don't have any stories."

"How about you, Danielle?" Jennifer starts to walk down the aisles. "I don't remember elementary school," Danielle remarks as she sticks out her tongue to her friend Jewel who is seated a few aisles over.

"Well let's get into some small groups and share any stories of school that have been embarrassing." Jennifer gestures to move the desks.

"Why do we have to work in small groups?" Jamal's challenge stops the students from rearranging the desks.

"Yeah, there aren't really enough of us here anyway." Damon looks around.

"OK, so let's give more examples then." Jennifer tries to get the conversation going again.

"School stories are boring. Let's do something else." Rubin looks around for approval.

"What about some bizarre thing you've seen on the subway." The room buzzes with gruesome stories of beheadings and dismemberment on the tracks and the students naturally begin talking to a smaller group than the whole class. Jennifer encourages this by suggesting, "Just keep telling the stories for the next ten minutes or so and then we will wrap up.

"Now, what I'd like you to do for tomorrow is write up one of those stories so that we can send them to the other eighth grade English class. They'll be sending their embarrassing stories to you."

"Can't we write about the subway? Those are RAD!" Other students nod approval at Abduhl's suggestion.

"Yeah, and can we write them in class tomorrow? I don't have time at home."

"Let's go to the lab to type 'em in. We could even do graphics of people getting shot and blood dripping."

"Hold it. Hold it. No, no, and no. I'm asking you to write about an embarrassing incident TONIGHT for homework. It's decided and the other class is doing the same. Then, tomorrow we'll switch our incidents with the other class and read theirs while they read yours. It's settled."

After class Jennifer suggested that "things tended to get out of hand. Maybe I shouldn't have ever let them get going with the subway stories. They got out of control." Jennifer felt that she lost the group. Additionally she began worrying because she'd made this arrangement with another teacher. "It sounded like a good idea at the time. Now, I'm wondering. The students aren't really into this and only thirteen out of twenty students were in class today. I'm not sure how to handle the situation. Not everyone will do these stories if anyone does. Maybe I should have said we will do them together in class or the computer lab. I'd set the agenda in advance and that didn't take into consideration the students. The bottom line is attendance. That seems simple, but it is a big deal."

Jennifer's cooperating teacher, Ms. Nixon, reacted to Jennifer's reflections. "You see, Jennifer, it's what I warned you about giving them an inch and they take a mile. You can nearly lose the purpose of your lesson if you let students take over. First it was that they didn't want groups. Then it was the topic, then homework, and finally that they wanted to do these on the computer. It just keeps getting more and more out of control." Ms. Nixon's comment is a reminder that the aphorism "Give them an inch and they'll take a mile" is alive and well in schools. The message behind Ms. Nixon's comments is more than just a message about what she believes is a truism about students. It is also a caution to Jennifer that she can't lose the reins of control in the classroom and that the discourse about keeping students "in their places" is intact in schools.

Jennifer thought for a few seconds before responding to Ms. Nixon: "I want to be flexible enough in my teaching to make alterations when something is clearly not going to work. Is that being too soft? Frankly, I didn't care what kind of stories they told. It's just that it was suggested by the other teacher. What I really wanted was for the classes to exchange stories, and they did get excited about the subway stories. I also wanted to give them an audience outside the class and that's what got me in trouble. I wanted this activity to make storytelling comfortable and enjoyable and fun." It's clear that Jennifer seeks to unsettle the privileging of a teacher agenda over a student agenda, as if a dichotomy must exist. If the teacher is aware of what is going on, any move made will be replied to with some student action, even when that action appears inaction. As MacIntyre (1984) puts it so succinctly, "the problem with real life is that moving one's knight to QB3 may always be replied to with a lob across the net" (p. 98). So, the point is: In the discourse on teaching we have some fairly consistent ways of preparing for, describing, and evaluating the "lob across the net."

Of course Ms. Nixon had a different take on the student response. "I think you let the class control your plans. I believe in flexibility, but you need to write out each lesson on what you plan to teach so the students don't throw off your strategy. No matter what comes up, the students should leave the class 'knowing' certain things that you determine they should know." Ms. Nixon is passing on the discourse of "us versus them" oppositions as part of the discourse on teaching. But what of discourses dealing with "empowerment," "negotiation," and "liberation"?

Problems develop when any regime of truth is postulated without sufficient awareness that politics and advocacy reside in any discourse. Simplistic pedagogy simplifies and bifurcates the issues. We might try to explicate a regenerative pedagogy for teacher preparation that forges links between the various discourses that are occurring in the classroom at any given time. One way of doing that might be to consider how to help teachers identify the relations of power in the classroom, to have a way of examining what it is we have been initiated into, what have been accepted as truisms, and what it is we have been unable to ask. There is little doubt that classroom life can perpetuate some of the discourses that appear unproductive. Consider, for example, the following segment from another one of Jennifer's classes.

9:20 A.M., November 1

Jennifer asks students to discuss Naomi Shihab Nye's poem "Late."
Cher says, "I don't know, but it has images of childhood play."
Ron adds, "I don't get this part about the "shadowy baby."
Ronnette reads her favorite lines which are an image of a basement.
"I hear you talking about what takes place in the poem. Is there a difference in what takes place and what the poem means?"
"Yeah," Ron says. "You know like the actual stuff stands for something like in metaphor or when we studied symbols. There's probably somethin' like lurkin' under the words."
Jennifer suggests that the class break into small groups to discuss whether there is more meaning than is on the surface.
Tanya refuses. "We don't EVER accomplish anything in small groups."
Jennifer asks Tanya to get into one of the groups. "You're making it difficult for everyone to concentrate. Please, just join a group and do what you're asked."

"Slavery is over!" Tanya exclaims.

One student says to Tanya, "Ease off. Cool it. You always make a big deal out of nothin'." Tanya explodes at him. "You just love bein' a slave, huh? Play into Ms. Martin's hands. Brown nosin' takes on new meanin' with you."

Jennifer asks Tanya to be quiet. "If you can't join a group and be productive then just sit there quietly by yourself. Nobody really cares, if you don't make a scene."

Tanya slides down into her desk and puts her coat up over her head.

"Tanya," Jennifer persists, "If you don't work in a group you at least can write or read on your own. This isn't going to be a time for you to sleep."

"I'm not your slave," Tanya emphasizes again.

"No, you're my student though, and I expect you to use class time."

Jennifer states afterward that she was clueless as to how to deal with the situation. "Tanya threw the race card at me and my white guilt came through. I had to remind myself this wasn't about race, but about her responsibility to be a student if she is going to be in school. The only thing that mostly works with these students is a teacher-centered performance. They really listen up when I read to them or talk to them. But chaos and hostility result when I try to get them to work together on any kind of student-centered work. Why do they resist?"

What Jennifer failed to take into account is student resistance to approaches that reconfigure student and teachers' roles in the classroom. Tanya doesn't believe that she profits from group work. That students will flourish in student-centered classrooms and enjoy the freedom to work within much less defined structures is not as predictable as might be assumed from the professional literature. Jennifer had a more positive view of student-centered environments as a result of what she had read and the methods classes she was taking in her preparation program. She was not prepared to face resistance from students when, as she saw it, she was just trying to transfer power to them to enable them to take control of some of their learning.

One of the lessons Jennifer learned, however, was that students do take control over their own learning, but not always through the structures created by the teacher. Tanya is a case is point. She does exert power in both her resistance and in her allusion to slavery. Her frustration results at least partially from her perceived belief that nothing is accomplished in groups. One of the things that Tanya said to me after class was, "Why doesn't Ms. Martin just teach? She's just lettin' the kids take over and nothin' gets done that way. She knows stuff I don't know and I'd like her help directly in learnin' it."

On the other hand, Jennifer said to me after class that she thought she handled the situation "quite well. I needed to really come down on Tanya and not let her get away with things. The whole class becomes more receptive and seems to be more attentive and focused when they see I mean business. Sometimes maybe it just takes these kinds of incidents to show them that the teacher cares and expects a lot from them." What Jennifer doesn't do here is examine what motivated Tanya to respond in the way she did. Why does Tanya feel enslaved by this intended student-centered moment? As Tanya's sentiments indicate, she still feels the tyranny of being forced to work with a small group. While it is entirely possible that Tanya conceptualizes knowledge as a commodity in her discourse on school and expects to get that knowledge from the teacher who possesses it, she has brought the expectations of the discourse as she knows it to bear on how she will conduct herself in class. A question remains about how to deal with such a situation. I suggested to Jennifer that she talk with Tanya about the incident and try to structure the conversation so that both of them had a chance to explain to the other what was motivating their actions and reactions.

As the previous classroom incident illustrates, there are multiple grounds of resistance operating at any given moment. Recognizing these adds impetus to characterizing the classroom as a place of fragmentation, mixed intentions, and multiple events that will be interpreted in various ways by the participants. One way of studying resistances is to interrupt the narrative of the event by trying to extricate what forms of resistance are nestled within any given moment. To grapple with this concept, I include the following incident that occurred while Jennifer was student teaching.

9:30 A.M., October 28

I arrive early at the locked door of Room 307. Students begin to arrive, followed by Jennifer. "Sorry I'm late. I had to stop to ask the principal to come and unlock the door." Jennifer looks haggard before the day has begun. "Ms. Nixon called me last night. She won't be in today." A chorus of questions from students: "Where's Ms. Nixon?" "Ms. Nixon out today?" "You gonna teach Ms. Martin?" Then: "Whatdayaknow." "Awwwwwesome." "Shee-it!" Kids start running up and down the stairs. I was toying with the idea of intervening when a middle-aged woman appeared. "Who are you?" she asked Jennifer. "I hope you're not another substitute. They do that sometimes. Hire two. I'm Miss Kent."

Jennifer extended her hand, "I'm Jennifer Martin."

"Jennifer, her first name's Jennifer," Semia shouts to the class that's mostly congregated by the stairwell where some are still sliding down the hand rail.

Jennifer responds to the substitute, "I'm the student teacher assigned to this class and this," she points in my direction, "is my supervisor."

"You're joking," Miss Kent says bobbing her head up and down. "Why would you ever want to do this. These kids are all animals. My friend was hit with a chair at East last year. They all have switchblades, and they know you know they have 'em. You can't do anything. These kids might be all right, but you get in East or any of those schools and you'll be back where you came from in a year."

"Well, I don't know," Jennifer began but was interrupted.

"I have a lesson all planned. Read them the article about Joe Fernandez in today's *Times* and have them write an essay about it. You know, three paragraphs—beginning, middle, and end. It's all planned." Miss Kent looks at Jennifer and then at me.

"Actually we're right in the middle of a novel," Jennifer explains, "and I'm teaching it anyway, so you can take a break and just watch."

"No such thing," says the substitute. "I'm in charge. I teach my lesson." Mercifully, the principal arrives to unlock the door. The substitute and students bolt through the open door. Jennifer and I follow.

Miss Kent begins. "Down now. We're starting now."

"Talk LOUD-ly," Semia shouts.

Miss Kent persists, "Be Quiet. Quiet NOW."

"Why ain't Ms. Martin teaching? She's s'posed to be."

"I said quiet. Just be quiet."

Miss Kent begins to read the article haltingly, and through the din of student voices, "Fernandez capped a career. . .Who knows what capped means?"

Michael punctuated the classroom noise with sound effects patterned after the sounds of Nintendo.

"Capped means to put a lid on," Cher responds. Those listening begin to laugh.

Miss Kent, undaunted, began to read again, "abrasive style . . . Does anyone know what abrasive means?" Solomon shook his head. Miss Kent went to the board and wrote "abrasive" leaving out the "r."

"You an English teacher?" Dominique shouts. "English teacher s'posed to know how to spell."

Miss Kent looks at the board and back at the students. "Class, maybe Miss Martin can tell us what abrasive means!" She's nearly shouting by now. "Maybe Miss Martin can tell us how to spell it. She's going to *be* an English teacher after all."

The class is silent. Jennifer starts talking about sandpaper, how it is graded by the grit which is the degree of abrasion. Solomon shouts, "You don't get it, Ms. Martin. You're s'posed to tell us about how bad we're actin'. We be bad enough to be abrasive. We be a degree of grit ourselves."

The substitute interrupts. "That's about enough. Just read the rest of the article and write your essay. If you don't hand the essay in, you'll get an "F" for the day.

"What degree of grit is F grade, Ms. Martin?" Semia yells across the room and belly laughs.

I don't have the words to describe the layers of understanding on the discourse of schools that are embedded in this scene. The narrative reconstruction does not do justice to the complexity and tone of what went on before and during class. What took place made me sad. Always an optimist, I love these kids for their wisdom about how to defend themselves against mean-spiritedness. However, why are anger, resentment, power struggles, and abusive verbal bantering a part of the discourse in schools? My impulse here is to let the scene tell its own stories of resistance as well as let it reveal how embedded are the sanctioned discourses of the classroom. I've reread transcripts of this session as well as the written version many times, and each time I find still more to think about.

The discourse on teaching revealed through these events carries many examples of how the various participants are constituted: perceptions on teachers, substitutes, and students. What is obscured is the process through which each of these subjects became defined and represented as they are in the discourse of schools. The problem is that this is not a single case of such perceptions; it is too often the stereotypical view of each group. And, they act out their parts for the most part consistent with the role defined by the stereotype.

As Jennifer said after class, "I was trying not to get into the substitute's contempt for kids nor to let her vocabulary lesson become a venue for delivering homilies. I was going to resist that. But the kids expected it and in some ways taunted me like I was too stupid to take the cue from Miss Kent. Why wouldn't they see or did they know that I was trying to support them?" I asked Jennifer a question: "Do students accept that teachers use content to sermonize and demean or did their reactions illustrate a form of resistance?" I can't answer that for students. I suggested Jennifer ask her students the next day. A discussion in which everyone shares their various perceptions of the day's events might be important in revealing how the discourse on teaching defines and constitutes many of the roles any of us take in schools. "Why Do We Have to Do Groups?" seems a metaphor to the various discourses of resistance that place participants in the classroom in particular positions that serve to perpetuate the discursive practices of representation.

"Creating Him in My Own Image"

Cooperating teachers, with varying degrees of zeal, are put in a position where they are centrally involved in disseminating the discourses on teaching to their student teachers. Depending on the role that both the cooperating teacher and student teacher assume, the partnership may amplify or submerge either voice. Discussions between the two often reveal how potentially oppressive or open the relationship might be in providing space for the student teacher to construct some of his or her own discursive practices. Mr. McMurtrey and John had very different philosophies about what was important to teach in the discipline itself as well as differences about how to teach content. John wanted to engage the students in conversation, assuming, as he suggested, "that students who are enjoying the stories and participate actively will learn about literature. If they're passive and bored, they'll forget or not get involved." John wrote in an October log entry:

> Accordingly, I ask open-ended questions like: "What would you do if you were in Huck's shoes?" Moreover, interpretive points are addressed as they crop up in the conversation. I let the students guide the conversation.

As John perceived it,

> Mr. McMurtrey prefers a more structured and detailed approach. His points follow one another logically, and his questions are information-oriented. "Where did Huck and Jim plan to flee to?" He insists upon detailed lesson plans and lists of unit goals in advance. As I tried to fit my techniques with his methods, my spontaneity decreased and student discussion tailed off. He made suggestions designed to stimulate student participation (some quite valuable) but we never really got it back. It seemed that the more informational and teacher-oriented the class was, the more he liked it. I was not allowed to read to the students just for fun, nor could I let them read anything in class. "Pleasure reading is extracurricular, and homework is done exactly where the word says—at home." I'm sure he enjoys literature, but it seemed that much of his method turned the course into work. Work, of course, is not to be shunned, but if delight is expelled from literature, it becomes drudgery. And little, I feel, is learned by drudgery.

When I talked with Mr. McMurtrey about his perceptions of John's philosophy and practice during an October meeting, he suggested:

> Well, I know that John wants or thinks he wants the students to think for themselves so he's pretty loose with the kinds of questions he asks. I see the kids getting confused, not really knowing

what's going on or why. That isn't helpful to them. They get way off track and have trouble understanding why they are discussing at all. John's open-minded and takes every answer as equal. I think if one of the students said that Huck is really an alien from outer space, John would pursue the interpretation. I mean there's a limit. He calls it open-minded. I call it silly.

Ultimately, these two people don't think alike about teaching. That does not, in and of itself, warrant that the student teacher and cooperating teacher relationship will be ineffective or dysfunctional. To be sure, both John and Mr. McMurtrey believe they know something about teaching and that they have important contributions to make to their students' education. As John wrote, "In the end you teach life—your own life. You teach kids that the world is inviting, fascinating, and fun-filled, or forbidding, boring, and grim. Our very personality gives kids an option, a way of being, that they may accept or reject." Mr. McMurtrey told me that he viewed teaching as "creating an impression of what's important. I want students to know that learning is demanding. I demand silence, attention, and discipline because that's how learning takes place. I want students to know that learning requires that they are serious and work-oriented." Noting these two very different ways of thinking about teaching forecasts some of the problems they might have as they share the responsibilities in the classroom.

John says, "I'll never be like Mr. McMurtrey. He has a right to be himself, but I won't be that way." Mr. McMurtrey says of John, "Well we have a lot to teach him about what really counts. In this semester I won't be able to create him in my image, but you can bet after he's taught thirty years like I have he'll be more like me than he would ever imagine could be possible." As I chronicled the differences in their perceptions as well as how Mr. McMurtrey perceived his role as cooperating teacher, I should have been able to predict that an exchange similar to the following one would take place between the two of them. But, as has been said before, Monday morning quarterbacking has its advantages when the outcome is already known. During the first week of November, I was the observer of the following exchange between Mr. McMurtrey and John:

> "Some of the students are coming to me and saying they're losing respect for you. That you don't make them behave, that you don't seem to be teaching them anything about literature." Mr. McMurtrey directs his remarks at John but keeps glancing toward me as if to acknowledge my presence. We are sitting together at the round table in the back of the classroom.
>
> "Well, nobody's going to please everybody, so I can't worry too

much about it." John juts out his chin and repositions his body so that he leans further away from Mr. McMurtrey.

Mr. McMurtrey pursues the idea, "What do you mean, you can't worry about it?"

"I mean that I accept the fact that not everybody is going to like me." John begins to put his books and papers in his briefcase as if getting ready to end the conversation.

"Five students have talked to me in private about you, and they don't like . . ."

"Two can play that game! You want to hear what students say to me about you? Nobody's universally popular. Not you. Not me. Nobody."

"So now you're attacking me? You're the guest in this classroom." Mr. McMurtrey slams his hand on the table.

"Guest? Guest? I thought I was teaching here." John taps his clenched fist on the table.

"You're learning to teach. Much of what you are doing is still inadequate, so you need to be knocked down a peg sometimes. You resist my suggestions. How will you learn to teach if you don't model or even listen? You're a little too certain of yourself."

And so it went. It ranged over several topics and thirty more minutes. As I sat listening, I was reminded that this was the cooperating teacher who one of our student teachers indicated the year before had "taught me how to teach. Mr. McMurtrey has a passion for literature, loves the kids, and was so supportive as I was learning to teach. I learned how to teach under his guidance."

Neither John nor Mr. McMurtrey were willing to suggest that it might be important to talk about their different philosophies. Mr. McMurtrey was convinced that he should tell John how to teach. As he stated to John and me, "I've been around the block more than most people. I know what needs to be done with the students, and John could learn something if he remains open to it." John was concerned that, as he told both of us, "I walked into this semester's student teaching with all these ideas that I definitely wanted to try. After about ten minutes, you (directed to Mr. McMurtrey) told me my ideas were misguided and that I should depend on you for help." John asked if he could read some of the comments he'd jotted down during early discussions with Mr. McMurtrey. John quoted Mr. McMurtrey: "I'm not sure you want to do that. It's too long and hard to cover over the course of the next few weeks." "The story you've chosen isn't relevant." "Oh, yes, well, I guess you could do it, but I think it's a bad choice." "You need to be better prepared and the reason you don't get finished is because you haven't planned enough." "Just try it my way and you'll see." As John finished reading these comments, he said, "I feel that I need to please myself first as a teacher. If you listen to these comments it sounds like my first job is to please you" (referring to Mr. McMurtrey).

Mr. McMurtrey responds: "Well, I meant to help you figure out what is appropriate literature and that you need to plan more carefully or you don't get anywhere." John replied, "But I want to try it my way." What didn't happen in the conversation to this point was an attempt to share what each understood as their basic beliefs about teaching and learning literature.

The lack of self-examination was broken when John suggested that "It would be more helpful if you explained how to plan. I'm not certain I know. I think I've planned and then you say I haven't. I need to know what you mean." Mr. McMurtrey indicated, "I sometimes feel like you (referring to John) are a duck in a pond and you paddle out into the middle of a lesson and the ducklings join you because they know they should. Then you all tread water. It's like you're stuck in the middle out there without anywhere to go. I know students don't have a clue and are waiting for you to lead them and you don't." John explained his actions by suggesting that he thinks "students must be given the freedom to explore topics and the ideas that interest them. Once they are given the leeway to do so, the teacher should act as a coach to direct their learning."

Mr. McMurtrey responded: "Students need direction. Group work doesn't help them learn and neither do unfocused discussions. In any of those situations it is important for the teacher to have a specific agenda in mind. Teach elements of characterization through the discussion or identify how metaphor supports theme and then keep hitting on that one issue and bringing the students back to it when they stray."

John thought for a moment before responding: "Now, that's helpful. I see what you mean about having a point and bringing students back to it. I don't know how to do that without it seeming rigid, but I can give it a try." Mr. McMurtrey added that he felt that "kids are not going to get all the endless stuff in any piece of literature. These kids need to have one line of thinking drawn out, explained, and discussed to take something away from the reading that they will remember." John paused a moment before stating, "OK, but I need help on establishing goals. You have told me to plan, but I guess I really don't know how. I'd appreciate your help in conceptualizing how to teach a particular piece of literature. Then I'll give it a try that way."

By the end of this discussion, Mr. McMurtrey and John were beginning to have a conversation rather than throwing barbs at each other as they had done earlier. It was unclear where this discussion might lead them in their relationship and whether or not John's request for help would be of a kind that he needed to inform him about his own teaching life. Obviously the notion of imitation and resemblance has a long history, as Foucault (1970) suggests, in Western culture:

> It was resemblance that largely guided exegesis and the interpretation of texts; it was resemblance that organized the play of symbols, made possible knowledge of things visible and invisible, and controlled the art of representing them . . . And representation—whether in the service of pleasure or of knowledge—was posited as a form of repetition: the theatre of life or the mirror of nature . . . (p. 17).

Representation, resemblance, and repetition are all part of the discourse in learning to teach, as the case of John and Mr. McMurtrey highlights. What is conventional and convenient often leads to an educational discourse that emphasizes what "has been done" and what "ought to be emulated or continued." Emulation is a form of rendering that relies on producing resemblances of an act, event, image, or symbol. Similitude often drives the visions of education particularly when, as we have seen, not only students but also teachers have resisted ways of creating practices and developing philosophies beyond the familiar. Educational practices are covered with blazons and signatures and other marks of the past. That is to be valued as well as critiqued. Yet, to compose is to find a way beyond past signatures and marks and to act and interpret, as well as to write, new events and words.

The controversies to which the search for the regime of truth about teaching have given rise are well known and documented as issues. It is upon the projected surface of these controversies that individual teachers and particularly those individuals learning to teach find norms of adjustment that permit them to produce and compose teaching events and practices. The discourse must be supple enough to allow for reconfigurations in the territory where knowledge about teaching is located. This is important for several reasons. First, it allows for the development of one's own consciousness about teaching. Second, it enables analysis that probes the contingency of one's own and other's texts of teaching. Third, it suggests that practices can be reworked. What John attempts to do in his present situation is find spaces within the cracks of Mr. McMurtrey's less-than-supple articulations. Particularly for cooperating teachers and teacher educators there are important implications that include acknowledging the need to step outside their own discursive order to allow their colleagues and those entering the profession to think about the issues through new or different discursive practices.

Tricks of the Trade

As Regina Riggs said several times, "There is so much to learn all at once. The number of times I've thought about what I said before, you know, about not even knowing how hard to press the chalk has become a metaphor to me. I'm learning this doesn't come through books or classes, but through experience." Regina indicated that little things count, like learning to "have students copy the homework when they first enter the room, to get them settled, or checking homework assignments at the beginning of class, to make students accountable for homework, are things my cooperating teacher says are the most important tricks of the trade." The practical, manual aspects of learning to teach carry within them a discourse that cannot be ignored due to the power these have to shape teachers' ways of knowing and acting. What does Regina know from the two examples she gives? Are practices of students copying homework assignments or checking homework the knowledge that Regina should construct about teaching? Is the language of "making students accountable" and "tricks of the trade" the discourse that will help Regina compose a teaching life?

The challenge for Regina Riggs is to develop a means of inquiry that prepares her to deal with the daily pedagogical struggles without disguising them in the "tricks of the trade" discourse. Rather than sustaining old contestations with versions of proven truths, it's important for teachers to critique and possibly disrupt certain propositions that have been allowed to stand beyond dispute. Submitting this discourse to some scrutiny may help me demonstrate how Regina and her cooperating teacher pattern this "tricks of the trade" discourse.

11:25 A.M., November 5

Regina starts the class with "U-turns," a timed exercise she uses in the writing workshop. "OK," she says turning to the chalkboard. "You have two minutes to write as much as you can about 'I know.'" She scrawls it on the board. After two minutes, she writes "I don't know" beneath it. She asks students to write for two more minutes on this U-turn. "Now I want you to dig for diamonds. Find something special in what you've written and make it into a poem, a paragraph, or a drawing."

Eugene Kim has been sitting with blank paper in front of him. He's tapping his pencil on the side of his desk.

Regina walks over to him. "Why aren't you writing?"

"It's stupid," Eugene blurts out.

"OK, well, just give it a try—you never know what you'll come up with." Ms. Riggs turns to talk with Martha who sits in front of Eugene.

Eugene clenches his fists and swipes the papers on his desk onto the floor: "This is so stupid! This is ridiculous! Who's going to read this shit? Nobody will ever read it! This is not writing."

"Eugene, I'm just asking that you try this. If it doesn't work for you, that's fine. You know you can always work on your own writing for the rest of this period. I'm just asking that you give this a shot."

"We've done this before! We keep doing it over and over again. It's just so stupid! No one's ever going to read this. What's the point?" Eugene pushes his notebook onto the floor. It falls with a loud thump. Joseph is suppressing giggles and Nick does too, until they see Regina glaring at them.

"The reason why we're doing this, Eugene, is to develop your writing, to make it easier for you to brainstorm through writing. All writers need to keep their skills sharp. Eugene, you have a right to express your opinion but not to disrupt the class. Just do it." Regina walks away.

Eugene picks up the papers that have scattered across the floor. He stomps out of the room.

Regina laments afterward that writing is difficult to teach. She believes that Eugene made a valid point, but she thinks the activity she assigned helps the students develop writing fluency. She also wondered how, after this incident, she might renegotiate a relationship with Eugene. As she suggests, "I've talked with Eugene about publishing a literary magazine out of the writing students do in the class. He's a good writer and needs to be stretched, but doesn't he still need to do the assignments? What would happen if all students did their own thing? I get frustrated with direct confrontations like this. I don't think students have the right to be so argumentative and just walk out of class. I think, on one hand, I need to do something to acknowledge that he did wrong, but, on the other hand, I want to have a truce."

Regina's cooperating teacher, Ms. Murphy, suggested that there is "always a contest between your authority as a teacher and the student's need for power. One of the tricks I've learned is to make small concessions in order to protect my power when I need it." The view of authority relationships between teacher and pupils on a common sense level points to both Regina and Ms. Murphy's beliefs that they need to maintain control over students. Their prescribed construct of power leads to practices that perpetuate teacher control. Regina, as she struggles with how to handle the situation with Eugene, asks questions about how to negotiate Eugene's needs with her own and what the fragile relationship of power is if students are allowed to "rebel against authority." Ms. Murphy's responses do not cause Regina to probe more deeply into issues of power relations and how those might be examined. The presupposition that there is a "way" to give minor concessions "to get what the teacher wants" simply reinforces the discursive practices of social control over organization of the space and distribution of activity and power by a central monitoring power—the teacher. Since orthodox behavior earns rewards and deviance doesn't, both teachers and students internalize and put into practice a series of practices that lead students to maintain a norm. Eugene may have temporarily broken the norm, but he will "get back on track" again. In effect, students and teachers have discursive practices that encourage and control each other's normative performances. The power is strong enough to discourage deviant discourse. So, Regina is learning the "tricks of control" rather than interrogating fully and carefully how and where control and power reside in a discourse on schools.

Another observation of Regina's might seem more difficult to incorporate into the comparison I have been seeking to draw between the means through which interaction is structured in the classroom and the power relations that result. Students often describe how their status is that of object. At this particular middle school, students labeled their relationships with teachers using the following descriptions: "My view is unimportant"; "We're just prisoners"; "Teachers decide and we're s'posed to perform"; "Small and unequal"; and "Invisible." Denied status through interactions that create such object distinctions strips away the sense of agency and identity. One seventh grader in this middle school told me that "students don't really exist. It's like we're there, and they just tell us to do this stuff to keep us busy and quiet." It is important to be clear here about just how the discourse and the messages within it get translated into power relationships. Regina, after describing how the students seem disinterested in "almost all aspects of class," said:

> Jamie told me about her reaction to a poem we'd read in class when I ran into her in the hallway. "One of my favorite poems this year was 'Portrait of Georgia' because it was so descriptive in so few words, and yet it also made you think and so wasn't very simple. I think I liked it so much because we went over it again and again. I like to hear everyone's suggestions and opinions. One small poem had so much in it." Now Jamie showed a very different reaction when we were studying this in class.

Regina went on to describe how Jamie's reaction was unexpected. Jamie had made a point in class of saying to everyone, "I'm just not into this poem." Ms. Murphy listened to Regina's comments and then offered her "take" on the difference in Jamie's reactions in and out of class. "It isn't highly unusual for students to have a public reaction that's different from their private reaction. After all, students can't reveal that they like something going on in class. They can't afford to show they are on 'our' side. Most of them like to keep the separation. They'll grandstand for each other about how disinterested they are in what's going on in class or how boring the work is. They have peer pressure to do that, and most of them don't want to be perceived in collusion with the teacher."

This incident underscores that students have their own "tricks of the trade" as they produce a student discourse of power. In Jamie's version, the actual message ("I'm not interested in this poem" and "This is one of my favorite poems") carries other messages. The teacher, as Ms. Murphy explains, learns how students create their own power plays. The students obviously know how teachers control the situation. There is a constant resistance to the struggle of the other (student or teacher) to attain power, and Regina is being initiated into an overt knowledge of this. As she said, "I'll have to remember that what students say about the work isn't necessarily what they mean." The valorization of the struggle on both sides confines the notion of resistance as a purely territorial need to challenge the other's power. To what ends and what purposes is this necessary or productive in schools? But the discourse of power is evident, and its perpetuation constant.

Regina writes in her journal:

> So many things about school seem like medieval relics: chalkboards and washing them, roll books, detentions and calls home, and talking to a kid in the hallway when they need a talking to. Psychology would say that talking in the hallway—separating peer from peers, removing the instigator from the scene—works. It worked with Chad today. I had to talk with him and another student in the hallway about cheating on a quiz. I chose to do it during class rather than after class because the students have only two minutes of passing time (another relic), and I knew that talking to him during class would give me time to work this through with him.
>
> Anyway, Chad turned in a quiz with a wrong answer exactly duplicating that of a girl who sat near him. The students sit at long tables, in groups, which research says is great for their learning. Hm . . . I wonder.
>
> "I dunno. That's what I thought," said Chad. This kid is not a cool liar: his twitching hands and darting eyes screamed guilt. Anne was also shifting uncomfortably from foot to foot. I walked down the hall a little way with her, and said that I could tell from her other responses that she read the book. I told her that academic integrity was a two-way street. Being aware of cheating, or allowing someone

else to cheat was as much a blot on one's honor as doing the cheating. I sent her back to class. Now I was left with Chad who was banging his sneakered heels against the side of the desk he sat on in the hall. I approached him and he instantly assumed the glazed-over stare of a kid who knows he's going to get yelled at. I didn't yell. I was very quiet. "Why didn't you read?" I asked him.

"I duno," Chad said. "I just don't like English any more."

"Really?" I asked.

"I dunno. I don't feel like reading. With Ms. Murphy we did myths and stuff and now it's just not fun."

I see," I said. "You think it's my fault."

"I dunno" were his last words.

Chad's strategy is to make Regina responsible for his lack of interest in the class and hence the incident of cheating. It is reasonable also to suppose that Regina believed that the key to Chad's problem was her: "I did feel guilty because I'm taking Ms. Murphy's place and maybe he did work better with her. That doesn't give him the right to cheat though, so I'm struggling with what to make of this incident." The significant feature of how Chad has deflected responsibility is the way in which it both constitutes Chad as the victim of circumstance and renders the cheating incident null. The perceived problem is Regina's incapacity to motivate Chad rather than the incident of cheating itself. Ms. Murphy considered the incident Chad's deliberate attempt to "squirm out of the situation. These kids know how to pull at the strings of our vulnerabilities." With this comment, Ms. Murphy dismissed Chad's behavior as just another trick of the trade.

The incident was a revealing instance of the competitive nature of conversation. Both Regina and Chad were seeking to control the situation by presenting their competing views on what had taken place. Taken at face value, there is no give-and-take in the conversation. Each person has bracketed off a version of the incident—Regina referring to the cheating incident and Chad discussing his disinterest in the class. The conversation ends with Chad in the dominant position. Regina has not answered his charges and the silence she renders by cutting off the conversation may signal her acceptance of responsibility for Chad's actions. The incident is a reminder that all the players in the school culture write and rewrite versions of reality to fit their own purposes. It is through different accounts of teachers' and students' discourses that the power relations in the classroom are shaped. After analyzing many conversations among students, student teachers, and teachers, I have found that the intersecting discourses mostly work to perpetuate present power structures and initiate student teachers into the subtleties of how to take up the role of teacher in the discourse. To understand more fully how student teachers are socialized by the interplay of these discourses researchers will need to engage in careful scrutiny of the political issues of technique and content as well as the development of critical consciousness about teaching as student teachers engage in the pedagogical struggles that are their primary concern during the student teaching experience.

A final poignant entry in her journal characterizes how pedagogical struggles dominated much of Regina's thinking:

> I went to the school thinking that a writing workshop should be like what Nancie Atwell describes. Atwell describes how she is lucky enough to teach the same students twice daily, and therefore her "curriculum" consisted of one class period of reading workshop and one of writing workshop. The content of both of these class periods was completely determined by the students. Students were "required" to have reading conferences with classmates, but this talk about texts served to report about books and to recommend them or not to other readers, not to engage in dialogue about a shared reading experience.
>
> I described to Ms. Murphy why I would like to have a model like this. I told her it sounded ideal and then she explained to me how one year she had tried something similar—she didn't do any shared texts that year. The kids mostly came to class and read and conferenced and wrote. What I missed in her description is what I see in the classroom now—talk, activity, shared energy, *and* independent work. I mentioned this to Ms. Murphy and she nodded her head. "One of the things that I've learned through the years is never to just buy into what someone else suggests. You have to look at things in many ways." Ms. Murphy led me to wonder: Wouldn't it get a little lonely, coming to school every day to read your own book and write your own piece, and get up in the author's chair occasionally and read to the class? What about tackling issues and ideas and learning together? I believe the Atwell model ignores the responsibility teachers have to acquaint students with different styles of learning and reading and writing.
>
> Ms. Murphy says she's learned that a writing curriculum varies between structured assignments and individual works, interspersing directed prompts with unstructured opportunities. "You have to know how to help them and have an idea of what they can and need to accomplish, otherwise they don't make much progress," Ms. Murphy confided. "I've been there too. I've tried many things and finally I think I keep struggling to find ways of doing it better." I started thinking about ways to take the best of what I've seen and also think about what I do well and care about—I'd like to start from there and see where it takes me.

As Regina struggles with the puzzlements of pedagogy here, she generates issues out of her struggle with at least three different versions of classroom workshops—Atwell's, Ms. Murphy's, and her own. What was particularly noticeable was her use of multiple perspectives rather than being overpowered by one dominant tradition, whether it be that of Atwell or Murphy. Here, Regina works through her own pedagogical concerns, which has a potentially powerful effect of helping her create something new rather than merely echo other's versions of the dominant discourses.

Regina begins to construct a language of possibility out of her examination of the many contradictions and inconsistencies in various versions of workshop approaches. This seems a small and precarious step into territory where Regina has not been before. What seems useful here is that Regina contemplates a different set of questions rather than deliberates on whether Atwell or Ms. Murphy have the "right" approach. It is through a different account, Regina's account, that her pedagogical struggle will continue and be shaped. The next step will be to "play out critique in the real" as Foucault suggested (1981, p. 13). Doing so will require that Regina plan, act, observe, and reflect on her attempts at "playing it out." Hopefully, she has been supported in her efforts to engage in these ways of studying her teaching through her preparation program. Such habits of constructing practice might be the most important trick of the trade that Regina can learn.

Regenerating Versions of Teaching

The political assumptions that underlie the rhetoric of initiation into the teaching community are much broader than these incidents portray, but the accounts describing Beverly, Jennifer, John, and Regina's particular cases demonstrate the discourses located in the classroom that serve to generate or control their versions of teaching. While much of the educational literature espouses a rhetoric that promotes student teacher decision making, reflection, collaboration, intuition, and negotiation, there is a tendency in practice to undermine the preparation of teachers by shackling them to parent practices. This apprenticeship tradition seems no less true today than it has been during the last decade or more when heated criticism exposed the student teacher as a passive recipient of a predefined pedagogy.

The incidents that I have reported in this chapter contain many critical components of power—from cooperating teachers who say "we know from experience" to the students' resistance or open hostility involving "why do we have to do it that way" and beyond to the student teachers' belief that their experience was "being controlled from above." The student teachers had less power than anyone else in these classrooms because they did not have equal access to or equal influence in shaping the discourse of either teachers or students. More often than not, influences outside themselves shaped their purposes and practices.

While this lack of power is troublesome, I learned that productive work could go on in environments where versions of teaching and learning were contested. An assumption cannot be made that the most productive experience for student teachers would be to work in environments where they matched or "fit in" with the cooperating teacher's philosophy. Such an arrangement might overlook or minimize difference in a way that does not allow either the cooperating teacher or the student teacher to compare their pedagogical choices and processes. Much of the initial experience for Beverly, Jennifer, John, and Regina seemed to bear out traditional power relations. The student teachers were never in charge and were caught between the role of student and teacher in varying degrees of apprenticeship, initiation, or opposition. Yet, all of them had some opportunities of talking about or knowing schools in ways they hadn't before, and these opportunities usually came when some conflict or tension arose. Hence, the issue of productive oppositions constitutes occasions for the construction of knowledge.

What emerges out of this consideration is the potential to create discussions of difference based on a discourse in which multiplicity of action and belief contradict and cohere simultaneously. The traditional way of educating student teachers has been to work within a discourse of agreement: to maintain connection and consistency, excluding the most divisive forces of difference. Specifically, I am recommending that we rescue the discourse on teaching from the bonds of accepted and agreed upon principles. I don't think it is necessarily productive for student teachers to believe that they have "come a long way" when they fit the traditional conceptions of the teaching community. We must think again about the discourses that are perpetuated through the initiation of other students and teachers into the discursive practices of school. I'd like to consider another of Foucault's (1982) principles of power. He applies the concept of the political "double-bind" to education by suggesting:

> Take for example an educational institution: the disposal of its space, the meticulous regulations which govern its internal life, the different activities which are organized there . . . all these things constitute a block of capacity-communication-power. The

activity which ensures apprenticeship and the acquisition of apti-
tudes or types of behavior is developed there by means of a whole
ensemble of regulated communications (lessons, questions and
answers, orders, exhortations, coded signs of obedience, differen-
tiation marks of the 'value' of each person and of the levels of
knowledge) and by the means of a whole series of power processes
(enclosure, surveillance, reward and punishment, the pyramidal
hierarchy) (pp. 218–219).

The big challenges in composing a teaching life will be to work
within and beyond the "ensemble of regulated communications."
And, how are Beverly, Jennifer, John, and Regina composing their
teaching lives as I write this chapter some three years after their student teaching experience? Beverly began teaching in an alternative
school not many blocks from where we walked the streets to these
student teachers' first placements. Beverly thrived in the school,
and the students were nurtured by her tough yet tender way of expecting them to succeed. Beverly began another degree program,
finding that "it's important to stay in the conversation." She indicated that continuing in the program gave her the opportunity to think
more carefully about what she was doing with students. "I'm learning to relax and deal with the teaching in the ways I think are best."
As she elaborated the issues, it became increasingly clear that this
community that supported and challenged her gave her confidence
in what she does in the classroom: "I always think about what I'm
doing, and I enjoy the intellectual stimulation as well as how that
informs my teaching. I'm not trying to earn another degree and get
out of what I'm doing. I want the conversations and community."

Jennifer moved to California and began teaching in a high school.
"So far," she wrote during the middle week of her first November,
"I'm elated with the students and their willingness to give things a
try. Many times I fall on my face, but the kids and I are working together. Of course there are rugged days. I'm dead tired!" Jennifer
found that the teachers in her school were developing some innovative programs, but that factions created pockets of resistance and
competition that she hadn't expected. "They talk about each other
and are genuinely nasty if someone is perceived successful in changing the way things have been." At the end of Jennifer's second year
of teaching, she wrote a letter: "What seems to fall away is the stress
with the workload and the ways of handling routines. I have that
down and concentrate more on how to expand my ideas of curriculum, to teach the literature better and with more complexity, and to
think about how to stretch my high school writers into more careful
consideration of their revisions. As far as faculty tensions, I've

learned to look the other way and avoid choosing sides. The best way to do that is never, I mean NEVER, go into the faculty room."

John located himself in the mountains of Colorado where he teaches at a private boarding school. I taught with him for two weeks in his high school English classes during his second year there. When I arrived, the students were reading *The Odyssey*. "They're loving it, and they are storytelling each of the books in *The Odyssey*, preparing a storytelling by sections. We're trying to really give a rendition of the oral tradition."

I suggested that we add one other dimension. "What if," I suggested, "we get them to work on their own odyssey pieces as well?" As they continued to read and give oral interpretations, we got them thinking about versions of the journeys of their lives. The advantage of a boarding school is the disadvantage—you have the kids with you day and night. The way it turned out we had many extra writing sessions, conferences, and peer response time together during those two weeks. These kids made journeys like I'd never imagined. That's always the gift of teaching. Here are two of their versions of *The Odyssey*:

To Feel the Gods

There are mists and light
Wheel tracks and footprints
Inside me
I can feel them
I know they're there.

There is hair in my face
an itch on my nose
I can feel them
I know they're there.

There are books and tin cans
A lightbulb, candleflame,
flower, sunshine, moonglow,
My soul
Can travel anywhere.
                    —Erin Frazer

You Could

You could fall in love
with Butte, Montana—the all
night M and M Cigar Store

and Cafe. Miners hover
over keno like tanningers
ruffling and pecking
at their share of lady
luck—the stone weight
of one number missing.
Booze with girls who'll
moonlight for any price.

Butte Montana—six
miners trapped when you
hit town. Terror zips words
shut. What ever happened to
the richest strike on earth?
Waiting through the clink,
clink on metal softening earth's
frozen jaw. Lizzie waits in blue
brocade, stands vigil. When rescuers
find spine crushed against granite,
Lizzie chokes back rage. Alone.

Butte. Arriving there, twenty-five
below zero, the world freezes into
ice fishing. Lines of matchsticks huddle
against the horizon. Joe Lydon's son
practices spitting sideways on the ice.
Just like his father. He says he'll buy
a Toyota Celica. Says he'll split
this town.

You could fall in love
with Butte, Montana. Row
after row of Victorian gingerbread,
clapboard, eviction papers jitter
with the wind's beat. Coal dust
sticks like oil in the pores
of everything.

                                    —Reynold Marks

As so often happens with a group of students, I am somehow implicated in their work if I have listened to and accept the alternatives
they provide.

Regina was hired to teach seventh grade English in a middle
school in a rough neighborhood. She turned in her attendance and
grade book by the end of October and took a position in one of the
large educational publishing houses in the city. "I thought I could

do it. I thought I could make a difference, but I didn't realize how the poverty and waste and violence could overcome my desire to make a difference. I couldn't face it day after day. I just couldn't find the hope that I needed to sustain the energy required. I hope that working in publishing is a different way to meet my commitment to these kids. I can't endure it this way."

Epilogue

"Remember your stories," Kim Stafford said to a group of students in Wallowa County. "They can save your life a little at a time." As Beth, Jane, Joe, Avis, Stephen, Sarah, Ben, Beverly, Jennifer, John, and Regina were kind enough to let us experience with them, teachers are continuously reading and writing the texts of their teaching lives. All of them yearn for form and significance, yet they also demonstrate the power of imagination to engrave practice with their personal signatures. Traditions in education have largely dictated content and form and created a world dulled by habitude. And, once more, I'll emphasize that the dialectics of probability and possibility create a healthy tension, as these teachers' frustrations and elations have illustrated.

We enter into spaces of uncertainty when we teach. I often think of teaching in simile: it's like standing on the threshold of a door that opens into nothing short of a void. I stand there a moment—falter, teeter, and sometimes return to the side of the threshold where I can plant my foot on *terra firma*. Less often, I step into the white space. As I wrote the various chapters of this book, I was reminded again of how difficult it is to enter the slippery world of teaching where nothing remains stable except the instability. It is through a family story told for over three decades at holiday dinners that I can magnify that feeling.

A distant cousin named Hank frequently opened the glass doors on the bookcase in his living room and took out his great grandfather's turn of the century *Historical Atlas*. He curled up on the couch and studied maps of the world—the squiggles of ink that represented continents, coastlines, rivers, national boundaries, the peaks of mountains, and juts of earth that stretched out toward the sea. He liked to hear the names of exotic places, and he mouthed them just loudly enough to resonate into his throat and off his tongue—Siam, Persia, Saxony, Anatolia, Prussia, Serbia, Baluchistan, Abyssinia. He learned the earth intimately through this naming. He gained access and control over the terrain through close study, and he knew the indentations, curves, twists, and stretches of shaded green, blue, pink, and purple. He repeated names, night after night, year after year. He did all this before he was in fourth grade. He had gone so far as to name and sketch imaginary land masses in journal after journal. Within this world even the flora and fauna were sketched, named, and given place on the land. Hank often climbed Buck's hill, the highest perch from which to gaze over the landscape of his rural Idaho home. From there he could imagine the whole world stretched out and familiar. He navigated through familiar waters and walked terrain that he could name. The names were beautiful. Rivers, seas, forests, mountain peaks—Garonne, Tyrrhenian, Abittibi, Fiscellus.

In fifth grade, Mrs. Anderson, the librarian at Washington School, received the *Atlas of World History* in her two boxes of new books. That was 1957. Mrs. Anderson beamed when she held out a blue leather binder filled with glossy and highly colored maps. Hank turned pages. He looked for order, shape, and names of the world with which he'd grown familiar and of which he'd taken possession. He turned more pages and found new names—Soviet Union, Iran, Ethiopia, Thailand, and Turkey.

He found names given to lands that had been deep green and nameless—islands, lakes, rivers that he'd named for himself. Hank kept finding, with each new page, worlds terrifying in their unfamiliarity. His head zigzagged and his heart raced, and, as he stood up to catch his breath, he fainted. "Right there," one of our grandmothers said at every holiday dinner as she shook her hand back and forth. "How can anybody be so stubborn about change. It took some convincing for him to open an atlas after that. He still kept sketching every little thing he saw around him, but he didn't look outward much anymore. Couldn't tolerate change—then or now." Hank would sit across the table smiling as the story was told. As an architect, he was still imagining the poetics of space, naming and forming his new-found landscapes.

Within anyone's story are multiple stories—stories of resistance to change, of comfort in familiarity, and of the need to name and create. There are other stories as well. Two generations of grandmothers felt the story was important to tell. I believe that they told it for its double-edged complexity. Although resistance to change is viewed critically, this is also the story of family pride in a boy with such full possession of his imagination that he created a world enriched by his own visions. In some ways, it is the fear of stepping over the threshold into the unknown that may keep classrooms and the teaching and learning that go on there so familiar. I was struck by this particularly when, several years ago now, I sat in the desk of my first grade daughter on Back To School Night:

My six-year-old's teacher is talking about the children's upcoming experiences. I'm looking around at pictures the children have drawn, mostly blue skies with a lone tree, full of green squiggles, searching the horizon. Multi-colored houses with trap door eyes stare out. In one, a stick figure child reaches toward a ray of sun; another stick has a red triangle skirt covering a large circle tummy. A blue bow perches atop the yellow waves of hair. All twenty 8½ by 11-inch squares of white have house, sky, tree, and sun. None of the drawings look conspicuously foreign, no pink houses or green skies. I'm wondering why I don't see rain clouds, a favorite pet dog, a rocket ship, or a waterfall. Craters of the Moon in bas-relief, with its eerie desolation, would be an oasis against all this sameness. I hear my inner voice screaming out, in all my roles as parent, teacher, and student of education: Where is the "I" in school?

I finger through the book atop Katie's desk, trying to ease the voice within. I find phonics skill worksheets and dumbed down stories about children who "ride the bike," "go for a hike," and "like Mike." I leaf through pages that describe animals whose names cannot be more than three or four letters maximum. So, this is school. Not much has changed since my older children began their formal education in this same room nearly ten years before Katie. I'm thinking that schools have the power to generate ways for students to understand what the world is and what it might become. But, I'm also thinking that too often school is a place that leaves the real world outside and carries on a dull, uninspired, monotone voice, a world that doesn't exist let alone excite. I'm wondering whether it will profit our children if they know the basic facts yet cannot feel, make sense of or question their experiences and attitudes. We have the power as teachers to cripple the "I" or not to.

For my children, school has been a gradual denial of self which in turn meant a denial of thinking and feeling and acting. Many of us don't need to be convinced that by the time students arrive at the end of their high school years they have become masters at saying what the teacher thinks they ought to say. On the other side, school could be a place where individual voices are encouraged. As I think back on Katie's entrance into the world of school, I remember the pages of copied sentences on her desk: "Susan plays ball." "The dog likes his bath." At home, in her journal, she wrote: "Is what they write on the bathroom walls really true?" What will happen to our questioning, curious, probing Katie? I see school taking the "I" away from her. I hear her voice becoming softer, more distant—graphite on white paper—without life, without a mark or symbol that stamps Katie's signature of mind on her work and world. Will her natural, inquisitive writing be polluted by school where the emphasis is not on developing her unique voice? I lament again: Where is the "I" in school?

I left that Parent's Night with more resolve as teacher than as parent. I want my classroom free of the meaningless claptrap of exercise stuff that bears no resemblance to life and learning. I can't teach the merest fraction of what children teach themselves about life, language, science, or math if they are inquisitive, experimental, and turned on to learning. But I can influence their interchanges with the world by being in a position to nurture the kind and quality of learning experiences they will have.

That is why I teach writing. It crept up on me as the logical outcome of my love of language and the evocation of story that my grandmother had performed on me. Words, for me, are the central nervous system of ideas. Because of their power to carry image, rhythm, movement, and sound, I'm convinced that words penetrate the very fiber of imagination. I try to help students pay attention to language, to listen and see with abandonment. I encourage them to grasp words in their hands, sniff them, breathe them in, or place the sounds and rhythm of words to their ears. Words are like gems turned slowly in the light, opening the landscapes within the mind to reflect angles and multitudinous ways of seeing and hearing human experience. Writing is an adventure. And there is some churlish satisfaction when the writing takes on a life of its own and comes down to earth, finds legs and walks around. Explaining all this reminds me how important it is not to rush the writing—it deserves lingering over. And sometimes in the rush to process or produce writing, students do not have the time or space to live with their words and imaginings.

I hope to help students see that writing is a construction site amidst the dust and rubble, and that writers clutch a ragged blueprint of an idea that must be crafted. Nearby are piles of new pine boards with the smell of pitch, strong and seductive, and a bagful of shining nails, a hammer, a saw and mitre box. These are tools of crafting and carpentry is the art. We writers have our own tools for designing, sawing, hammering, mitering, and sanding. It never quits surprising me, the power of the craft. This is my job as a teacher of writing: to help writers attune to the power of their eyes and ears, to help them learn the craftsmanship of the trade, and to help them trust imagination. Writing is a journey and an odyssey and laboriously hard work.

I would like to stress that through the student writing I have gained insight as a teacher into the richness—the small, near sacred geography hidden away from textbooks and curriculum guides. Dizzied by images of national literature and the worship of the canon, we sometimes forget the "I" in school. I need to remind myself often to pay heed to the literature my students write about the physical and spiritual landscapes of their lives. The literature they write offers a record of the ways in which they connect to a place and make it home, rooted in their lives and rhythms of the land that they feel under their feet and hear pounding in their hearts and imaginations. To preserve the wonder is the province of the classroom teacher. My role is to invite students into writing the stories that shape their identities. The thing I love most is that I can still evoke those students when I have an appetite to remember the days we shared together in class. I'd like some of them to have the last say in this book:

> My grandfather would cage fish for spawning. He'd take a hen fish and knead her belly until the eggs would spill forth like jelly into the bucket he'd carried there. Kneading again and again, he'd bring forth eggs until he'd let her go, back into the water. Then he'd uncage the male. He knew just the right movements to release a trickle. A thousand eggs were fertilized, sent back into the waters where the river doesn't roar. He had two purposes in the last of his life: to fish and to keep the river populated. In a way it's like a hand from God, something natural and unnatural at the same time.
>
> Sarah McMahon, age 14

> Early this morning I watched the calves herded into the range corral for branding. The irons were heated by a sagebrush bonfire to a red hot glow. Inside a smaller pen, Byron threw each calf to the ground, looping a rope around its back feet that was tied to a post. Once the front legs were tied, the calf was stretched out, much like a torture rack of the Middle Ages. Each calf would bawl pitifully, struggle to get up as the branding iron pressed into its hide. The stench rose and a breeze blew it my way.
>
> These calves represent our shelter, our bread and our home. The branding makes them legally ours. The brand defends our property much like a good fence does. Yet brands, like words, are only the symbol of an idea.
>
> Eric Downing, age 14

> ### Monuments
>
> It's like walking into a museum
> where stone has been cracked open
> to let the spirits walk on earth
> again.

Imagine the mother, holding
the dying infant in her arms.
All that's left now:
Lettie Burns Martin
September 7, 1893–September 12, 1894.
What did father say to mother? To
baby Lettie lying too still? Who dug the earth
away, preparer for the box of bone and flesh?

Ernesto Martinez, dead at forty-two.
He loved the random joy of dance
and drink and cards. I know it by his name.
Beside him dark-haired girls who listen
now to unheard beats. Ernesto
doesn't come again, he's trapped
in earth so heavy it takes love and memory
to break him free.

Stones grow here like flowers in a garden,
cropping up like weeds too fast, too soon
for those who stand upon the hill shaded
still by maple, birch, and ash.

I pity them the memories I can't sow
for them in life, in love, in constant
competition with the loss. Monuments
of stone so deep I dare not love for
fear of what is lost in love. This
country of monuments has a silent
solace of its own, retreats into the dark
of night, the spade to clink again
another day.

                                  Leticia Monroe, age 17

Mall Rats

The rain doesn't mind a rainy day but me and Robert, James, and
Joe use one to our advantage. We hit the road, screech the tires,
turn a quick right on 105. The mall stands like some circus tent,
filled with cubicles of pleasure. We take our pictures first—standing in those booths, grinning like gorillas when the light flashes.
A gruesome foursome looking like we own the block. It's ice cream
next cause girls in tight pink blouses dip our favorites out—cookie
dough with fudge topping and she gives me that smile that shows
her tongue and teeth. We stake our claim on a bench near The Wiz
and watch the girls go by. Eight billion girls paw through earrings,

white blouses, and belts on the bargain tables and there we sit making comments until Russell and Walter come by with some girls they've met who hang on every word. Robert impresses them by striking a book full of matches and then he stomp, stomp, stomps on the flame when everybody's getting nervous and the girls are squealing.

Joe will talk your ear off if you let him, so I head for some peace at the Arcade—red wallpaper, glittering lights, sounds of winning, clinks of quarters—my brain explodes in light. I start thinking that I'm losing my mind with boredom. I head over to the food court and grab a coke. I see the guys sitting with a girl from school, one of those with fingernails that click, click against the plastic of her cup. Joe's going on about how his brother climbed this mountain in Australia last year and made it sound like he marched straight up this hill and overtook the top. I know his brother nearly died of food poisoning and they had to bring him down on some pieced together stretcher. I don't say anything cause I'm not trying to impress this girl. Not true. I'm thinking the silent type might be a relief in this place. So she's saying to me now, "Tyrone, what you thinkin'? You got the downs?" Her eyes are dark as that fudge topping and sparkling with little glitters of light. I'm thinking how I'll ask her out. Tell her she can fix my blues. "Let's blow this place and leave these mutts behind. You and me breezin' down 105 with the top down. You and me at the movie. Let's go." It didn't happen. I couldn't get the words out. I sat there like some stone statue in the park and sipped my coke. She looks back at Joe, "What's with him? Sometimes he's soooo boring." I'm thinking how I'd rather be flying a kite against a strong wind, diving into the surf and feeling the sting of salt water, or shooting hoops with my dad. I say, "Let's go." Above the protests, I hear myself saying, "I'm the driver. I says it's time to go." That's that. We're out of there.

Tyrone Nixon, 17

My hope for all of us, and especially for Beth, Jane, Joe, Avis, Stephen, Sarah, Ben, Beverly, Jennifer, John, and Regina is that we continue to focus on how to let the learning loose in the classroom.

Bibliography

Anderson, S. 1930. "Sophistication." *Winesburg Ohio*. New York: Charles Scribner's Sons, 39–62.

Apple, M. 1985. *Education and Power*. New York: Routledge.

Applebee, A. 1974. *Tradition and Reform in the Teaching of English: A History*. Urbana, IL: National Council Teachers of English.

Aronowitz, S., & J. Giroux. 1985. *Education Under Siege: The Conservative, Liberal and Radical Debate over Schooling*. S. Hadley, MA: Bergin & Garvey.

Atwell, N. 1987. *In the Middle*. Portsmouth, NH: Boynton/Cook.

Atwood, M. 1983. *Murder in the Dark: Short Fictions and Prose Poems*. Toronto: Coach House Press.

Austin-Ward, B. 1986. "English Teaching and English Teachers: The Perceptions of Sixteen Year Olds." *Journal of Educational Research 28* (1): 32–42.

Bakhtin, M. 1981. *The Dialogic Imagination*. ed. M. Holmquist, trans. C. Emerson, Austin, TX: University of Texas Press.

Barthes, R. 1977. *Image, Music, Text*. New York: Hill and Wang.

Barthes, R. 1974. *S/Z* trans. by R. Miller. New York: Hill and Wang.

Bateson, M.C. 1989. *Composing a Life*. New York: Plume.

Bennett, W.J. 1984. *To Reclaim a Legacy*. Washington, DC: National Endowment for the Humanities.

Berk, L. 1980. "Education in Lives: Biographical Narrative in the Study of Educational Outcomes." *The Journal of Curriculum Theorizing 2* (Summer): 88–212.

Berliner, D. 1986. "In Search of the Expert Pedagogue." *Educational Researcher 15* (7), 5–13.

Bertaux, D., ed. 1981. *Biography and Society*. Bevery Hills, CA: Sage.

Berthoff, A. 1984. *Reclaiming the Imagination*. Portsmouth, NH: Boynton/Cook.

Bettelheim, B. 1977. *The Uses of Enchantment: The Meaning and Importance of Fairy Tales*. New York: Vintage.

Bhabha, H. 1990. "The Third Space: An Interview with Homi Bhabha." In *Identity: Community, Culture, Difference*, ed. J. Rutherford, 207–221. London: Lawrence & Wishart.

Bleich, D. 1978. *Subjective Criticism.* Baltimore, MD: The Johns Hopkins University Press.

Bloland, D. 1983. *Classroom Models of the Teaching of English: Four English Teachers' Perceptions of Their Students in Relation to the English Curriculum.* (Unpublished doctoral dissertation, New York University).

Bloom, A. 1987. *The Closing of the American Mind.* New York: Simon and Schuster.

Boomer, G. 1988. *Metaphors and Meanings: Essays on English Teaching by Garth Boomer.* ed. Bill Green, Australia: Australian Association of Teacher Education.

Brewer, J. & A. Hunter. 1989. *Multimethod Research: A Synthesis of Styles.* Beverly Hills, CA: Sage.

Britton, J. 1987. "A Quiet Form of Research." In *Reclaiming the Classroom,* eds. D. Goswami & P. Stillman, 13–19. Upper Montclair, NJ: Boynton/ Cook.

Britzman, D.P. 1991. *Practice Makes Practice: A Critical Study of Learning to Teach.* New York: State University of New York Press.

Brophy, J. & T. Good. 1986. "Teacher Behavior and Student Achievement." In *Handbook of Research on Teaching*, ed. M. Wittrock, 328–375. New York: Macmillan.

Broudy, H.S. 1977. "Types of Knowledge and Purpose of Education." In *Schooling and the Acquisitions of Knowledge,* eds. R.C. Anderson, R.J. Shapiro, & W.E. Montagne. New York: John Wiley.

Brown, L. 1987. "Rendering Literature Accessible." In *Readers, Texts, Teachers,* eds. B. Corcoran & E. Evans. Portsmouth, NH: Boynton/Cook.

Bruner, J. 1986. *Actual Minds, Possible Worlds.* Cambridge, MA: Harvard University Press.

———. 1990. *Acts of Meaning.* Cambridge, MA: Harvard University Press.

Bullough, R.V. & A.D. Gitlin. 1989. "Toward Educative Communities: Teacher Education and the Quest for the Reflective Practitioner." *Qualitative Studies in Education, 2* (4): 285–298.

Cheever, J. 1980. "Torch Song." In *The Stories of John Cheever,* ed. John Cheever, 105–122. New York: Ballantine Books.

Clandinin, D.J. 1986. *Classroom Practice: Teachers' Images in Action.* London: Falmer Press.

——— & F.M. Connelly. 1987. What Is 'Personal' in Studies of the Personality?" *Journal of Curriculum Studies 19* (6), 79–102.

——— & F. M. Connelly. 1988. "Studying Teachers' Knowledge of Classrooms: Collaborative Research, Ethics, and the Negotiation of Narrative. *The Journal of Educational Thought, 22* (2A): 269–282.

——— & F.M. Connelly. 1991. "Narrative and Story in Practice and Research. In *The Reflective Turn: Case Studies in and on Educational Practice,* ed. D.A. Schon, 258–281. New York: Teachers College Press.

Clark, C.M. & M. Lampert. 1986. "The Study of Teacher Thinking: Implications for Teacher Education." *Journal of Teacher Education, 37* (5), 27–31.

Connelly, F.M. & D.J. Clandinin. 1985. "Personal Practical Knowledge and Modes of Knowing: Relevance for Teaching and Learning." In *Learning and Teaching the Ways of Knowing,* ed. E. Eisner, 174–178. Eighty-fourth Yearbook of the National Society for the Study of Education, Part 2. Chicago, IL: University of Chicago Press.

———. 1987. "On Narrative Method, Biography and Narrative Unities in the Study of Teaching." *Journal of Educational Thought 21* (3), 130–139.

___. 1988. *Teachers as Curriculum Planners: Narratives of Experience.* New York: Teachers College Press.

Corcoran, B. & E. Evans, eds. (1987). *Readers, Texts, Teachers.* Portsmouth, NH: Boynton/Cook.

Cruikshank, D.R. & J.H. Applegate. 1981. "Reflective Teaching as a Strategy for Teacher Growth." *Educational Leadership, 38* (7), 553–554.

Darling-Hammond, L. 1994. "Performance-based Assessment and Educational Equity." *Harvard Educational Review 64* (1): 5–30.

Denzin, J. 1967. *The Research Act,* 2nd ed. New York: McGraw-Hill.

Dewey, J. 1933. *How We Think: A Restatement of the Relation of Reflective Thinking to the Educative Process.* Chicago, IL: D.C. Heath.

Dickens, C. 1958. *David Copperfield.* New York: Washington Square Press. (Original work published in 1850 in London, England in monthly installments.)

———. 1966a. *Hard Times.* New York: Norton. (Original work published in 1854 in London, England in weekly installments in *Household Words Magazine.*)

———. 1966b. *Oliver Twist.* Harmondsworth, England: Penguin English Library. (Original work published in 1838 in London, England in *Bentley's Miscellany Magazine.*)

———. 1971. *Our Mutual Friend.* Harmondsworth, England: Penguin English Library. (Original work published in 1865 in London, England in monthly installments.)

———. 1982. *The Life and Adventures of Nicholas Nichelby.* Harmondsworth, England: Penguin English Library. (Original work published in 1839 in London, England in monthly installments.)

Dixon, J. 1967. *Growth through English.* New York: Oxford University Press.

Eagleton, T. 1983. *Literary Theory: An Introduction.* Minneapolis: University of Minnesota Press.

Eco, U. 1979. *The Role of the Reader: Explorations in the Semiotics of Texts.* London: Hutchinson.

Eiseley, L. 1975. *All the Strange Hours: The Evacuation of a Life.* New York: Charles Scribner's Sons.

Elbow, P. 1990. *What is English?* New York and Urbana, IL: Modern Language Association & National Council Teachers of English.

Ely, M., M. Anzul, T. Friedman, D. Garner, & A. Steinmetz. 1991. *Doing Qualitative Research: Circles within Circles.* New York: Falmer Press.

Erickson, F. 1986. "Qualitative Methods in Research on Teaching." In *Handbook of Research on Teaching,* 3rd ed. M.C. Wittrock, ed. 119–161. New York: Macmillan.

Everhart, R. 1983. *Reading, Writing, and Resistance.* New York: Routledge and Kegan Paul.

Feiman, S. 1979. "Technique and Inquiry in Teacher Education: A Curricular Study." *Curriculum Inquiry 9* (1): 63–79.

Foucault, M. 1977. *Power/Knowledge: Selected Interviews and Other Writings 1972–1977.* New York: Pantheon.

———. 1982. Afterward. In *Michel Foucault,* eds. H. Dreyfus & P. Rabinow. Brighton, England: Harvester.

———. 1981. "Questions of method: An interview with Michel Foucault." *Ideology and Consciousness 8*: 3–14.

———. 1980. *The Order of Things: An Archaeology of the Human Sciences.* New York: Vintage Books.

Freire, P. 1971. *Pedagogy of the Oppressed.* New York: Herder and Herder.

Freire, P. 1970. "Cultural Action and Conscientization." *Harvard Educational Review 40* (3): 452–477.

Fulghum, R. 1990. "A Bag of Possibles and Other Matters of the Mind." *Newsweek* (September): 91–94.

Gadamer, H. 1975. *Truth and Method.* New York: The Seabury Press.

Geertz, C. 1988. *Works and Lives: The Anthropologist as Author.* Palo Alto, CA: Stanford University Press.

Geertz, C. 1983. *Local Knowledge.* New York: Basic Books.

Giroux, H. 1981. *Ideology, Culture, and the Process of Schooling.* Philadelphia, PA: Temple University Press.

Giroux, H. & R. Simon. 1989. *Popular Culture, Schooling, and Everyday Life.* New York: Bergin & Harvey.

Goetz, J. & M. LeCompte. 1984. *Ethnography and Qualitative Design in Educational Research.* Orlando, FL: Academic Press.

Goldhammer, R., R.H. Anderson, & R. Krajewski. 1980. *Clinical Supervision of Teachers: Special Methods for the Clinical Supervision of Teachers,* 2nd ed. New York: Holt, Rinehart & Winston.

Goodson, I.F. 1991. "History, Context, and Qualitative Methods." In *Biography, Identity, and Schooling: Episodes in Educational Research,* eds. I.F. Goodson & R. Walker, 114–136. London: The Falmer Press.

Gore, J. 1987. "Reflecting on Reflective Teaching." *Journal of Teacher Education 38* (2): 33–39.

Green, B. 1990. "A Dividing Practice: Literature, English Teaching and Cultural Politics. In *Bringing English to Order,* eds. I. Goodson & P. Medway, 135–161. New York: The Falmer Press.

Greene, M. 1978a. "Wide-Awakeness and the Moral Life." In *Landscapes of Learning.* New York: Teachers College Press.

———. 1978b. "Teaching: The Question of Personal Reality." *Teachers College Record 80* (1): 23–35.

———. 1986. "Reflection and Passion in Teaching." *Journal of Curriculum and Supervision 2*: 68–81.

Grimmett, P.P., A.M. MacKinnon, G.P. Erickson, & T.J. Riecher. 1990. "Reflective Practice in Teacher Education." In *Encouraging Reflective Practice in Education,* eds. R.T. Clift, W.R. Houston, & M.C. Pugach, 20–38. New York: Teachers College Press.

Grumet, M.R. 1980. "Autobiography and Reconceptualization." *Journal of Curriculum Theorizing 2* (2): 155–158.

Grundy, S. 1987. *Curriculum: Products or Praxis.* New York: Falmer Press.

Harding, D. 1977. Response to Literature. In *The Cool Web: The Pattern of Children's Reading,* eds. M. Meek, A. Warlow, & G. Barton, London: The Bodley Head.

Hemingway, E. 1932. *A Farewell to Arms.* New York: Charles Scribner's Sons.

Holt-Reynolds, D. 1992. "Personal History Based Beliefs as Relevant Prior Knowledge in Coursework." *American Educational Research Journal 29* (2): 325–349.

Howe, F. 1984. *Myths of Coeducation.* Bloomington: Indiana University Press.

Hirsch, E.D. 1975. Letter. *College English* 37(2):13–14.

———. 1987. *Cultural Literacy.* Boston: Houghton Mifflin.

Hunsaker, L. & M. Johnson. 1992. "Teacher Under Construction: A Collaborative Case Study of Teacher Change." *American Educational Research Journal 29* (2):350–372.

Iser, W. 1978. *The Act of Reading.* London: Routledge and Kegan Paul.

Kagan, D.M. 1992. "Professional Growth Among Preservice and Beginning Teachers." *Review of Educational Research 62* (2):129-169.

Kantor, K. 1993. "From Our Miss Brooks to Mr. Moore." In *Images of Schoolteachers in Twentieth-Century America,* eds. P. Joseph & G. Burnaford, 175–189. New York: St. Martin's Press.

Kantor, K. 1990. "Both Sides Now: Teaching English, Teaching Curriculum." In *Teaching and Thinking About Curriculum,* eds. J. Sears & J.D. Marshall, 61–74. New York: Teachers College Press.

Kelly, G. 1955. *The Psychology of Personal Constructs.* New York: Norton.

Kilbourn, B. 1988. "Reflecting on Vignettes of Teaching." In *Reflection in*

Teacher Education, eds. P.P. Grimmett & G.L. Erickson, 91–111. New York: Teachers College Press.

Kincheloe, J.L. 1991. *Teachers as Reseachers: Qualitative Inquiry as a Path to Empowerment.* New York: Falmer Press.

King, S. 1984. "Imagery and the Third Eye." In *The Writers Handbook,* ed. Sylvia K. Burack, 74–79. Boston, MA: The Winter Press.

Kirby, D., T. Liner., & R.Vinz. 1988. *Inside Out: Developing Strategies for Teaching Writing,* 2nd ed. Portsmouth, NH: Boynton/Cook.

Knoblauch, C.H., & L. Brannon. 1988. "Knowing Our Knowledge: A Phenomenological Basis for Teacher Research." In *Audits of Meaning: A Festschrift in Honor of Ann E. Berthoff,* ed. L.Z. Smith, 17–78. Portsmouth, NH: Heinemann, Boynton/Cook.

Korthagen, F.A.C. 1985. "Reflective Teaching and Preservice Teacher Education in the Netherlands." *Journal of Teacher Education 36* (5): 11–15.

Lakoff, G. & M. Johnson. 1980. *Metaphors We Live By.* Chicago: University of Chicago Press.

Langer, S. 1957. *Philosophy in a New Key: A Study in the Symbolism of Reason, Rite, and Art.* Cambridge, MA: Harvard University Press.

Lanier, S. 1945. "The Marshes of Glynn. In *Sidney Lanier: Poems and Poem Outlines,* ed. C.R. Anderson, 119–122. Baltimore, MD: The Johns Hopkins Press.

Lense, E. 1986. "Marbles." *Zone 3* (Fall): 31.

Lester, N.B., & J.S. Mayher. 1987. "Critical Professional Inquiry." *English Education* 19 (4): 198–210.

Lincoln, Y., & E.S. Guba. 1985. *Naturalistic Inquiry.* Beverly Hills, CA: Sage.

Lortie, D.C. 1966. "Teacher Socialization: The Robinson Crusoe Model. In *The Real World of the Beginning Teacher.* Washington, DC: National Commission on Teacher Education and Professional Standards. (ERIC Document Reproduction Service No. ED 030 616).

MacIntyre, A. 1984. *After Virtue: A Study in Moral Theory.* South Bend, IN: University of Notre Dame Press.

MacKinnon, A.M. 1987. "Detecting Reflection-in-Action Among Preservice Elementary Science Teachers." *Teaching and Teacher Education 3* (2): 135–145.

Mayer, J.S.. 1990. *Uncommon Sense: Theoretical Practice in Language Education.* Portsmouth, NH: Boynton/Cook.

———. 1991. "New Lenses for Old Problems: What We Believe is What We See." In *Search and Re-search: What the Inquiring Teacher Needs to Know* eds. R.S. Brause & J.S. Mayher, 3–22. New York: Falmer Press.

——— & R.S. Brause, 1991. "The Never-Ending Cycle of Teacher Growth. In *Search and Re-search: What the Inquiring Teacher Needs to Know,* eds. R.S. Brause & J.S. Mayher, 23–41. New York: Falmer Press.

————, N. Lester, & G. Pradl. 1983. *Learning to Write/Writing to Learn.* Upper Montclair, NJ: Boynton/Cook.

McIntosh, P. 1981. "The Study of Women: Implications for Reconstructing the Liberal Arts Discipline." *The Forum for Liberal Education 4* (1): 1–3.

McNeil, L. 1986. *Contradictions of Control: School Structure and School Knowledge.* New York: Routledge.

Mead, G. 1934. *Mind, Society, and Self.* Chicago: University of Chicago Press.

Meek, M. 1988. *How Texts Teach What Readers Learn.* Avonset, UK: Thimble Press.

Miles, M. & A.M. Huberman 1994. *Qualitative Data Analysis,* 2nd ed. Beverly Hills, CA: Sage.

Miller, J.L. 1990. Teachers as Curriculum Creators. In *Teaching and Thinking About Curriculum,* eds. J. Sears & J.D. Marshall, 85–96. New York: Teachers College Press.

Momaday, N.S. 1989. *Ancient Child.* New York: Harpers.

Moss, J.F. 1984. *Focus Units: A Handbook for Elementary School Teachers.* Urbana, IL: NCTE.

Muller, H. 1967. *The Uses of English: Guides for the Teaching of English from the Anglo-American Conference at Dartmouth College.* New York: Holt, Rinehart and Winston.

Murray, D.M. 1985. *A Writer Teaches Writing,* 2nd ed. Boston: Houghton Mifflin.

Naidoo, B. 1986. *Journey to Jo'burg.* New York: Harper and Row.

Nelms, B. 1988. "Sowing the Dragon's Teeth." In *Literature in the Classroom: Readers, Texts, and Contexts.* Urbana, IL: NCTE.

Oberg, A. 1986. "Using Construct Theory as a Basis for Research into Teacher Professional Development." *Journal of Curriculum Studies* 19 (1): 55-65.

Orwell, G. 1950. *Shooting an Elephant and Other Essays.* New York: Harcourt Brace.

————. 1970. *Collected Essays, Journalism and Letters.* London: Harmondsworth Press.

———— & M.R. Grumet. 1976. *Toward a Poor Curriculum.* Dubuque, IA: Kendall/Hunt.

Perrone, V. 1991. *Reflections on Schooling and the Art of Teaching.* New York: Jossey-Bass.

Pinar, W. & M. Grumet. 1976. *Toward a Poor Curriculum.* Dubuque, IA: Kendall/Hunt.

Polkinghorne, D.E. 1988. *Narrative Knowing and the Human Sciences.* New York: SUNY.

Pope, M. & P. Denicolo. 1986. "Intuitive Theories—A Researcher's Dilemma." *British Educational Research Journal 12* (2): 153–165.

Popkewitz, T.S. 1984. *Paradigm and Ideology in Educational Research: The Social Functions of the Intellectual.* New York: Falmer Press.

Postman, N. 1988. "The Educationalist as Painkiller." *English Education* 20: 3-17.

Pradl, G.M. 1991. "Reading Literature in a Democracy: The Challenge of Louise Rosenblatt." In *The Experience of Reading: Louise Rosenblatt and Reader Response Theory,* ed. J. Clifford, 23–46. Portsmouth, NH: Boynton/Cook.

Probst, R. 1988. *Response and Analysis: Teaching Literature in Junior and Senior High School.* Portsmouth, NH: Boynton/Cook.

Reid, L. & R. VanDeWeghe. 1994. "Thoughtful Communities: Classroom Research in Higher Literacy." In *English Journal* 83 (1): 21–26.

Rich, A. 1977. *On Lies, Secrets, and Silence.* New York: W.W. Norton.

Richardson, V. 1990. "The Evolution of Reflective Teaching and Teacher Education." In *Encouraging Reflective Practice in Education,* eds. R.T. Clift, W.R. Houston, & M.C. Pugach, 3–19. New York: Teachers College Press.

Rockwell, Joan. 1974. *Fact in Fiction: The Uses of Literature in the Systematic Study of Society.* Brighton, Sussex: The Harvester Press LTD.

Rogers, C. 1969. *Freedom to Learn.* London: Charles E. Merrill.

Romano, T. 1987. *Clearing the Way: Working With Teenage Writers.* Portsmouth, NH: Heinemann.

Rosenblatt, L. 1978. *The Reader, the Text, the Poem: The Transactional Theory of Literary Work.* Carbondale, IL: Southern Illinois University Press.

Russell, T. 1988. "From Pre-service Teacher Education to First Year of Teaching: A Study of Theory and Practice." In *Teachers' Professional Learning,* ed. J. Calderhead. London: Falmer.

Ryan, K. 1970. *Don't Smile until Christmas.* Chicago: University of Chicago Press.

Sanders, D.P., & G. McCutcheon. 1986. "The Development of Practical Theories of Teaching." *Journal of Curriculum and Supervision 2* (1): 50-67.

Schaefer, R.J. 1967. *The School as a Center of Inquiry.* New York: Harper and Row.

Scholes, R. 1985. *Textual Power.* New Haven, CT: Yale University Press.

Schon, D.A. 1983. *The Reflective Practitioner: How Professionals Think in Action.* New York: Basic Books.

———. (1987). *Educating the Reflective Practitioner.* San Francisco, CA: Jossey-Bass.

———. 1991. *The Reflective Turn: Case Studies in and on Educational Practice.* New York: Teachers College Press.

Schubert, W.H., & W.C. Ayers, eds. 1992. *Teacher Lore: Learning from Our Own Experience.* New York: Longman.

Shavelson, R., & P. Stern. 1981. "Research on Teachers' Pedagogical Thoughts, Judgements, Decisions, and Behavior." *Review of Educational Research 51*: 455–498.

Shrewsbury, C.M. 1987. "What Is Feminist Pedagogy?" *Women's Studies Quarterly 15* (3 & 4): 6–13.

Smith, F. 1983. *Essays into Literacy.* Portsmouth, NH: Heinemann.

Smyth, J., ed. 1987. *Educating Teachers: Changing the Nature of Pedagogical Knowledge.* New York: Falmer Press.

Spence, D. 1982. *Narrative Truth and Historical Truth: Meaning and Interpretation of Psychoanalysis.* New York: Norton.

Spindler, G.D., ed. 1974. *Education and Cultural Process: Toward an Anthropology of Education.* New York: Holt, Rinehart and Winston.

Spivak, G. 1990. *The Post-colonial Critic: Interviews, Strategies, Dialogues.* New York: Routledge.

Stafford, W. 1989. *You Must Revise Your Life.* Ann Arbor, MI: University of Michigan Press.

Stenhouse, L. 1975. *An Introduction to Curriculum Research and Development.* London: Heinemann.

Stillman, P. 1984. *Writing Your Way.* Portsmouth, NH: Boynton/Cook.

Strauss, A. 1987. *Qualitative Research for Social Scientists.* Cambridge, UK: Cambridge University Press.

Sullivan, P. 1990. "Sullivan's Travels: Mr. Duerksen's Magic Word." *West* 4: 92–98.

Tabachnick, B.R., T.S. Popkewitz, & K.M. Zeichner. 1980. "Teacher Education and the Professional Perspectives of Student Teachers." *Interchange 10*: 12–29.

Taubman, P. 1993. "Canonical Sins." In *Understanding Curriculum as Racial Text: Representations of Identity and Difference in Education,* eds. L. Castenell & W. Pinar, 35–52. New York: SUNY.

Tchudi, S., S. Tchudi, S. Yesner, & J. Yesner. 1990. *Literature by Doing: Responding to Poetry, Essays, Drama, and Short Stories.* Lincolnwood, IL: National Textbook Company.

Tom, A.R. 1984. *Teaching as a Moral Craft.* New York: Longman.

Turner, V. 1980. "Social Dramas and Stories about Them." *Critical Inquiry* 7:141–168.

Van Maanen, J. 1983. *Qualitative Methodology.* Beverly Hills, CA: Sage.

Vinz, R. 1993. *Composing a Teaching Life: An Inquiry of Possibility in Literature Education.* Urbana, IL: National Council Teachers of English.

Vinz, R. & D. Kirby. 1991. "Landscapes of the Imagination: Readers Encounter Texts." In *Vital Signs 2,* ed. J. Collins. Portsmouth, NH: Boynton/Cook.

Vondraceck, F. 1990. "A Developmental–Contextual Approach to Career

Development Research." In *Methodological Approaches to the Study of Career*, eds. R. Young & W. Borgen, 37–56. New York: Praeger.

Vygotsky, L. 1986. *Thought and Language*, trans. A. Kozulin, Cambridge, MA: MIT Press.

White, H. 1980. "The Value of Narrativity in the Representation of Reality." *Critical Inquiry 7:* 5–27.

Winkler, K. 1986. "Flourishing Research in Marxist Theory Belies Signs of Its Demise, Scholars Say." *Chronicle of Higher Education 1:* 4–5.

Witherell, C., & N. Noddings. 1991. *Stories Lives Tell: Narrative and Dialogue in Education*. New York: Teachers College Press.

Wittgenstein, L. 1974. *Philosophical Investigations*, trans. G.E.M. Anscombe. Oxford: Basil Blackwell.

Woods, P. 1983. *Sociology and the School: An Interactionist Viewpoint*. Boston, MA: Routlege and Kegan Paul.

Zancanella, D. 1991. "Teachers Reading/Readers Teaching: Five Teachers Personal Approaches to Literature and Their Teaching of Literature." *Research in the Teaching of English 25* (1):532.

Zeichner, K.M. 1987. "Preparing Reflective Teachers: An Overview of Instructional Strategies Which Have Been Employed in Preservice Teacher Education. *International Journal of Educational Research 11* (5): 565–576.

Zeichner, K.M. & J.M. Gore 1990. "Teacher Socialization." In *Handbook of Research on Teacher Education*, ed. W.R. Houston, 329–348. New York: MacMillan.

———— & D. Liston. 1987. "Teaching Student Teachers to Reflect." *HER 57*: 23–48.

Zumwalt, K.K. 1982. "Research on Teaching: Policy Implications for Teacher Education." In *Policy Making in Education: 81st Yearbook of the National Society for the Study of Education*, eds. A. Lieberman & M.W. McLaughlin, 215–248. Chicago, IL: University of Chicago Press.